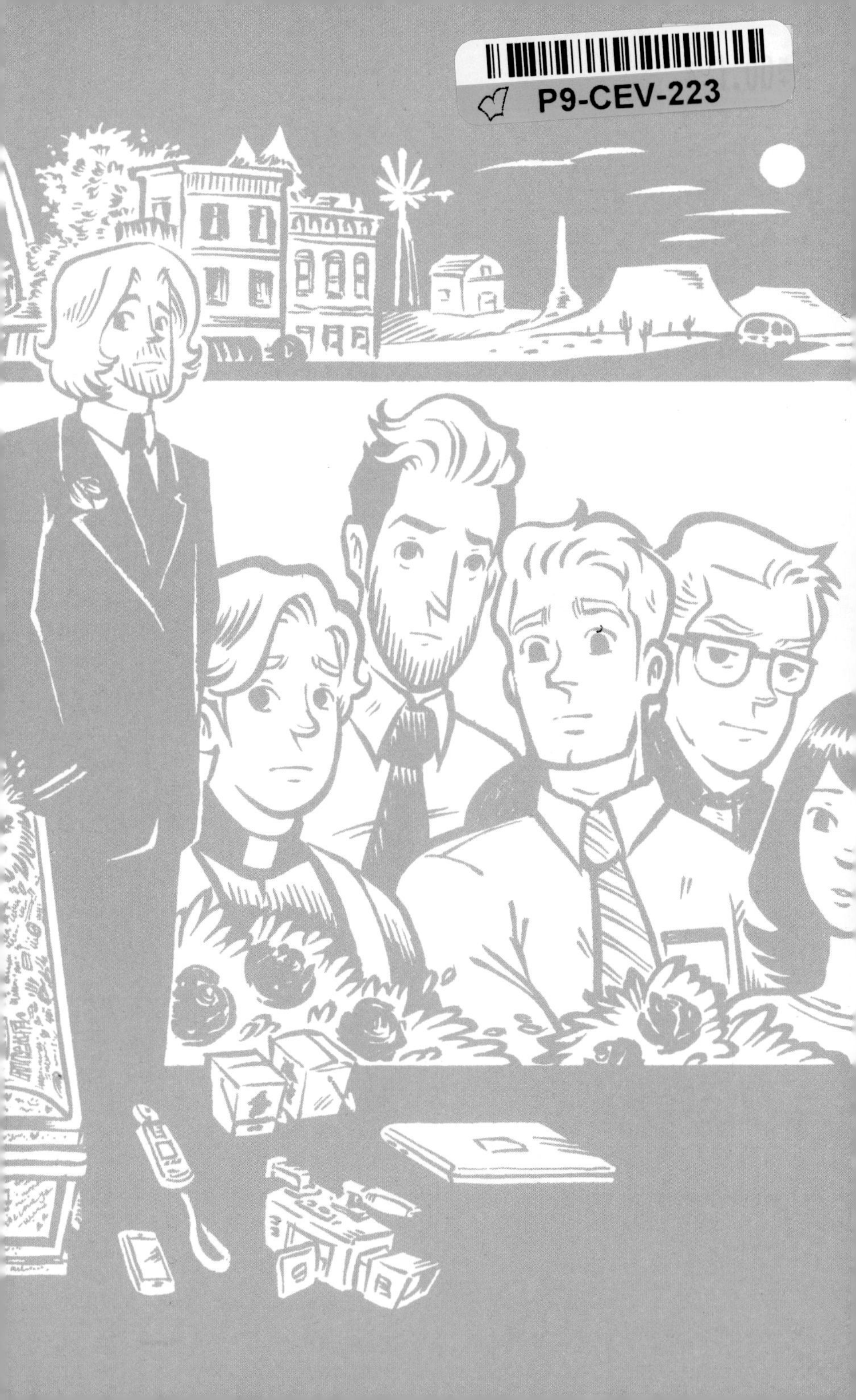

an ELEGY *for* AMELIA JOHNSON™

ROSTAN • VALEZA • KASENOW

ARCHAIA ENTERTAINMENT LLC
WWW.ARCHAIA.COM

Published by **Archaia**

Archaia Entertainment LLC
1680 Vine Street, Suite 912
Los Angeles, California, 90028, USA
www.archaia.com

AN ELEGY FOR AMELIA JOHNSON

March 2011

FIRST PRINTING

10 9 8 7 6 5 4 3 2 1

ISBN: 1-932386-83-1
ISBN13: 978-1-932386-83-7

Printed in Korea.

ARCHAIA ™

an ELEGY *for* AMELIA JOHNSON™

written *by* ANDREW ROSTAN
illustrated *by* DAVE VALEZA & KATE KASENOW
lettered *by* DAVE LANPHEAR

CHRIS ROBINSON & PAUL MORRISSEY, *associate editors*
STEPHEN CHRISTY, *editor*

An Elegy for Amelia Johnson created by
ANDREW ROSTAN & DAVE VALEZA

for JOSEPH LAWRENCE KACENGA

who never knew I would do this,
but believed that I could.

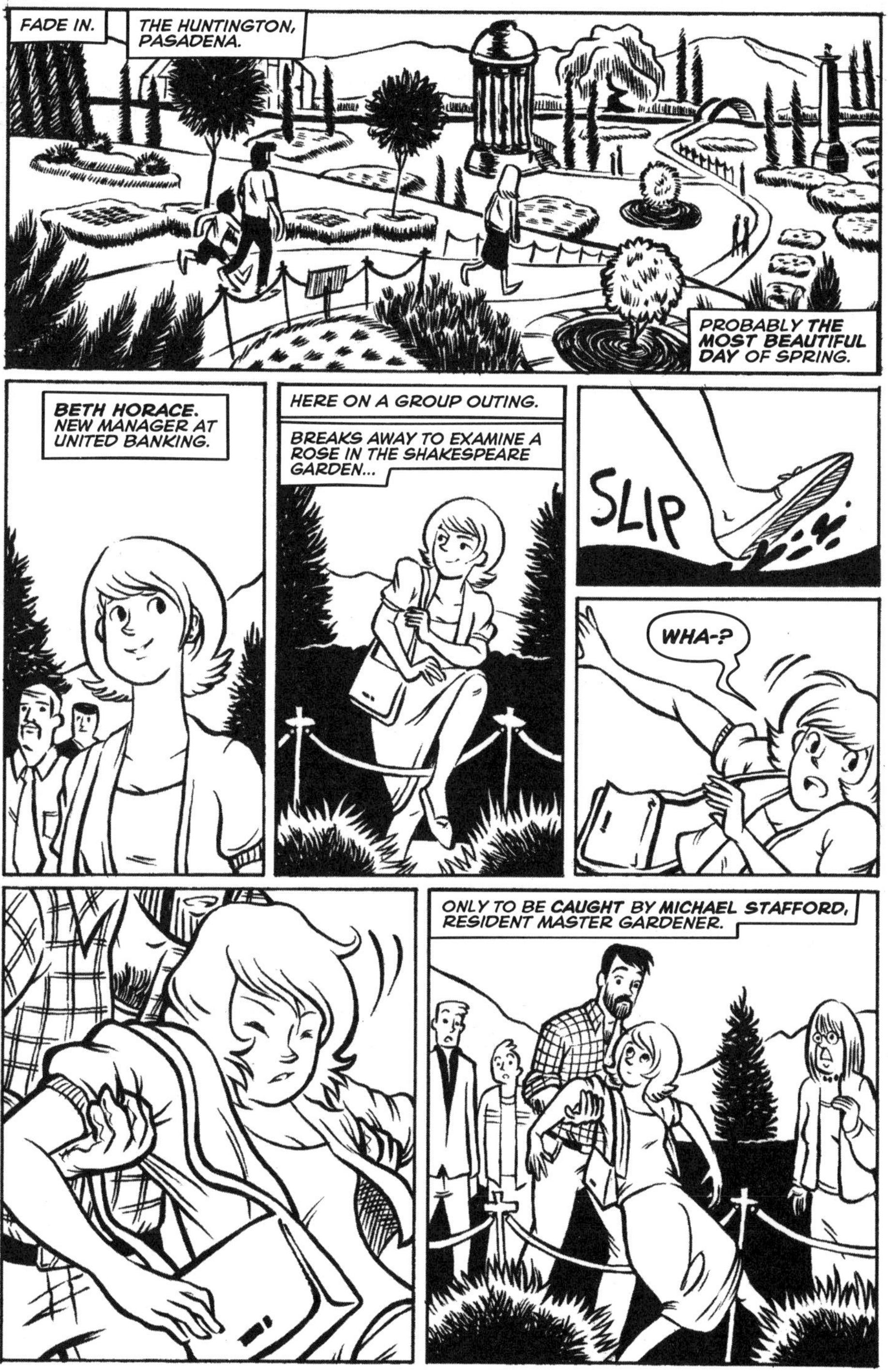
FADE IN.
THE HUNTINGTON, PASADENA.
PROBABLY THE MOST BEAUTIFUL DAY OF SPRING.
BETH HORACE. NEW MANAGER AT UNITED BANKING.
HERE ON A GROUP OUTING.
BREAKS AWAY TO EXAMINE A ROSE IN THE SHAKESPEARE GARDEN...
SLIP
WHA-?
ONLY TO BE CAUGHT BY MICHAEL STAFFORD, RESIDENT MASTER GARDENER.

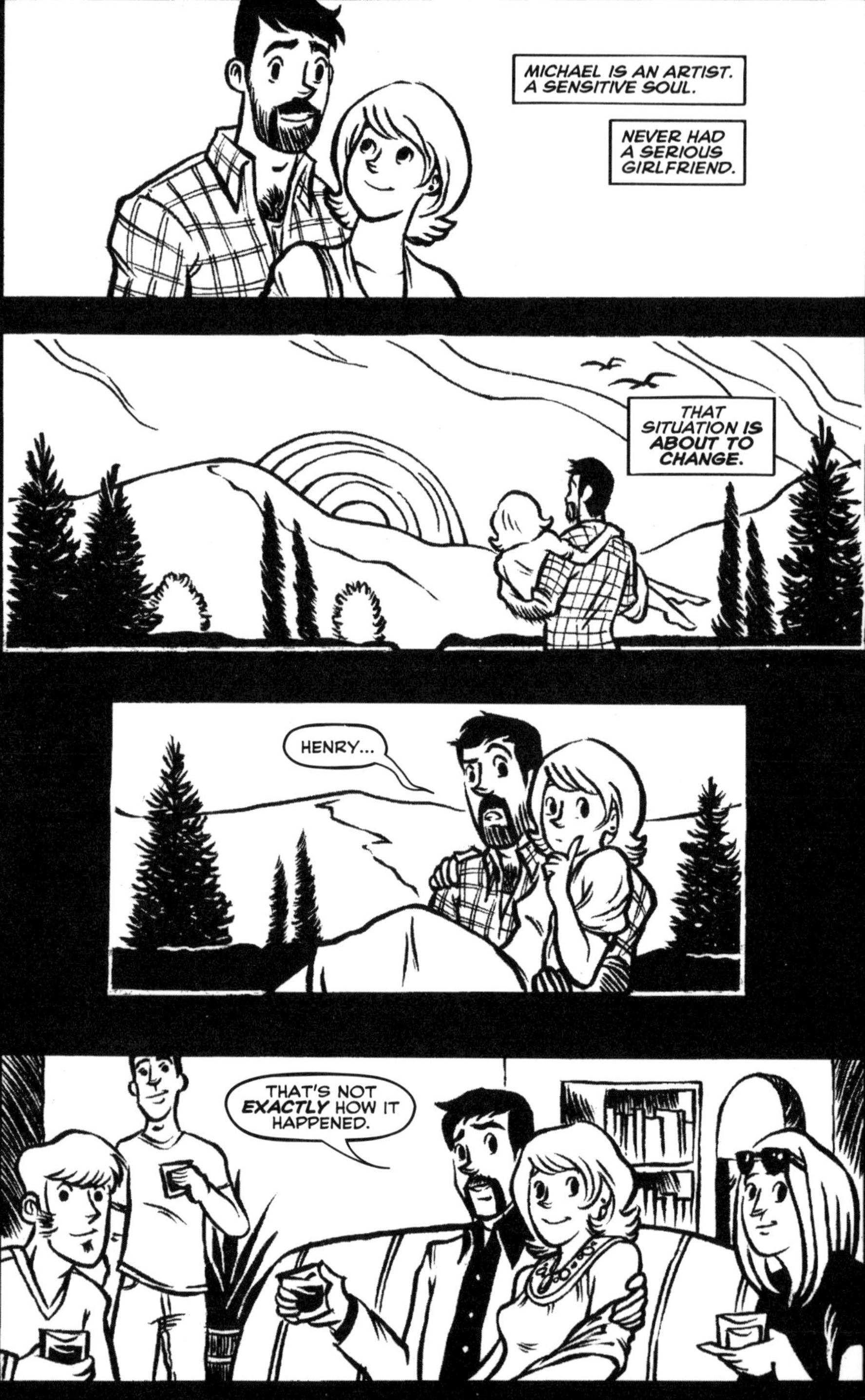
MICHAEL IS AN ARTIST. A SENSITIVE SOUL.
NEVER HAD A SERIOUS GIRLFRIEND.
THAT SITUATION IS ABOUT TO CHANGE.
HENRY...
THAT'S NOT EXACTLY HOW IT HAPPENED.

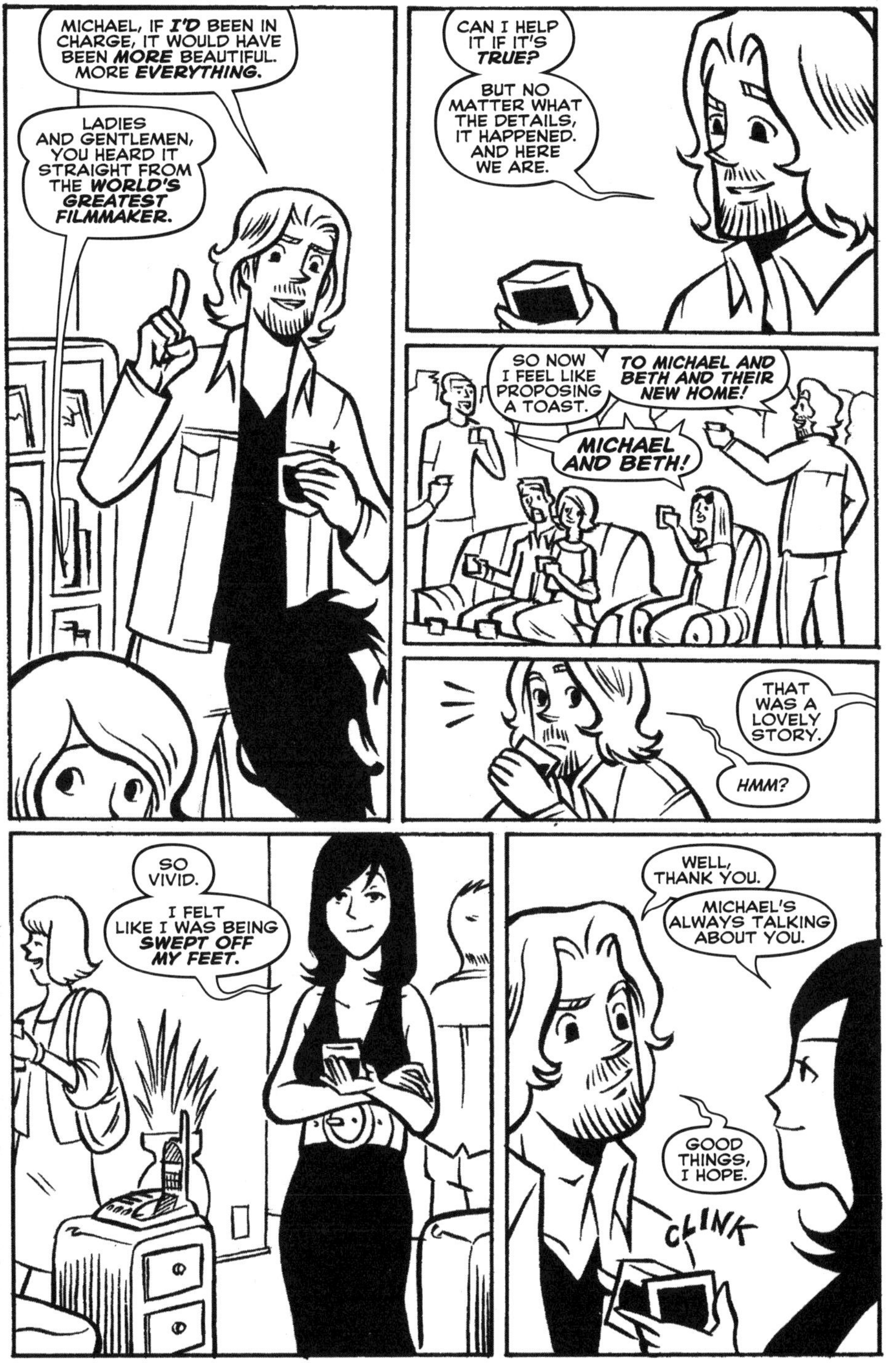

MICHAEL, IF I'D BEEN IN CHARGE, IT WOULD HAVE BEEN MORE BEAUTIFUL. MORE EVERYTHING.
LADIES AND GENTLEMEN, YOU HEARD IT STRAIGHT FROM THE WORLD'S GREATEST FILMMAKER.
CAN I HELP IT IF IT'S TRUE?
BUT NO MATTER WHAT THE DETAILS, IT HAPPENED. AND HERE WE ARE.
SO NOW I FEEL LIKE PROPOSING A TOAST.
TO MICHAEL AND BETH AND THEIR NEW HOME!
MICHAEL AND BETH!
THAT WAS A LOVELY STORY.
HMM?
SO VIVID.
I FELT LIKE I WAS BEING SWEPT OFF MY FEET.
WELL, THANK YOU.
MICHAEL'S ALWAYS TALKING ABOUT YOU.
GOOD THINGS, I HOPE.
CLINK

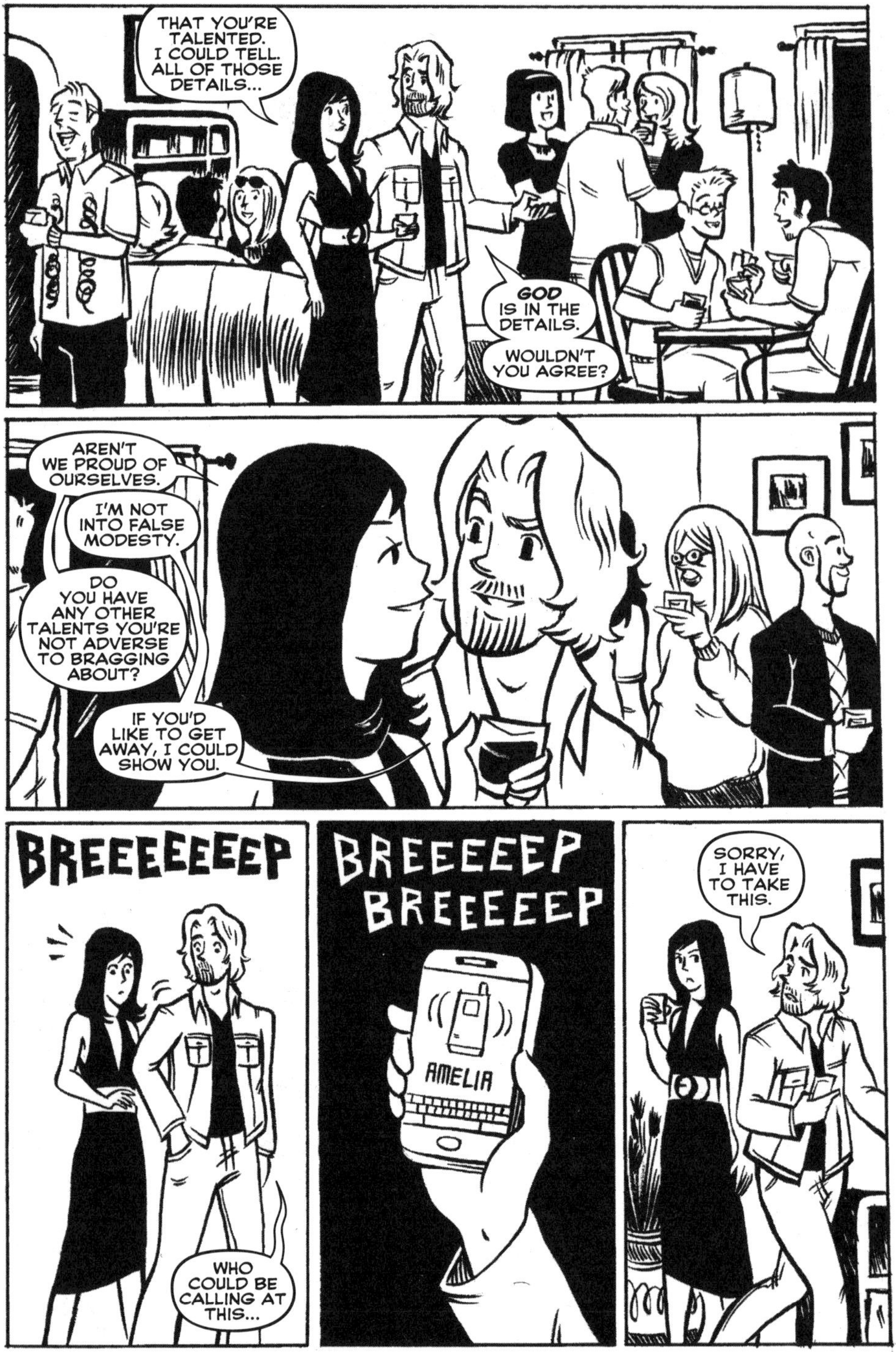
THAT YOU'RE TALENTED. I COULD TELL. ALL OF THOSE DETAILS...
GOD IS IN THE DETAILS.
WOULDN'T YOU AGREE?
AREN'T WE PROUD OF OURSELVES.
I'M NOT INTO FALSE MODESTY.
DO YOU HAVE ANY OTHER TALENTS YOU'RE NOT ADVERSE TO BRAGGING ABOUT?
IF YOU'D LIKE TO GET AWAY, I COULD SHOW YOU.
BREEEEEEEP
WHO COULD BE CALLING AT THIS...
BREEEEEP
BREEEEEP
AMELIA
SORRY, I HAVE TO TAKE THIS.

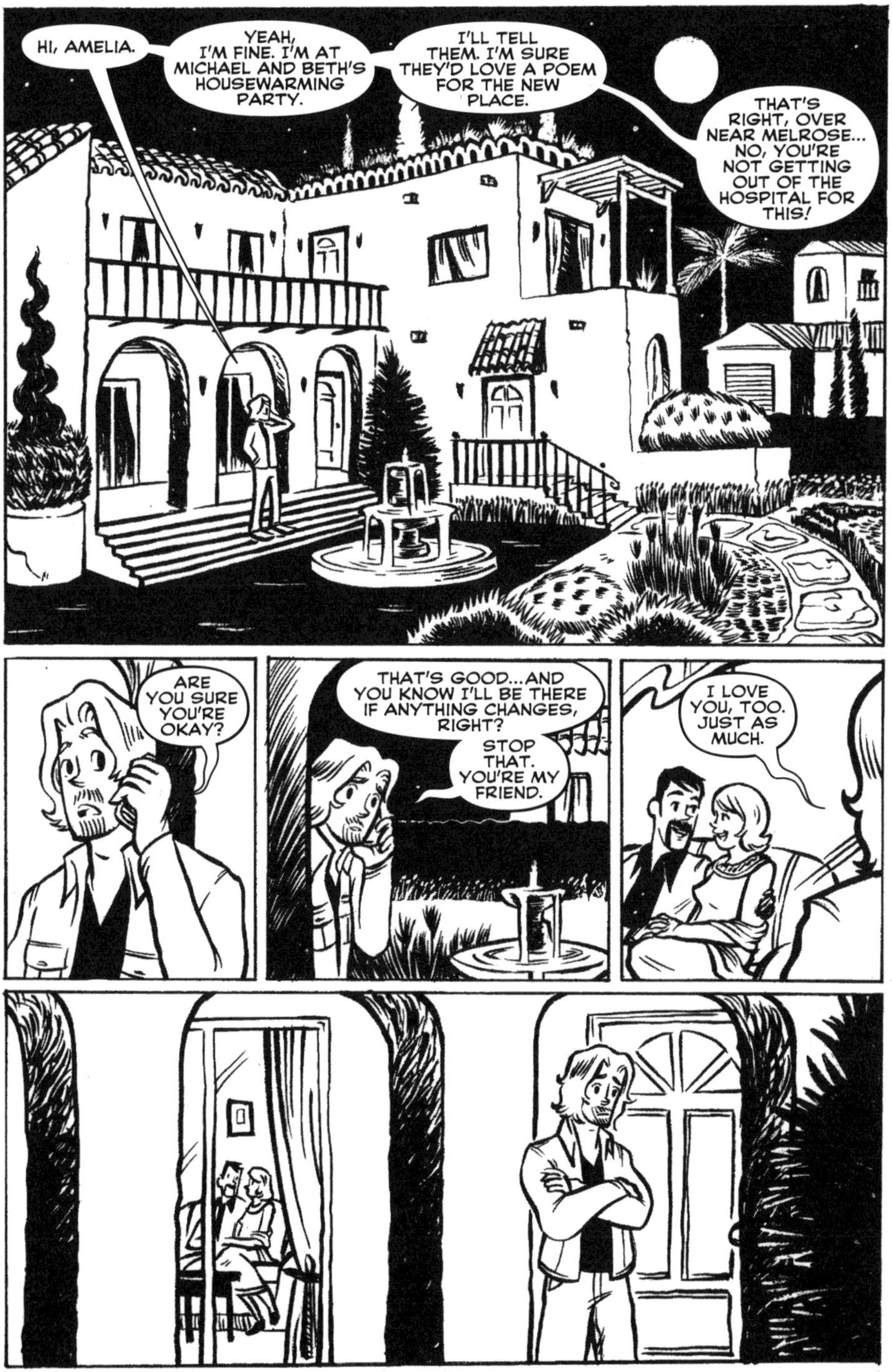
HI, AMELIA.
YEAH, I'M FINE. I'M AT MICHAEL AND BETH'S HOUSEWARMING PARTY.
I'LL TELL THEM. I'M SURE THEY'D LOVE A POEM FOR THE NEW PLACE.
THAT'S RIGHT, OVER NEAR MELROSE... NO, YOU'RE NOT GETTING OUT OF THE HOSPITAL FOR THIS!
ARE YOU SURE YOU'RE OKAY?
THAT'S GOOD...AND YOU KNOW I'LL BE THERE IF ANYTHING CHANGES, RIGHT?
STOP THAT. YOU'RE MY FRIEND.
I LOVE YOU, TOO. JUST AS MUCH.

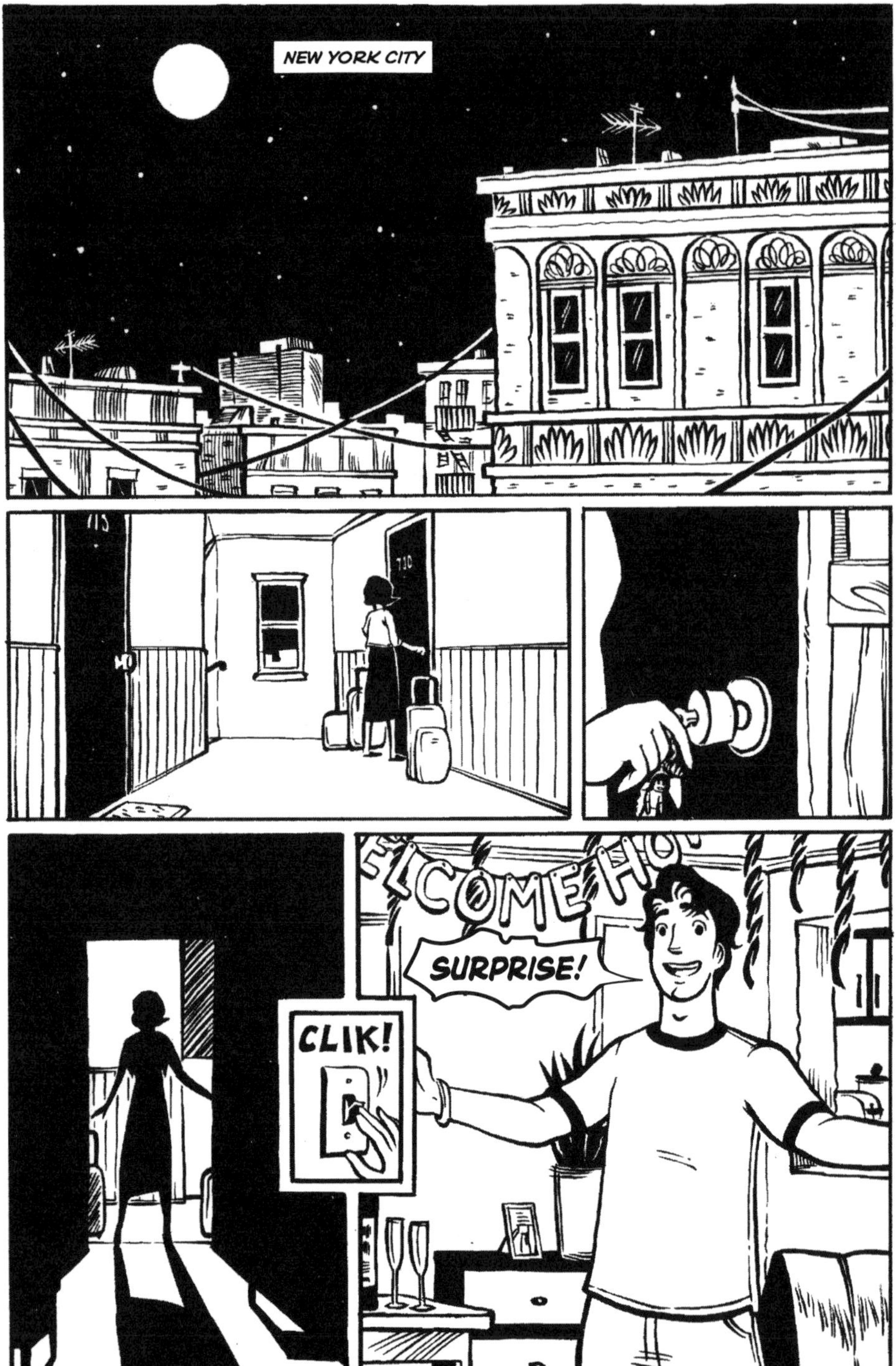
NEW YORK CITY
CLIK!
SURPRISE!

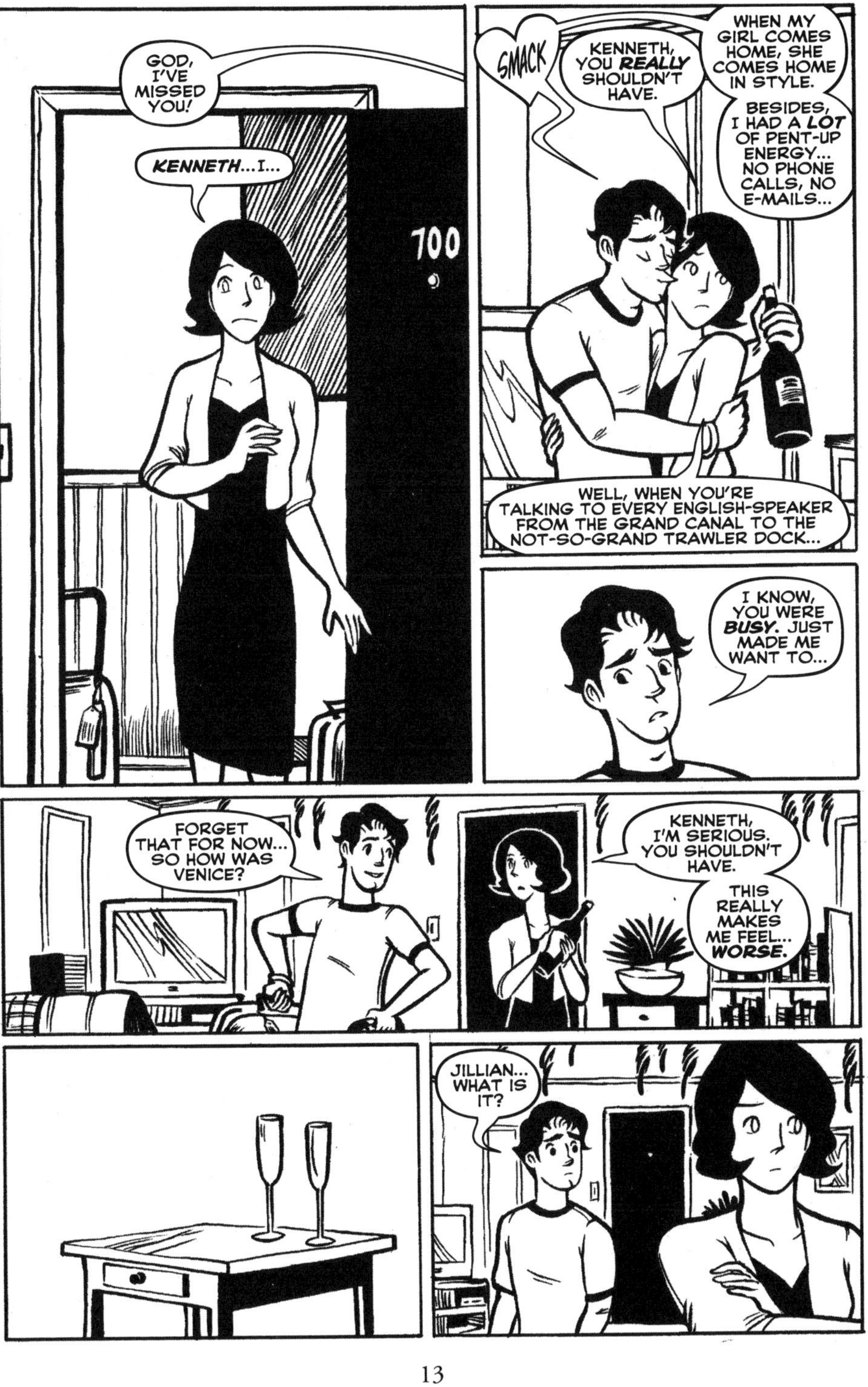
GOD, I'VE MISSED YOU!
KENNETH...I...
700
SMACK
KENNETH, YOU REALLY SHOULDN'T HAVE.
WHEN MY GIRL COMES HOME, SHE COMES HOME IN STYLE.
BESIDES, I HAD A LOT OF PENT-UP ENERGY... NO PHONE CALLS, NO E-MAILS...
WELL, WHEN YOU'RE TALKING TO EVERY ENGLISH-SPEAKER FROM THE GRAND CANAL TO THE NOT-SO-GRAND TRAWLER DOCK...
I KNOW, YOU WERE BUSY. JUST MADE ME WANT TO...
FORGET THAT FOR NOW... SO HOW WAS VENICE?
KENNETH, I'M SERIOUS. YOU SHOULDN'T HAVE.
THIS REALLY MAKES ME FEEL... WORSE.
JILLIAN... WHAT IS IT?

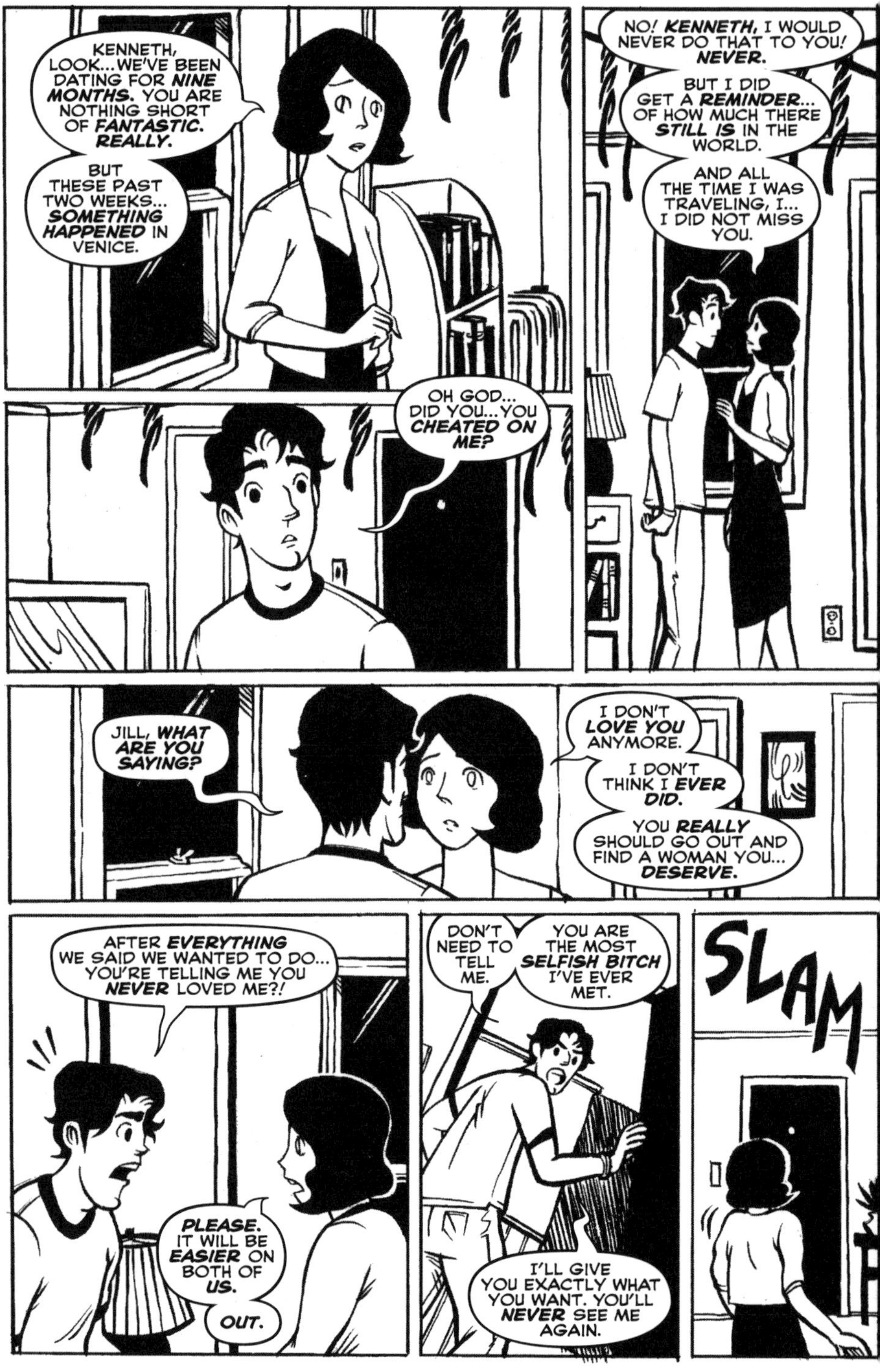
KENNETH, LOOK...WE'VE BEEN DATING FOR NINE MONTHS. YOU ARE NOTHING SHORT OF FANTASTIC. REALLY.
BUT THESE PAST TWO WEEKS... SOMETHING HAPPENED IN VENICE.
OH GOD... DID YOU...YOU CHEATED ON ME?
NO! KENNETH, I WOULD NEVER DO THAT TO YOU! NEVER.
BUT I DID GET A REMINDER... OF HOW MUCH THERE STILL IS IN THE WORLD.
AND ALL THE TIME I WAS TRAVELING, I... I DID NOT MISS YOU.
JILL, WHAT ARE YOU SAYING?
I DON'T LOVE YOU ANYMORE.
I DON'T THINK I EVER DID.
YOU REALLY SHOULD GO OUT AND FIND A WOMAN YOU... DESERVE.
AFTER EVERYTHING WE SAID WE WANTED TO DO... YOU'RE TELLING ME YOU NEVER LOVED ME?!
PLEASE. IT WILL BE EASIER ON BOTH OF US.
OUT.
DON'T NEED TO TELL ME.
YOU ARE THE MOST SELFISH BITCH I'VE EVER MET.
I'LL GIVE YOU EXACTLY WHAT YOU WANT. YOU'LL NEVER SEE ME AGAIN.
SLAM

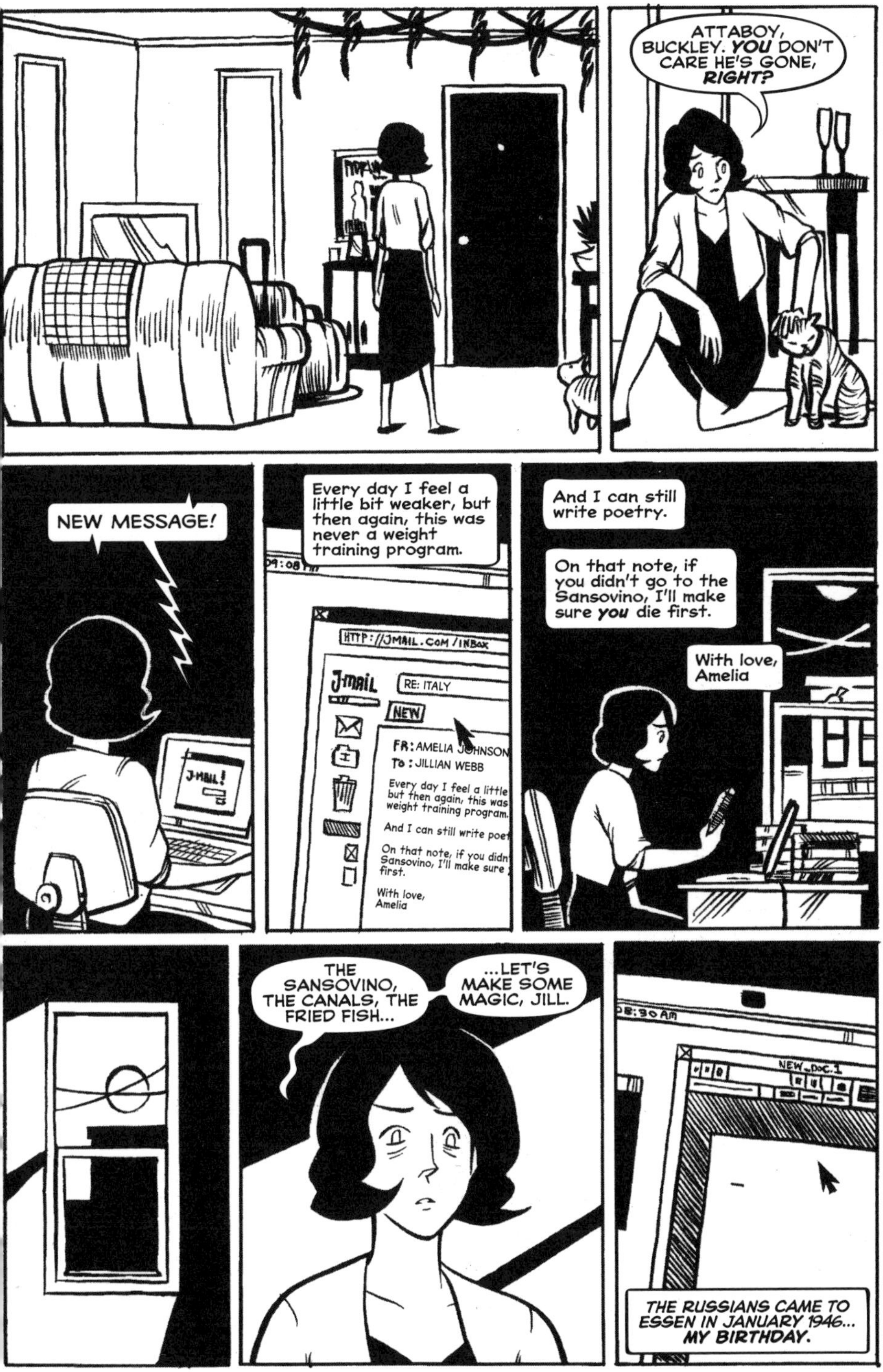
ATTABOY, BUCKLEY. YOU DON'T CARE HE'S GONE, RIGHT?
NEW MESSAGE!
Every day I feel a little bit weaker, but then again, this was never a weight training program.
HTTP://JMAIL.COM/INBOX
J-MAIL
RE: ITALY
NEW
FR: AMELIA JOHNSON
TO: JILLIAN WEBB
And I can still write poetry.
On that note, if you didn't go to the Sansovino, I'll make sure you die first.
With love, Amelia
THE SANSOVINO, THE CANALS, THE FRIED FISH...
...LET'S MAKE SOME MAGIC, JILL.
08:30 AM
NEW_DOC.1
THE RUSSIANS CAME TO ESSEN IN JANUARY 1946... MY BIRTHDAY.

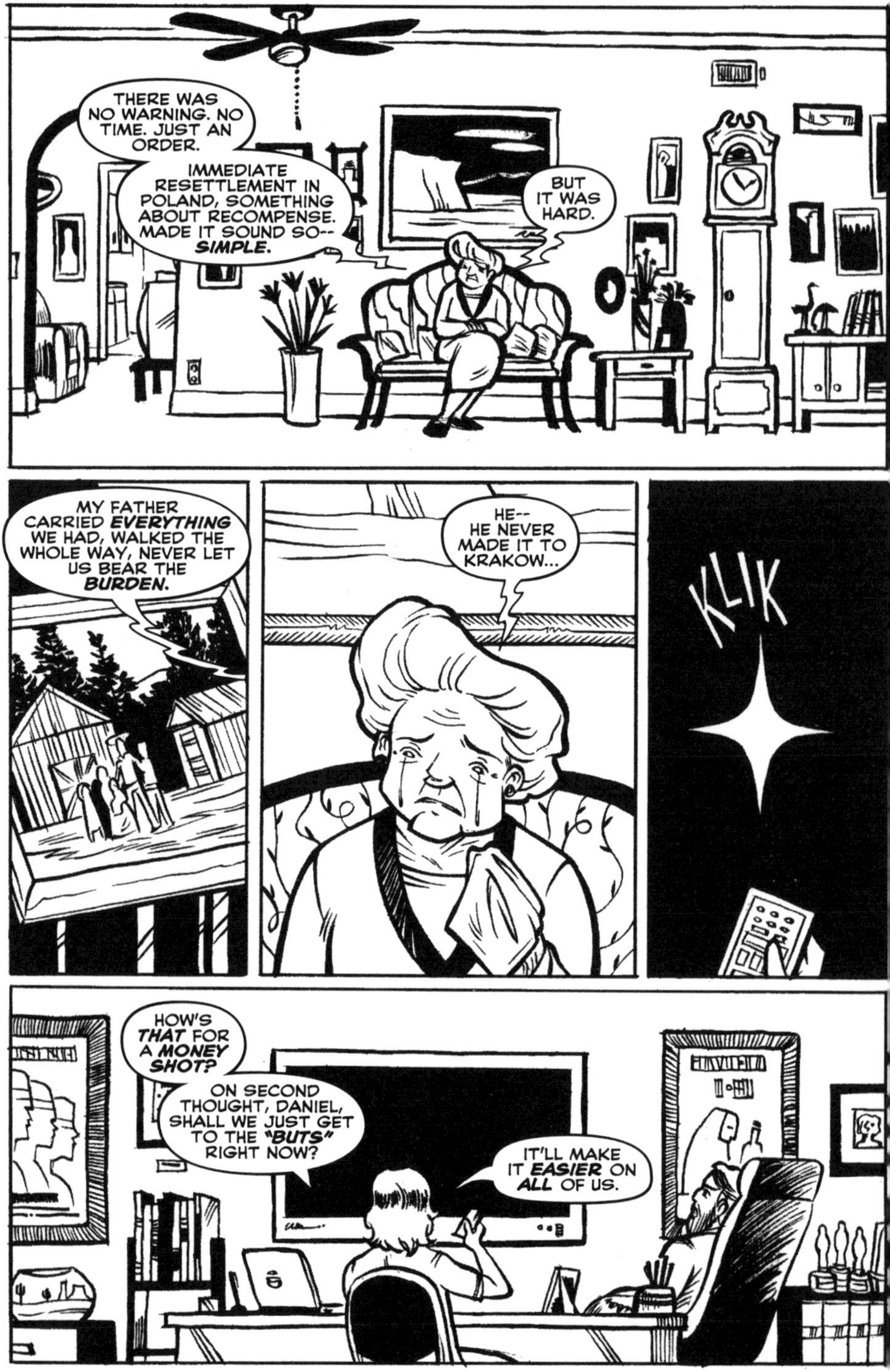
THERE WAS NO WARNING. NO TIME. JUST AN ORDER.
IMMEDIATE RESETTLEMENT IN POLAND, SOMETHING ABOUT RECOMPENSE. MADE IT SOUND SO-- **SIMPLE.**
BUT IT WAS HARD.
MY FATHER CARRIED **EVERYTHING** WE HAD, WALKED THE WHOLE WAY, NEVER LET US BEAR THE **BURDEN.**
HE-- HE NEVER MADE IT TO KRAKOW...
KLIK
HOW'S **THAT** FOR A **MONEY SHOT?**
ON SECOND THOUGHT, DANIEL, SHALL WE JUST GET TO THE **"BUTS"** RIGHT NOW?
IT'LL MAKE IT **EASIER** ON **ALL** OF US.

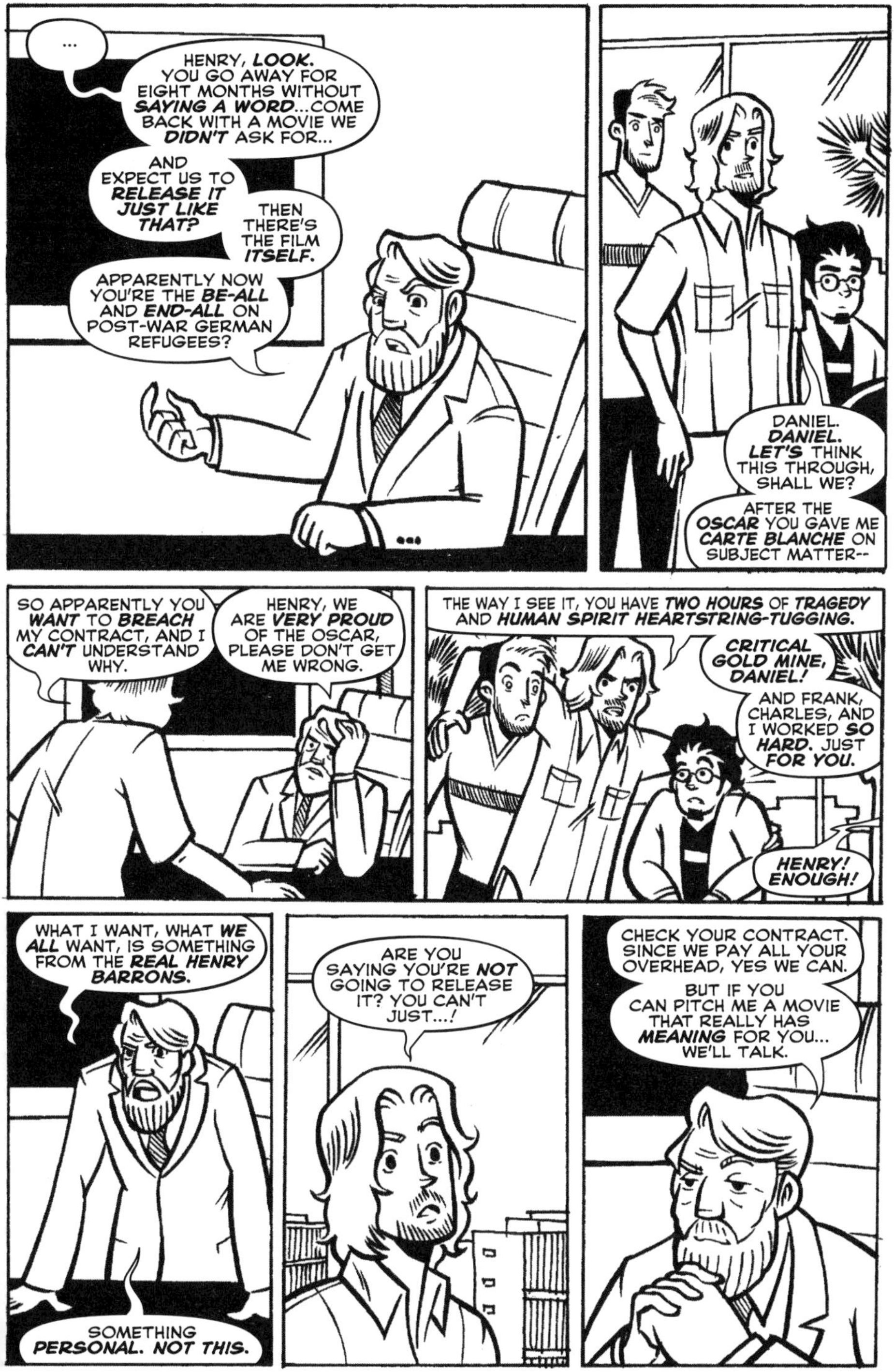
...
HENRY, LOOK. YOU GO AWAY FOR EIGHT MONTHS WITHOUT SAYING A WORD...COME BACK WITH A MOVIE WE DIDN'T ASK FOR...
AND EXPECT US TO RELEASE IT JUST LIKE THAT?
THEN THERE'S THE FILM ITSELF.
APPARENTLY NOW YOU'RE THE BE-ALL AND END-ALL ON POST-WAR GERMAN REFUGEES?
DANIEL. DANIEL. LET'S THINK THIS THROUGH, SHALL WE?
AFTER THE OSCAR YOU GAVE ME CARTE BLANCHE ON SUBJECT MATTER--
SO APPARENTLY YOU WANT TO BREACH MY CONTRACT, AND I CAN'T UNDERSTAND WHY.
HENRY, WE ARE VERY PROUD OF THE OSCAR, PLEASE DON'T GET ME WRONG.
THE WAY I SEE IT, YOU HAVE TWO HOURS OF TRAGEDY AND HUMAN SPIRIT HEARTSTRING-TUGGING.
CRITICAL GOLD MINE, DANIEL!
AND FRANK, CHARLES, AND I WORKED SO HARD. JUST FOR YOU.
HENRY! ENOUGH!
WHAT I WANT, WHAT WE ALL WANT, IS SOMETHING FROM THE REAL HENRY BARRONS.
SOMETHING PERSONAL. NOT THIS.
ARE YOU SAYING YOU'RE NOT GOING TO RELEASE IT? YOU CAN'T JUST...!
CHECK YOUR CONTRACT. SINCE WE PAY ALL YOUR OVERHEAD, YES WE CAN.
BUT IF YOU CAN PITCH ME A MOVIE THAT REALLY HAS MEANING FOR YOU... WE'LL TALK.

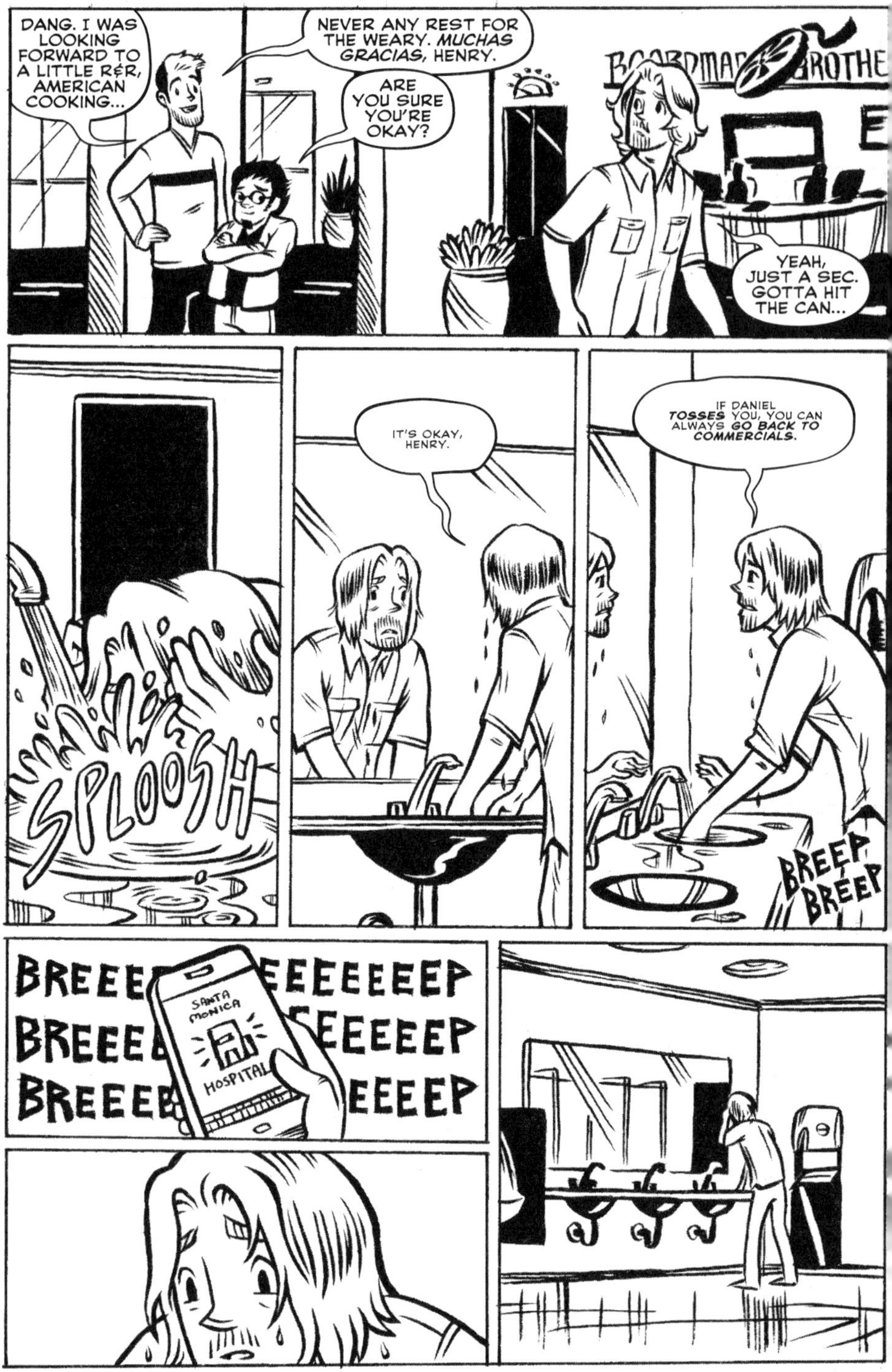
DANG. I WAS LOOKING FORWARD TO A LITTLE R&R, AMERICAN COOKING...
NEVER ANY REST FOR THE WEARY. *MUCHAS GRACIAS,* HENRY.
ARE YOU SURE YOU'RE OKAY?
YEAH, JUST A SEC. GOTTA HIT THE CAN...
SPLOOSH
IT'S OKAY, HENRY.
IF DANIEL **TOSSES** YOU, YOU CAN ALWAYS **GO BACK TO COMMERCIALS.**
BREEP BREEP
BREEEEEEEEEEEEEP
BREEEEEEEEEEEEP
BREEEEEEEEEEEP
SANTA MONICA HOSPITAL

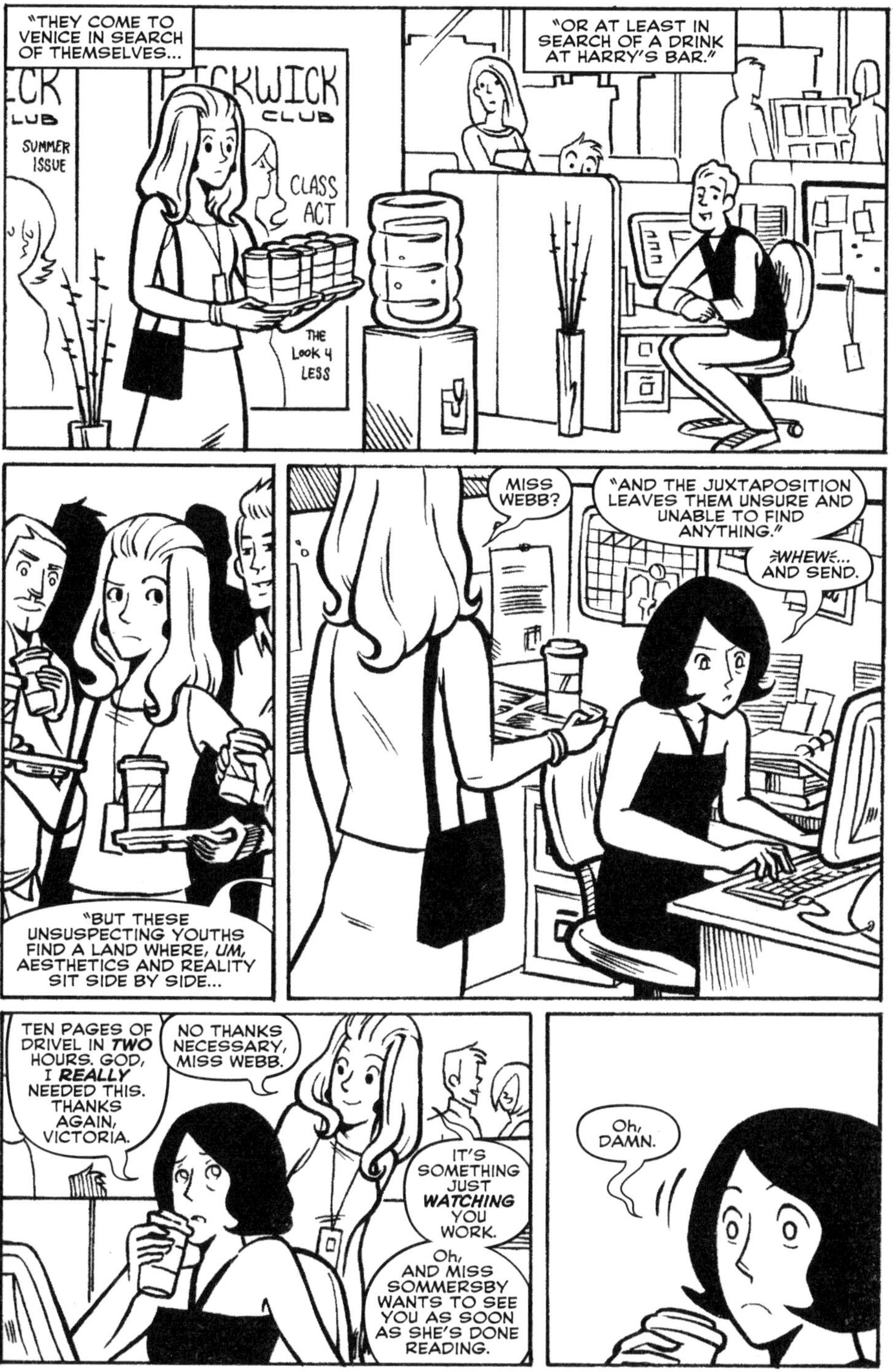

"THEY COME TO VENICE IN SEARCH OF THEMSELVES...
PICKWICK CLUB
SUMMER ISSUE
CLASS ACT
THE LOOK 4 LESS
"OR AT LEAST IN SEARCH OF A DRINK AT HARRY'S BAR."
"BUT THESE UNSUSPECTING YOUTHS FIND A LAND WHERE, UM, AESTHETICS AND REALITY SIT SIDE BY SIDE...
MISS WEBB?
"AND THE JUXTAPOSITION LEAVES THEM UNSURE AND UNABLE TO FIND ANYTHING."
WHEW... AND SEND.
TEN PAGES OF DRIVEL IN TWO HOURS. GOD, I REALLY NEEDED THIS. THANKS AGAIN, VICTORIA.
NO THANKS NECESSARY, MISS WEBB.
IT'S SOMETHING JUST WATCHING YOU WORK.
Oh, AND MISS SOMMERSBY WANTS TO SEE YOU AS SOON AS SHE'S DONE READING.
Oh, DAMN.

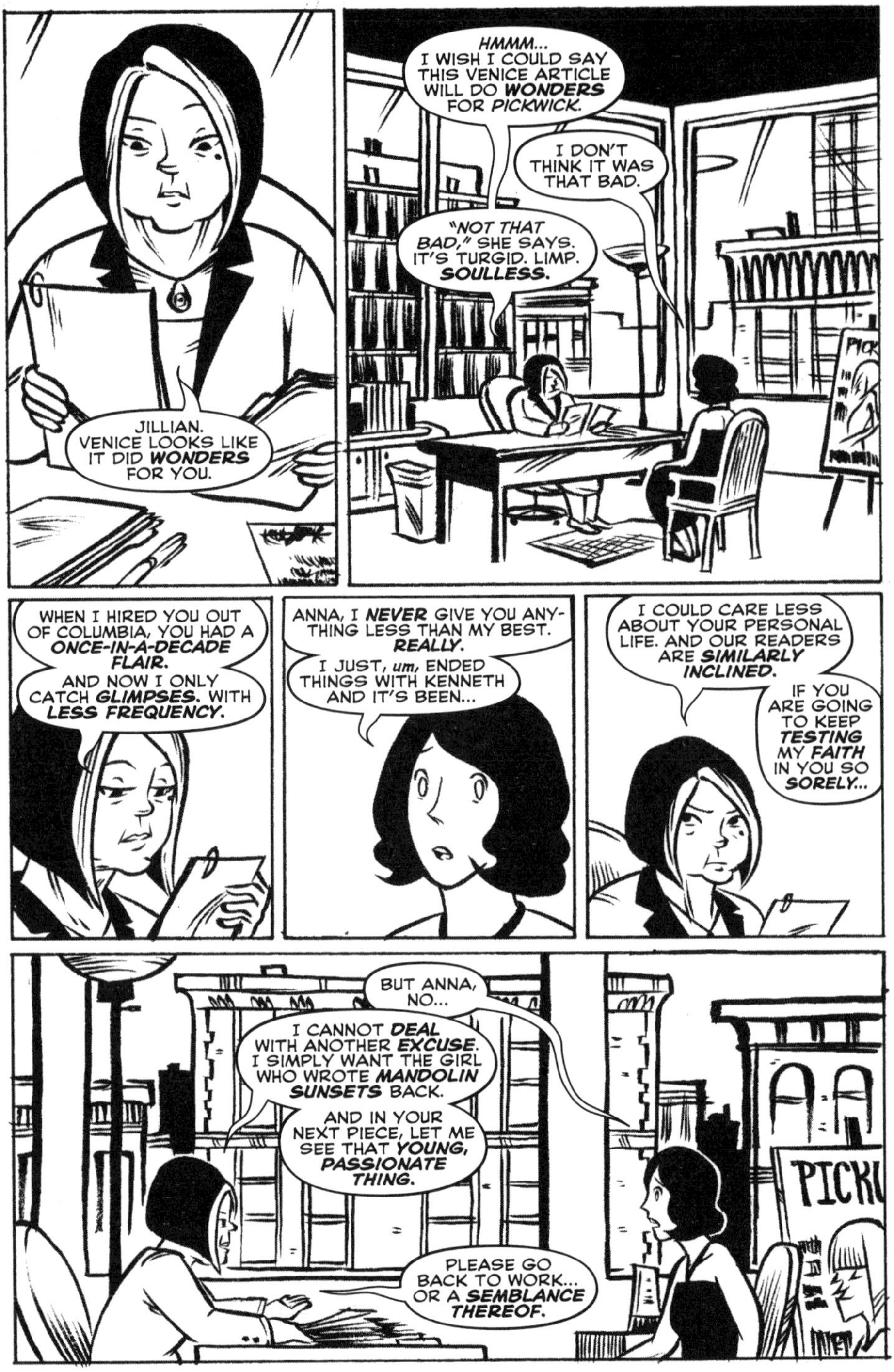
JILLIAN. VENICE LOOKS LIKE IT DID WONDERS FOR YOU.
HMMM... I WISH I COULD SAY THIS VENICE ARTICLE WILL DO WONDERS FOR PICKWICK.
I DON'T THINK IT WAS THAT BAD.
"NOT THAT BAD," SHE SAYS. IT'S TURGID. LIMP. SOULLESS.
WHEN I HIRED YOU OUT OF COLUMBIA, YOU HAD A ONCE-IN-A-DECADE FLAIR.
AND NOW I ONLY CATCH GLIMPSES. WITH LESS FREQUENCY.
ANNA, I NEVER GIVE YOU ANYTHING LESS THAN MY BEST. REALLY.
I JUST, um, ENDED THINGS WITH KENNETH AND IT'S BEEN...
I COULD CARE LESS ABOUT YOUR PERSONAL LIFE. AND OUR READERS ARE SIMILARLY INCLINED.
IF YOU ARE GOING TO KEEP TESTING MY FAITH IN YOU SO SORELY...
BUT ANNA, NO...
I CANNOT DEAL WITH ANOTHER EXCUSE. I SIMPLY WANT THE GIRL WHO WROTE MANDOLIN SUNSETS BACK.
AND IN YOUR NEXT PIECE, LET ME SEE THAT YOUNG, PASSIONATE THING.
PLEASE GO BACK TO WORK... OR A SEMBLANCE THEREOF.
PICK

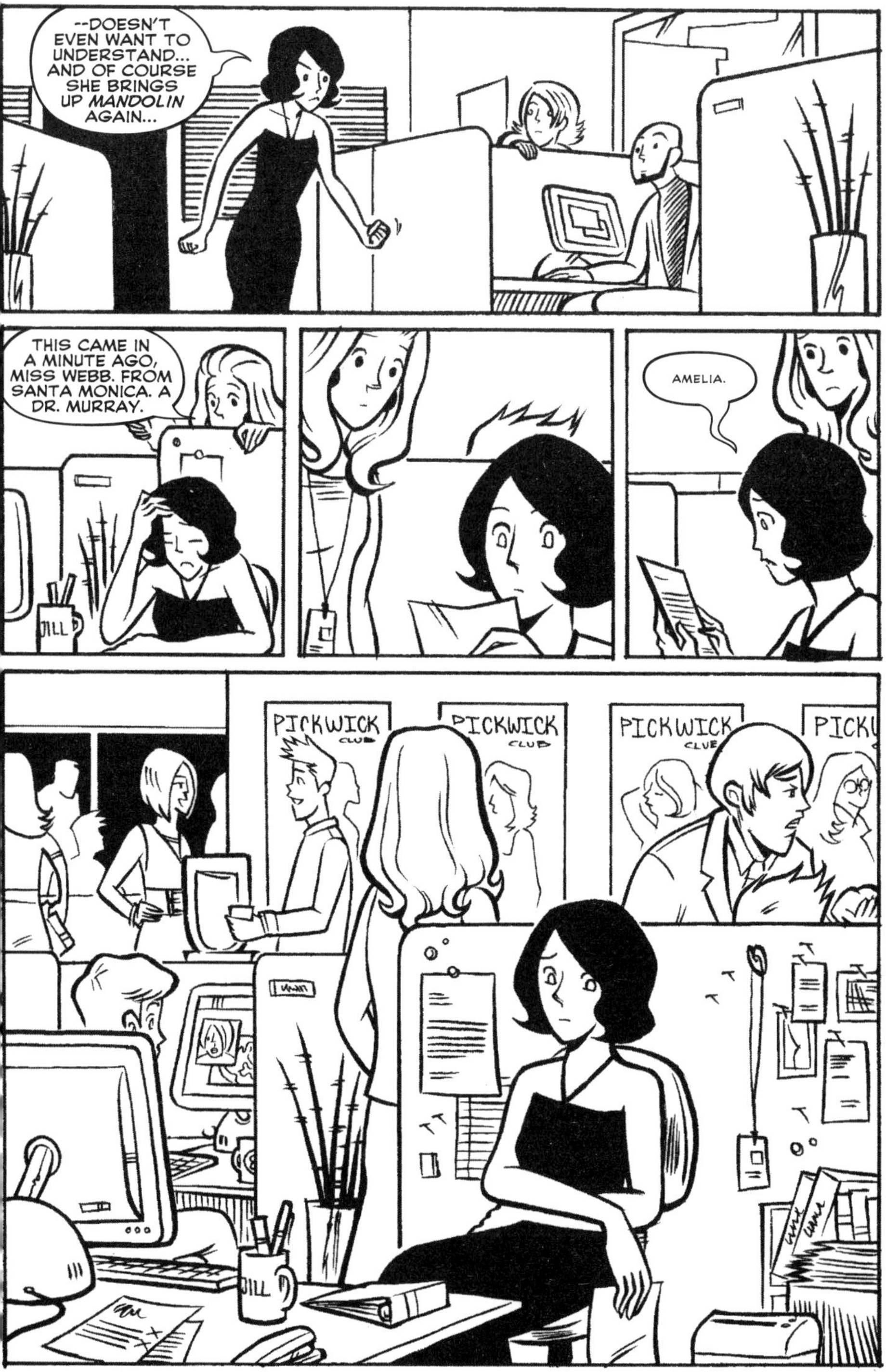
--DOESN'T EVEN WANT TO UNDERSTAND... AND OF COURSE SHE BRINGS UP *MANDOLIN* AGAIN...
THIS CAME IN A MINUTE AGO, MISS WEBB. FROM SANTA MONICA. A DR. MURRAY.
AMELIA.
JILL
PICKWICK CLUB
PICKWICK CLUB
PICKWICK CLUB
JILL

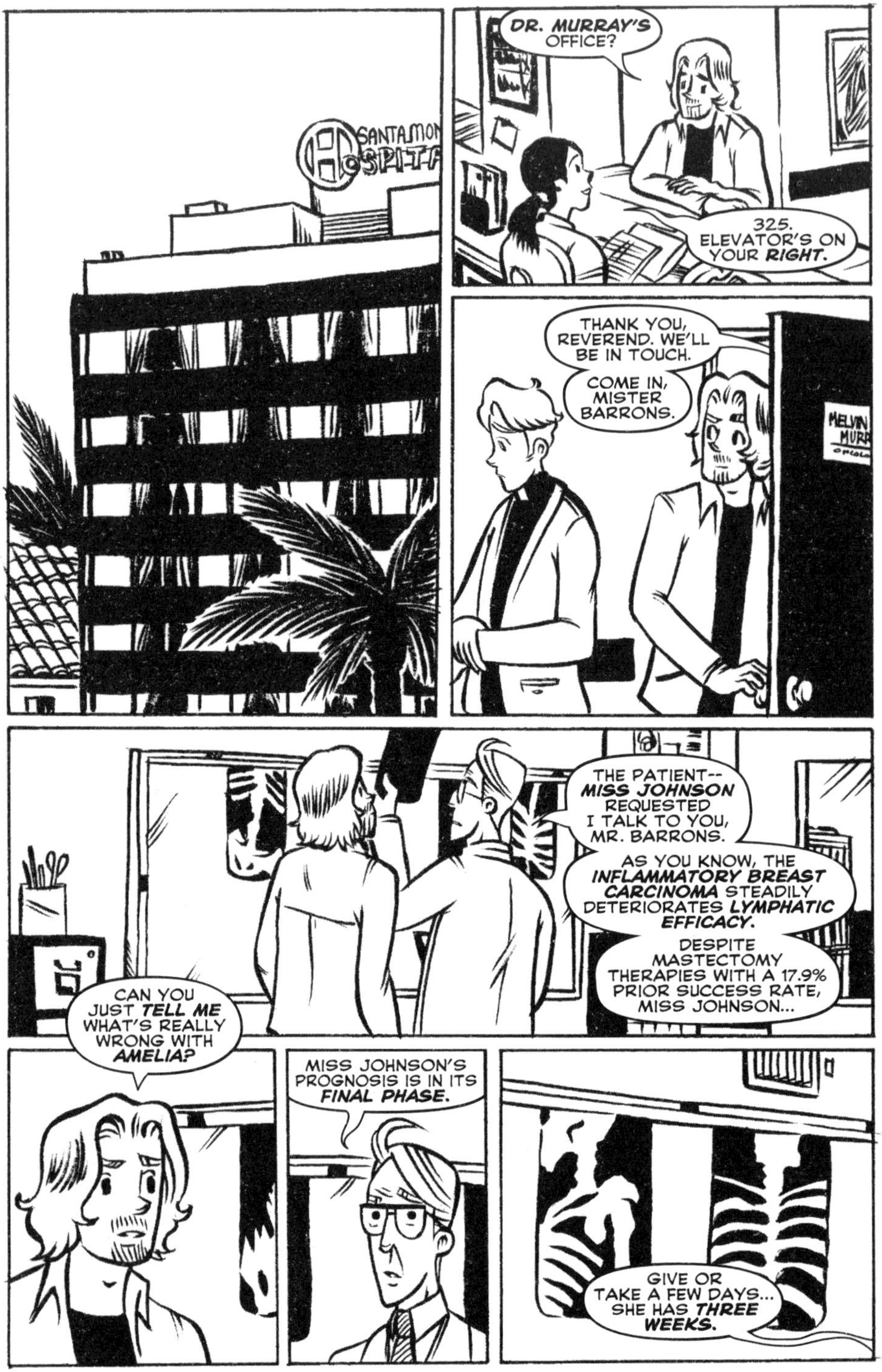
SANTAMON
HOSPITA
DR. MURRAY'S OFFICE?
325. ELEVATOR'S ON YOUR RIGHT.
THANK YOU, REVEREND. WE'LL BE IN TOUCH.
COME IN, MISTER BARRONS.
MELVIN MURR
THE PATIENT-- MISS JOHNSON REQUESTED I TALK TO YOU, MR. BARRONS.
AS YOU KNOW, THE INFLAMMATORY BREAST CARCINOMA STEADILY DETERIORATES LYMPHATIC EFFICACY.
DESPITE MASTECTOMY THERAPIES WITH A 17.9% PRIOR SUCCESS RATE, MISS JOHNSON...
CAN YOU JUST TELL ME WHAT'S REALLY WRONG WITH AMELIA?
MISS JOHNSON'S PROGNOSIS IS IN ITS FINAL PHASE.
GIVE OR TAKE A FEW DAYS... SHE HAS THREE WEEKS.

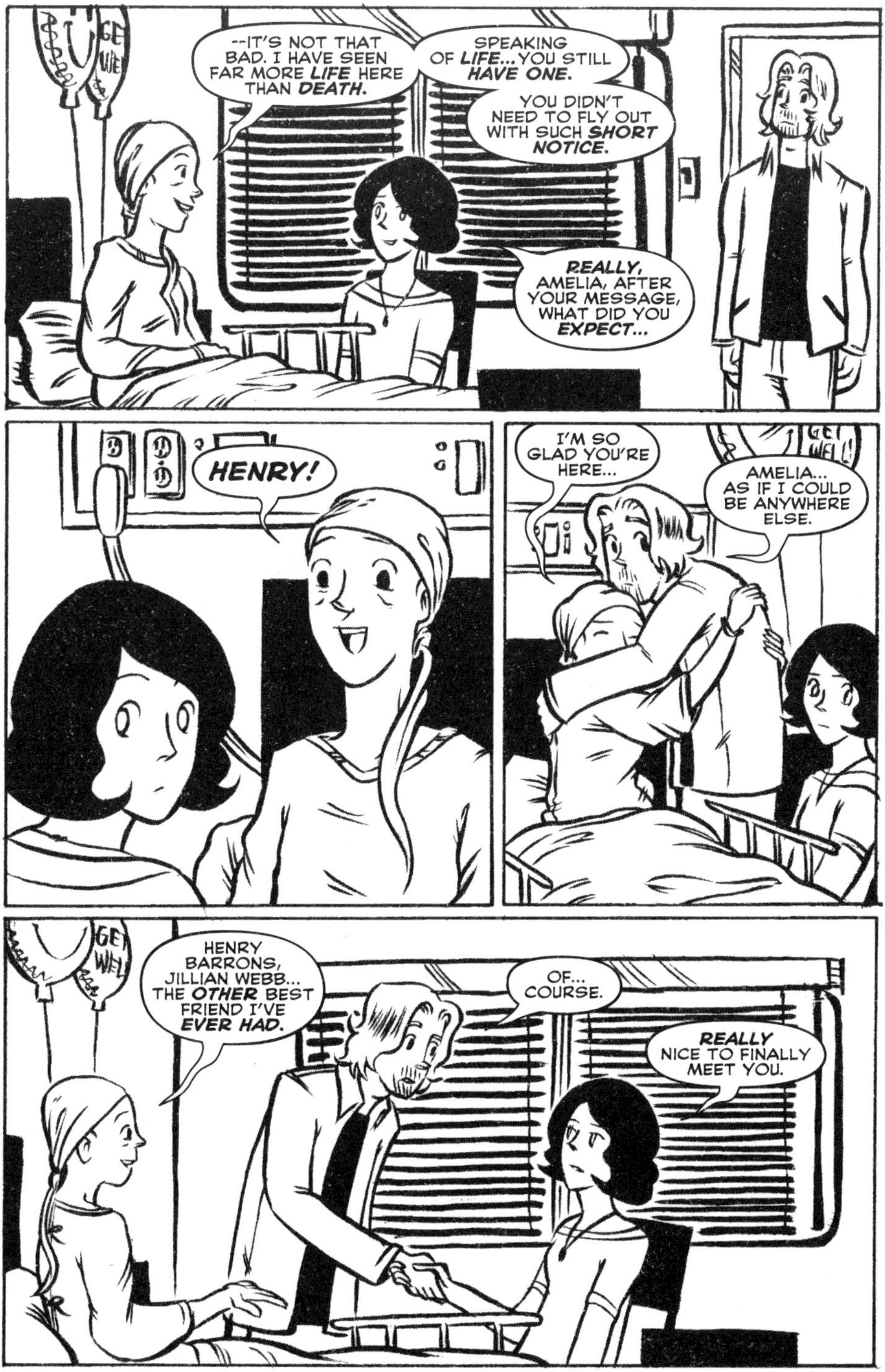
--IT'S NOT THAT BAD. I HAVE SEEN FAR MORE LIFE HERE THAN DEATH.
SPEAKING OF LIFE... YOU STILL HAVE ONE.
YOU DIDN'T NEED TO FLY OUT WITH SUCH SHORT NOTICE.
REALLY, AMELIA, AFTER YOUR MESSAGE, WHAT DID YOU EXPECT...
HENRY!
I'M SO GLAD YOU'RE HERE...
AMELIA... AS IF I COULD BE ANYWHERE ELSE.
HENRY BARRONS, JILLIAN WEBB... THE OTHER BEST FRIEND I'VE EVER HAD.
OF... COURSE.
REALLY NICE TO FINALLY MEET YOU.

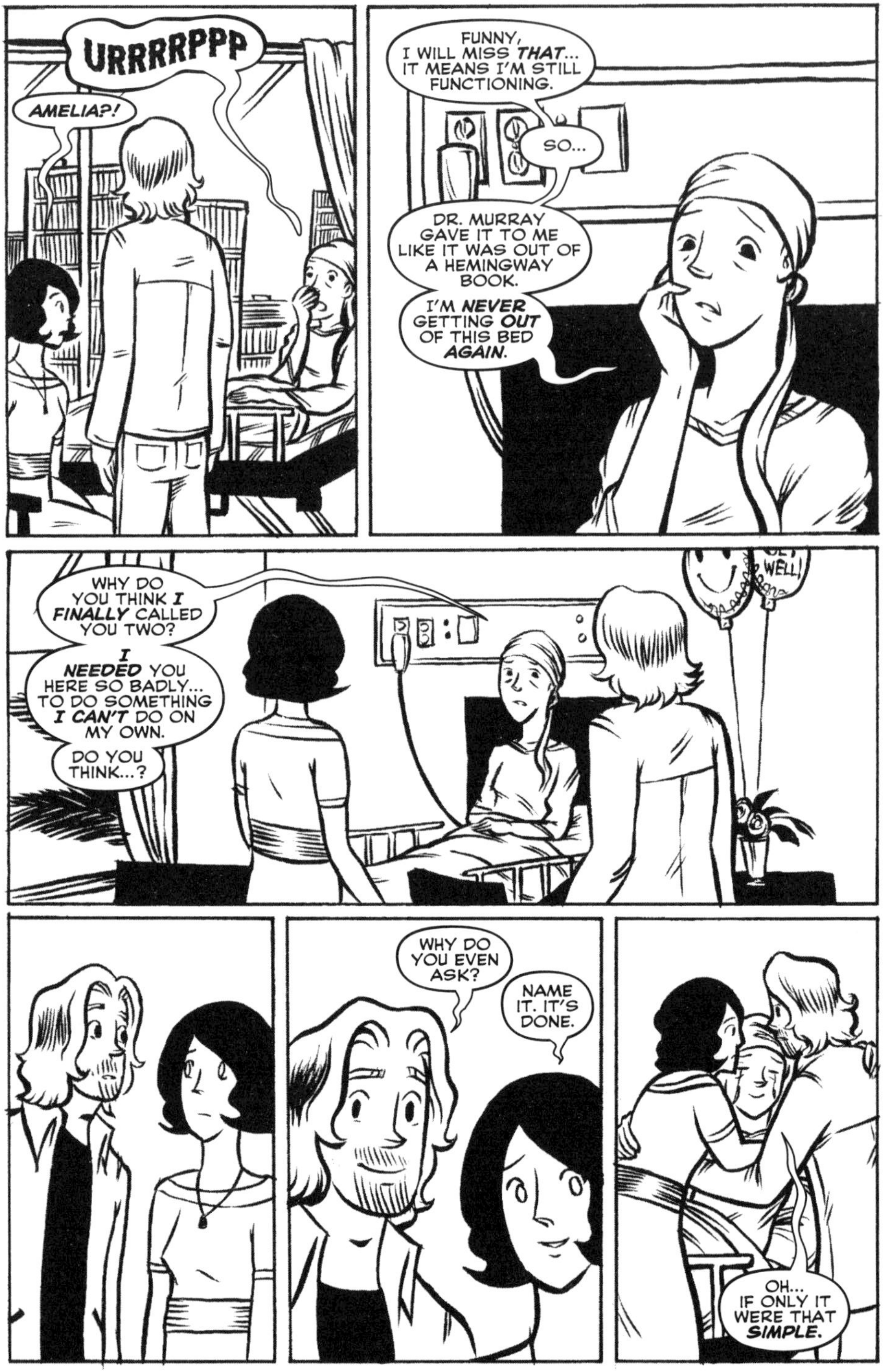
URRRRPPP
AMELIA?!
FUNNY, I WILL MISS THAT... IT MEANS I'M STILL FUNCTIONING.
SO...
DR. MURRAY GAVE IT TO ME LIKE IT WAS OUT OF A HEMINGWAY BOOK.
I'M NEVER GETTING OUT OF THIS BED AGAIN.
WELL!
WHY DO YOU THINK I FINALLY CALLED YOU TWO?
I NEEDED YOU HERE SO BADLY... TO DO SOMETHING I CAN'T DO ON MY OWN.
DO YOU THINK...?
WHY DO YOU EVEN ASK?
NAME IT. IT'S DONE.
OH... IF ONLY IT WERE THAT SIMPLE.

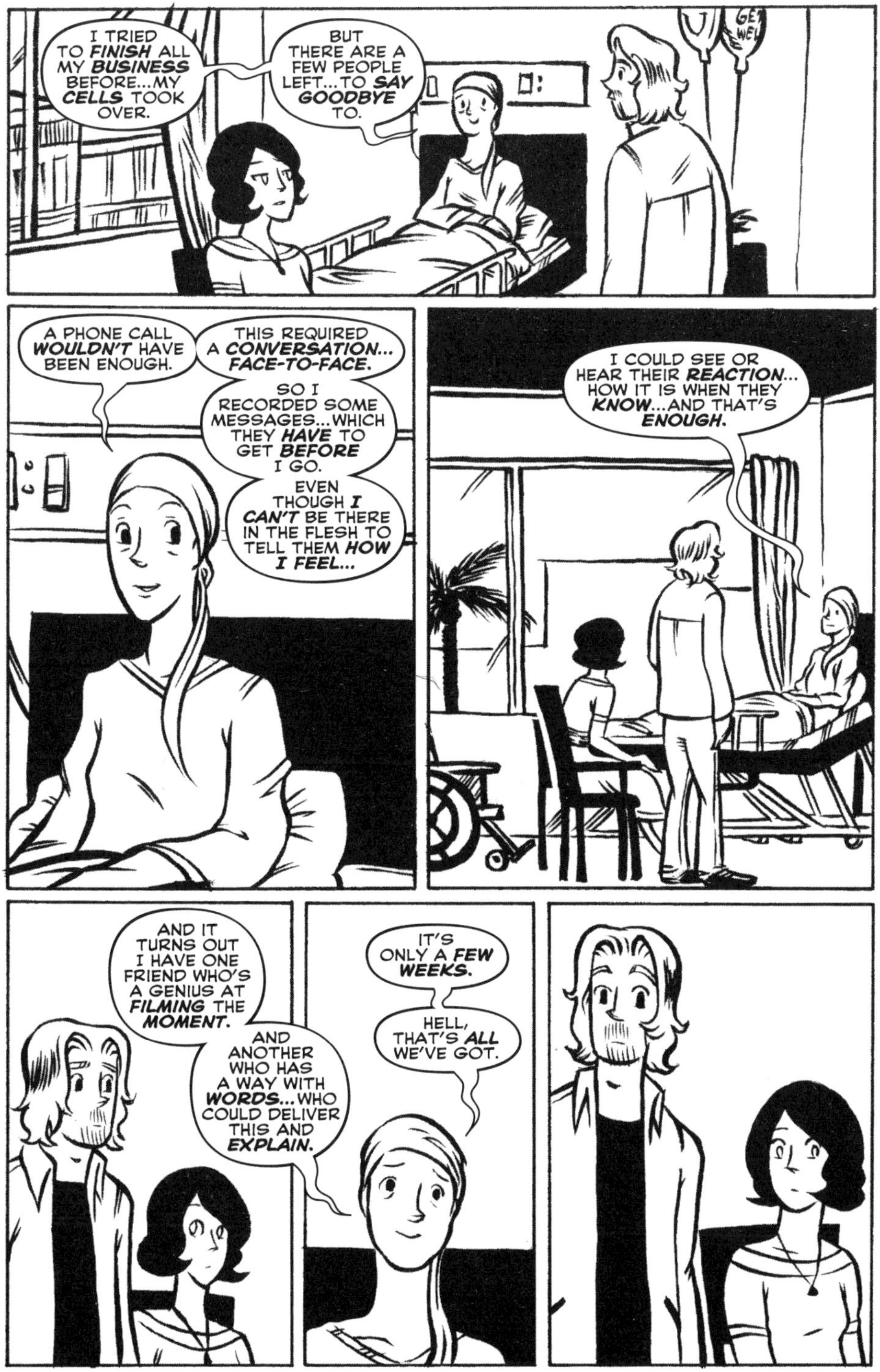
I TRIED TO FINISH ALL MY BUSINESS BEFORE...MY CELLS TOOK OVER.
BUT THERE ARE A FEW PEOPLE LEFT...TO SAY GOODBYE TO.
A PHONE CALL WOULDN'T HAVE BEEN ENOUGH.
THIS REQUIRED A CONVERSATION... FACE-TO-FACE.
SO I RECORDED SOME MESSAGES...WHICH THEY HAVE TO GET BEFORE I GO.
EVEN THOUGH I CAN'T BE THERE IN THE FLESH TO TELL THEM HOW I FEEL...
I COULD SEE OR HEAR THEIR REACTION... HOW IT IS WHEN THEY KNOW...AND THAT'S ENOUGH.
AND IT TURNS OUT I HAVE ONE FRIEND WHO'S A GENIUS AT FILMING THE MOMENT.
AND ANOTHER WHO HAS A WAY WITH WORDS...WHO COULD DELIVER THIS AND EXPLAIN.
IT'S ONLY A FEW WEEKS.
HELL, THAT'S ALL WE'VE GOT.

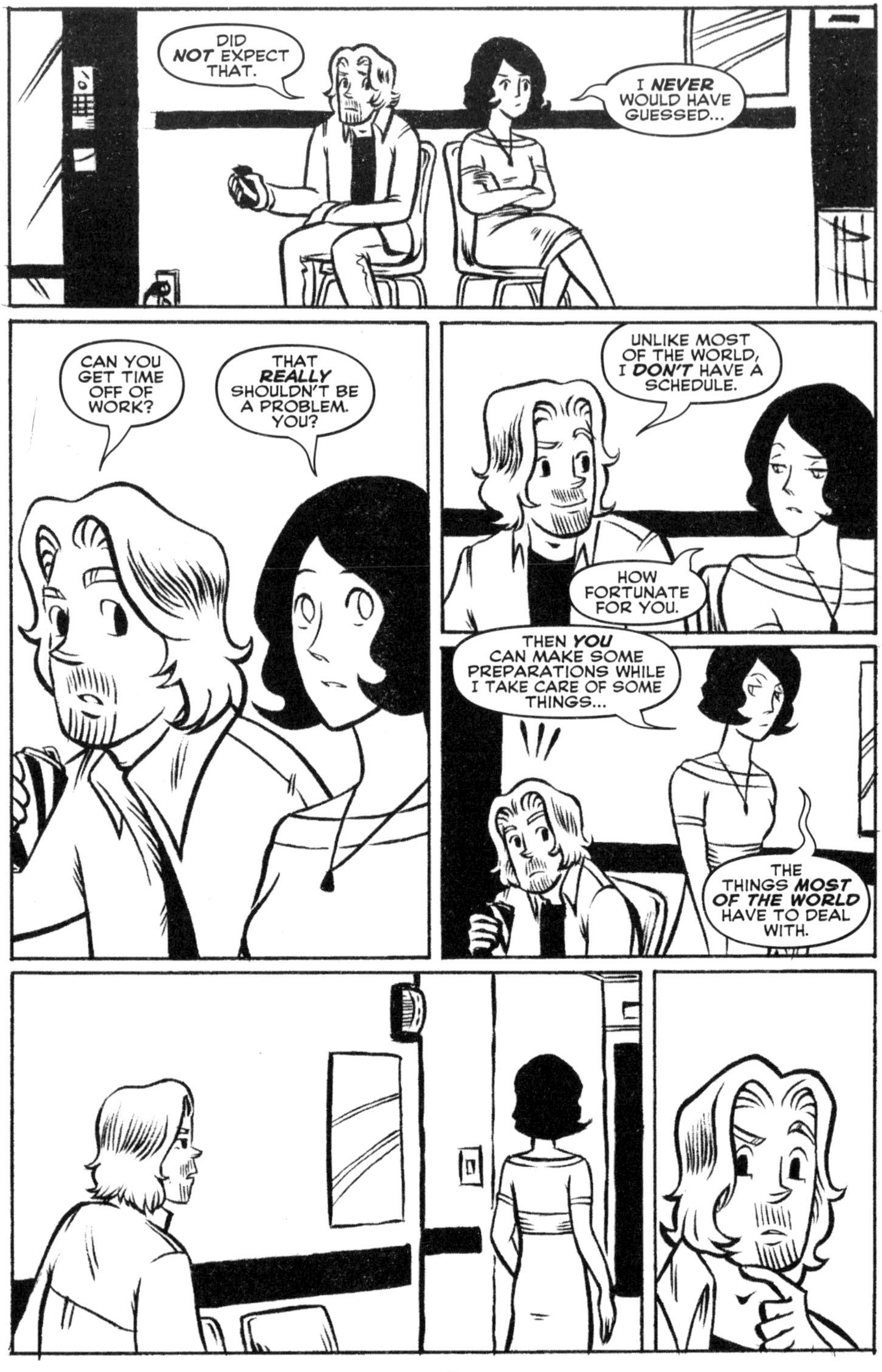
DID NOT EXPECT THAT.
I NEVER WOULD HAVE GUESSED...
CAN YOU GET TIME OFF OF WORK?
THAT REALLY SHOULDN'T BE A PROBLEM. YOU?
UNLIKE MOST OF THE WORLD, I DON'T HAVE A SCHEDULE.
HOW FORTUNATE FOR YOU.
THEN YOU CAN MAKE SOME PREPARATIONS WHILE I TAKE CARE OF SOME THINGS...
THE THINGS MOST OF THE WORLD HAVE TO DEAL WITH.

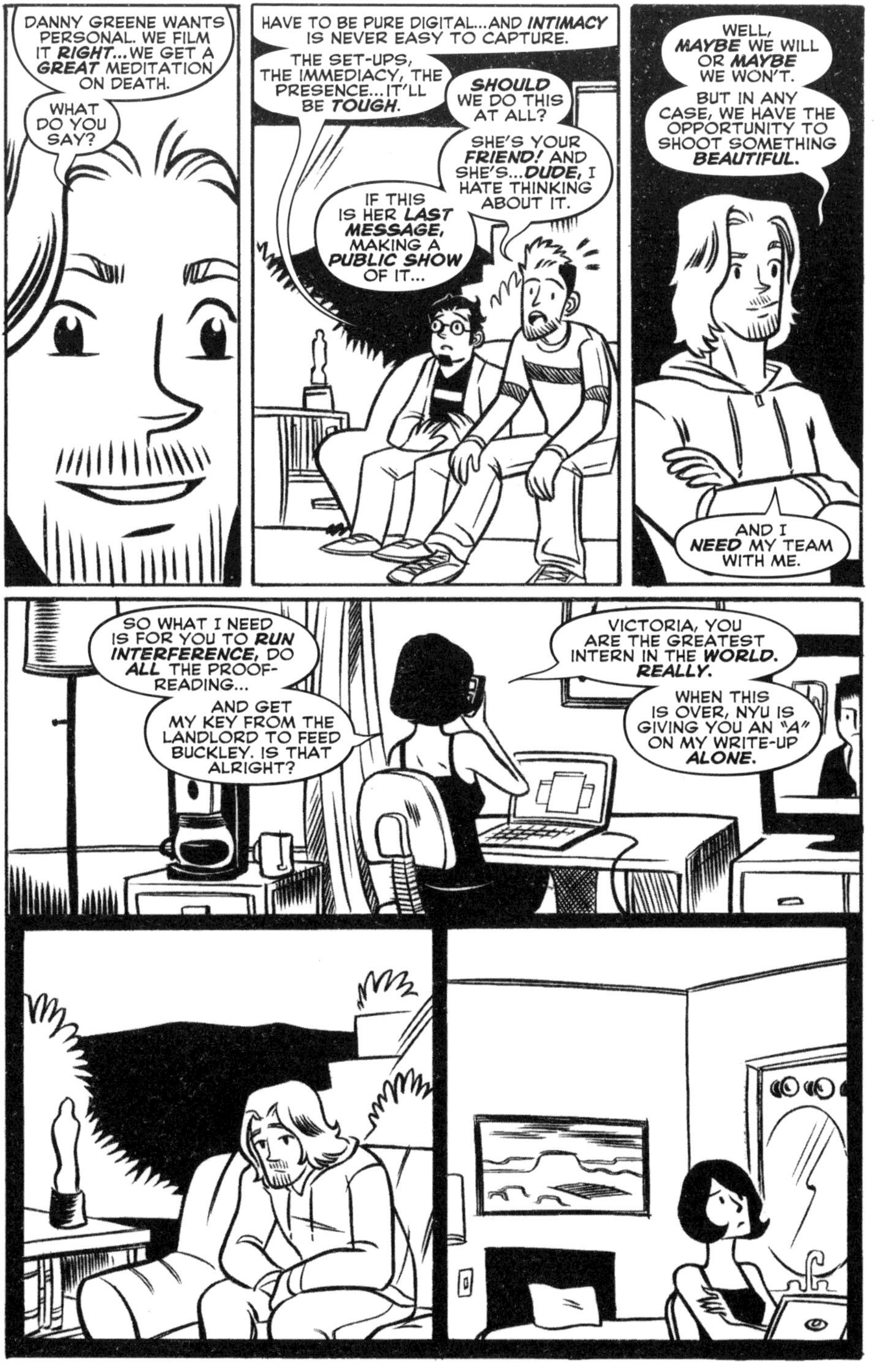
DANNY GREENE WANTS PERSONAL. WE FILM IT RIGHT...WE GET A GREAT MEDITATION ON DEATH.
WHAT DO YOU SAY?
HAVE TO BE PURE DIGITAL...AND INTIMACY IS NEVER EASY TO CAPTURE.
THE SET-UPS, THE IMMEDIACY, THE PRESENCE...IT'LL BE TOUGH.
SHOULD WE DO THIS AT ALL?
SHE'S YOUR FRIEND! AND SHE'S...DUDE, I HATE THINKING ABOUT IT.
IF THIS IS HER LAST MESSAGE, MAKING A PUBLIC SHOW OF IT...
WELL, MAYBE WE WILL OR MAYBE WE WON'T.
BUT IN ANY CASE, WE HAVE THE OPPORTUNITY TO SHOOT SOMETHING BEAUTIFUL.
AND I NEED MY TEAM WITH ME.
SO WHAT I NEED IS FOR YOU TO RUN INTERFERENCE, DO ALL THE PROOF-READING...
AND GET MY KEY FROM THE LANDLORD TO FEED BUCKLEY. IS THAT ALRIGHT?
VICTORIA, YOU ARE THE GREATEST INTERN IN THE WORLD. REALLY.
WHEN THIS IS OVER, NYU IS GIVING YOU AN "A" ON MY WRITE-UP ALONE.

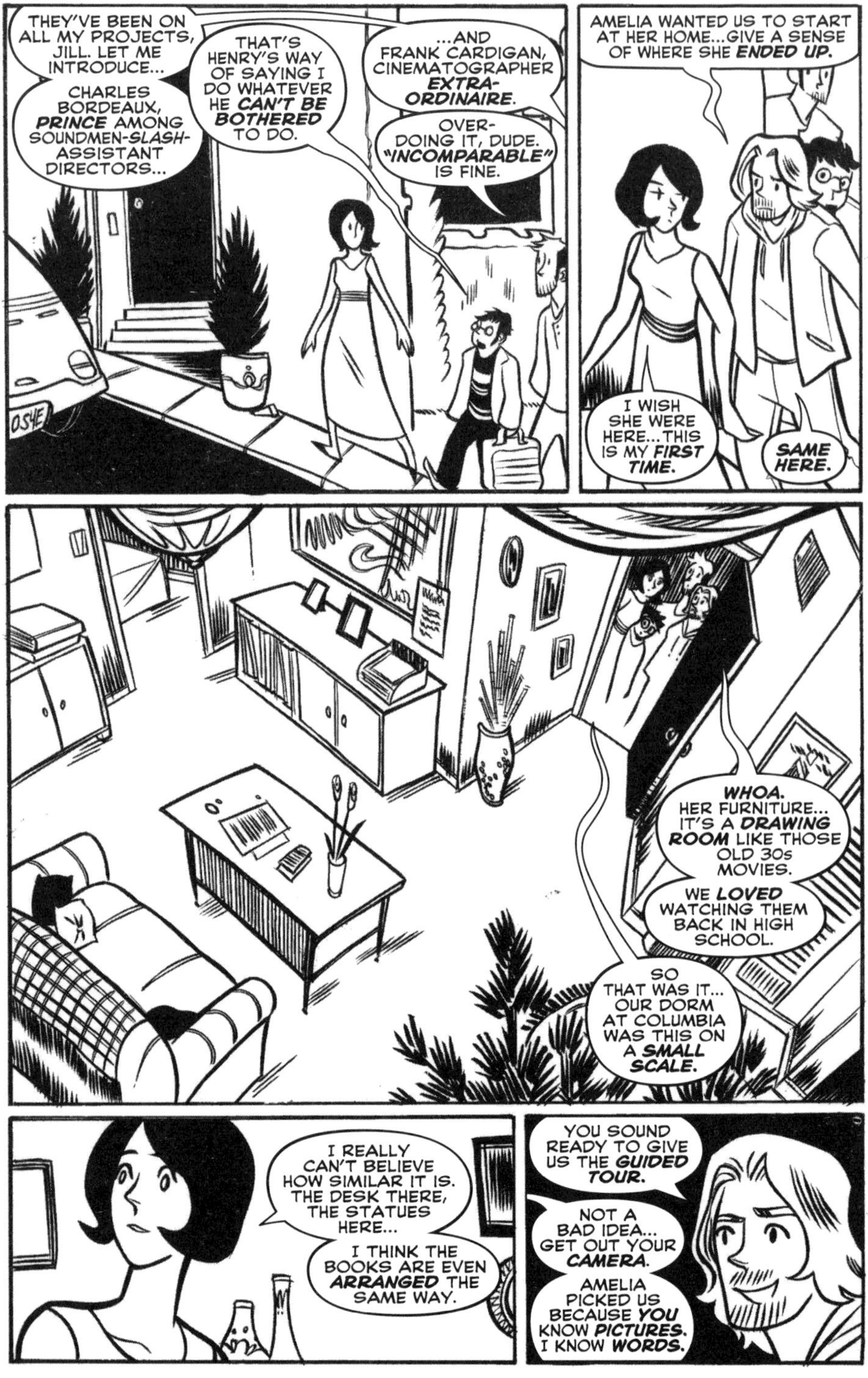
THEY'VE BEEN ON ALL MY PROJECTS, JILL. LET ME INTRODUCE...
CHARLES BORDEAUX, PRINCE AMONG SOUNDMEN-SLASH-ASSISTANT DIRECTORS...
THAT'S HENRY'S WAY OF SAYING I DO WHATEVER HE CAN'T BE BOTHERED TO DO.
...AND FRANK CARDIGAN, CINEMATOGRAPHER EXTRA-ORDINAIRE.
OVER-DOING IT, DUDE. "INCOMPARABLE" IS FINE.
AMELIA WANTED US TO START AT HER HOME...GIVE A SENSE OF WHERE SHE ENDED UP.
I WISH SHE WERE HERE...THIS IS MY FIRST TIME.
SAME HERE.
WHOA. HER FURNITURE... IT'S A DRAWING ROOM LIKE THOSE OLD 30s MOVIES.
WE LOVED WATCHING THEM BACK IN HIGH SCHOOL.
SO THAT WAS IT... OUR DORM AT COLUMBIA WAS THIS ON A SMALL SCALE.
I REALLY CAN'T BELIEVE HOW SIMILAR IT IS. THE DESK THERE, THE STATUES HERE...
I THINK THE BOOKS ARE EVEN ARRANGED THE SAME WAY.
YOU SOUND READY TO GIVE US THE GUIDED TOUR.
NOT A BAD IDEA... GET OUT YOUR CAMERA.
AMELIA PICKED US BECAUSE YOU KNOW PICTURES. I KNOW WORDS.

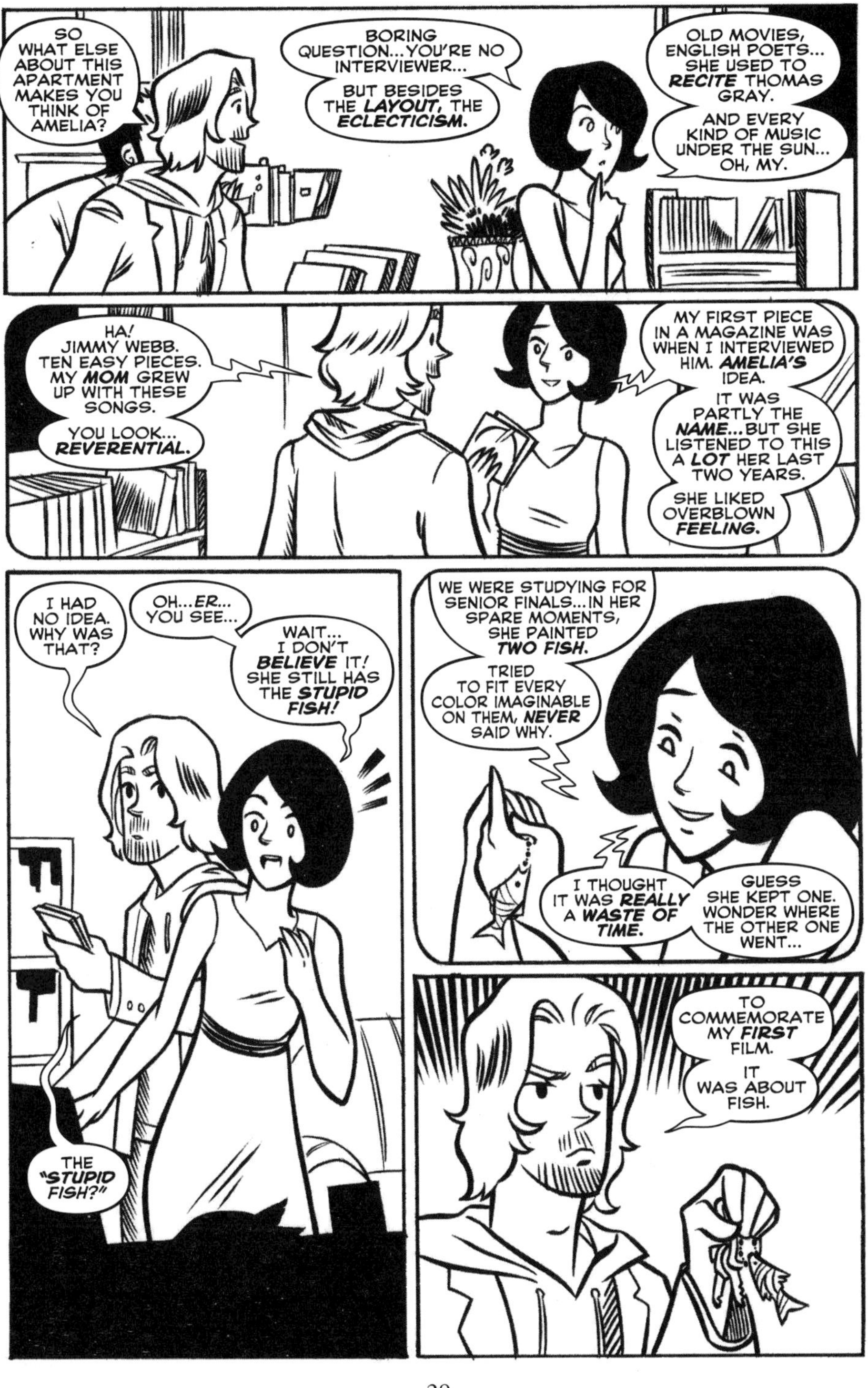
SO WHAT ELSE ABOUT THIS APARTMENT MAKES YOU THINK OF AMELIA?
BORING QUESTION... YOU'RE NO INTERVIEWER...
BUT BESIDES THE LAYOUT, THE ECLECTICISM.
OLD MOVIES, ENGLISH POETS... SHE USED TO RECITE THOMAS GRAY.
AND EVERY KIND OF MUSIC UNDER THE SUN... OH, MY.
HA! JIMMY WEBB. TEN EASY PIECES. MY MOM GREW UP WITH THESE SONGS.
YOU LOOK... REVERENTIAL.
MY FIRST PIECE IN A MAGAZINE WAS WHEN I INTERVIEWED HIM. AMELIA'S IDEA.
IT WAS PARTLY THE NAME... BUT SHE LISTENED TO THIS A LOT HER LAST TWO YEARS.
SHE LIKED OVERBLOWN FEELING.
I HAD NO IDEA. WHY WAS THAT?
OH... ER... YOU SEE...
WAIT... I DON'T BELIEVE IT! SHE STILL HAS THE STUPID FISH!
THE "STUPID FISH?"
WE WERE STUDYING FOR SENIOR FINALS... IN HER SPARE MOMENTS, SHE PAINTED TWO FISH.
TRIED TO FIT EVERY COLOR IMAGINABLE ON THEM, NEVER SAID WHY.
I THOUGHT IT WAS REALLY A WASTE OF TIME.
GUESS SHE KEPT ONE. WONDER WHERE THE OTHER ONE WENT...
TO COMMEMORATE MY FIRST FILM.
IT WAS ABOUT FISH.

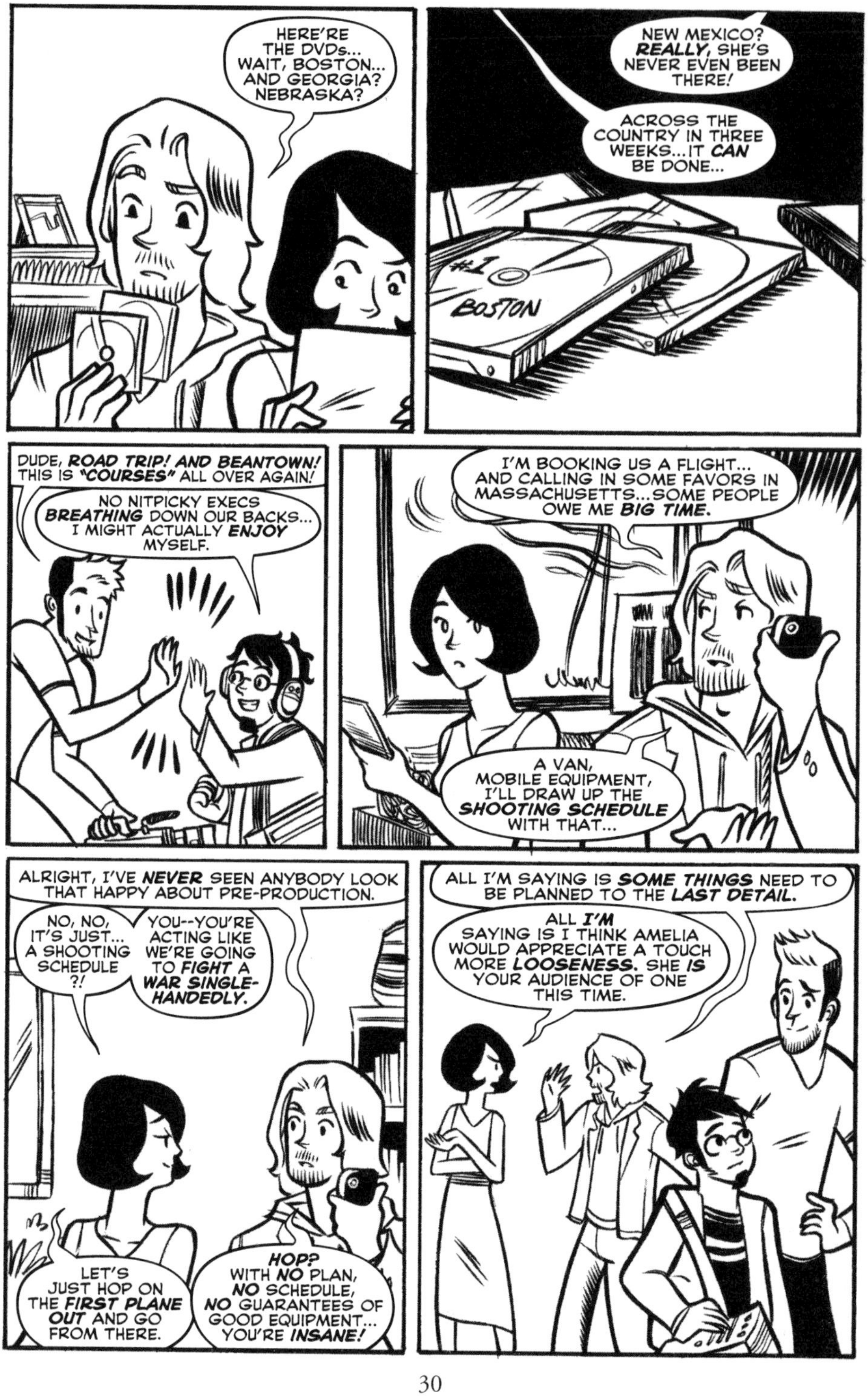
HERE'RE THE DVDs... WAIT, BOSTON... AND GEORGIA? NEBRASKA?
NEW MEXICO? REALLY, SHE'S NEVER EVEN BEEN THERE!
ACROSS THE COUNTRY IN THREE WEEKS...IT CAN BE DONE...
#1 BOSTON
DUDE, ROAD TRIP! AND BEANTOWN! THIS IS "COURSES" ALL OVER AGAIN!
NO NITPICKY EXECS BREATHING DOWN OUR BACKS... I MIGHT ACTUALLY ENJOY MYSELF.
I'M BOOKING US A FLIGHT... AND CALLING IN SOME FAVORS IN MASSACHUSETTS...SOME PEOPLE OWE ME BIG TIME.
A VAN, MOBILE EQUIPMENT, I'LL DRAW UP THE SHOOTING SCHEDULE WITH THAT...
ALRIGHT, I'VE NEVER SEEN ANYBODY LOOK THAT HAPPY ABOUT PRE-PRODUCTION.
NO, NO, IT'S JUST... A SHOOTING SCHEDULE ?!
YOU--YOU'RE ACTING LIKE WE'RE GOING TO FIGHT A WAR SINGLE-HANDEDLY.
LET'S JUST HOP ON THE FIRST PLANE OUT AND GO FROM THERE.
HOP? WITH NO PLAN, NO SCHEDULE, NO GUARANTEES OF GOOD EQUIPMENT... YOU'RE INSANE!
ALL I'M SAYING IS SOME THINGS NEED TO BE PLANNED TO THE LAST DETAIL.
ALL I'M SAYING IS I THINK AMELIA WOULD APPRECIATE A TOUCH MORE LOOSENESS. SHE IS YOUR AUDIENCE OF ONE THIS TIME.

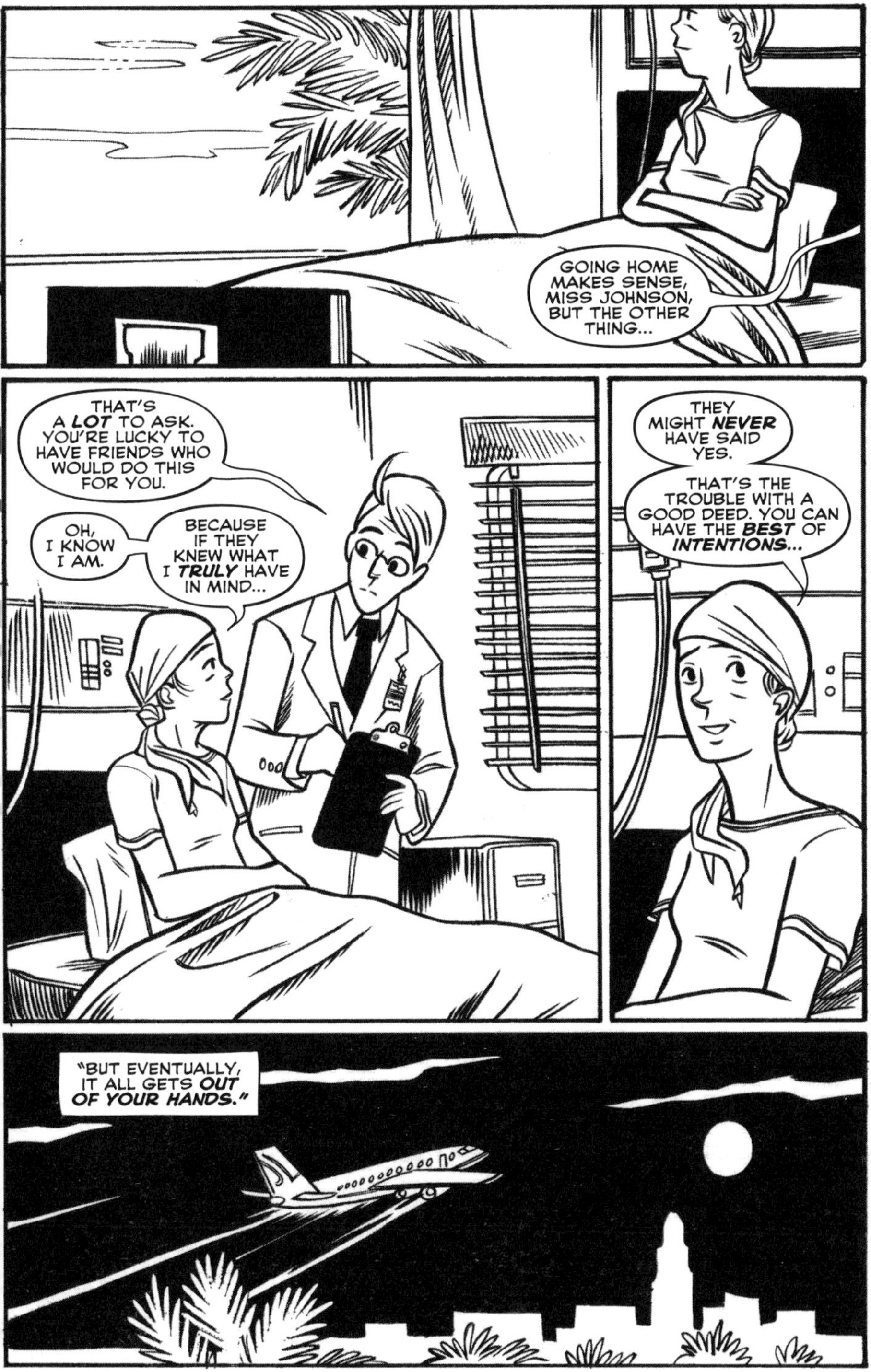
GOING HOME MAKES SENSE, MISS JOHNSON, BUT THE OTHER THING...
THAT'S A LOT TO ASK. YOU'RE LUCKY TO HAVE FRIENDS WHO WOULD DO THIS FOR YOU.
OH, I KNOW I AM.
BECAUSE IF THEY KNEW WHAT I TRULY HAVE IN MIND...
THEY MIGHT NEVER HAVE SAID YES.
THAT'S THE TROUBLE WITH A GOOD DEED. YOU CAN HAVE THE BEST OF INTENTIONS...
"BUT EVENTUALLY, IT ALL GETS OUT OF YOUR HANDS."

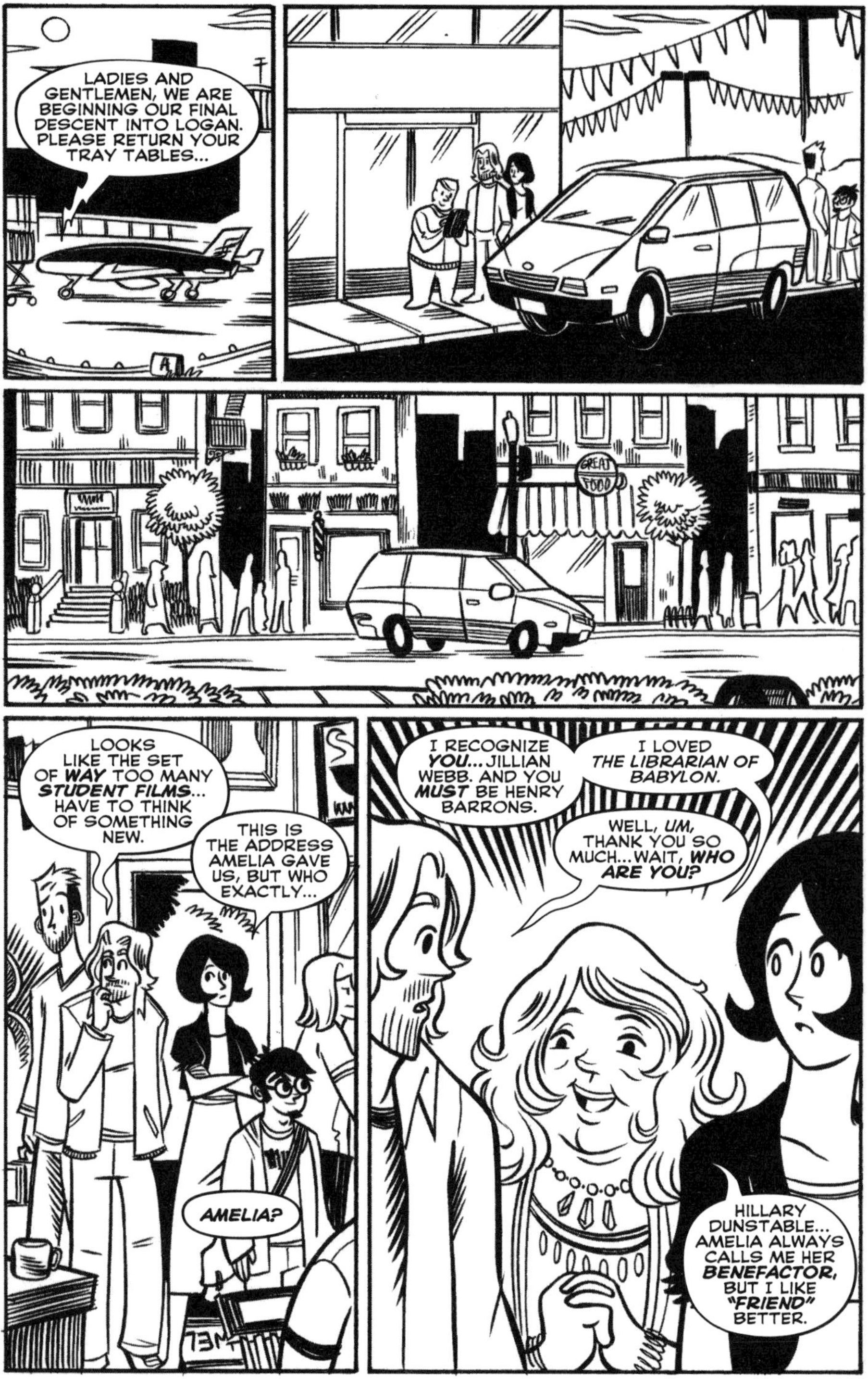
LADIES AND GENTLEMEN, WE ARE BEGINNING OUR FINAL DESCENT INTO LOGAN. PLEASE RETURN YOUR TRAY TABLES...
GREAT FOOD
LOOKS LIKE THE SET OF WAY TOO MANY STUDENT FILMS... HAVE TO THINK OF SOMETHING NEW.
THIS IS THE ADDRESS AMELIA GAVE US, BUT WHO EXACTLY...
AMELIA?
I RECOGNIZE YOU... JILLIAN WEBB. AND YOU MUST BE HENRY BARRONS.
I LOVED THE LIBRARIAN OF BABYLON.
WELL, UM, THANK YOU SO MUCH...WAIT, WHO ARE YOU?
HILLARY DUNSTABLE... AMELIA ALWAYS CALLS ME HER BENEFACTOR, BUT I LIKE "FRIEND" BETTER.

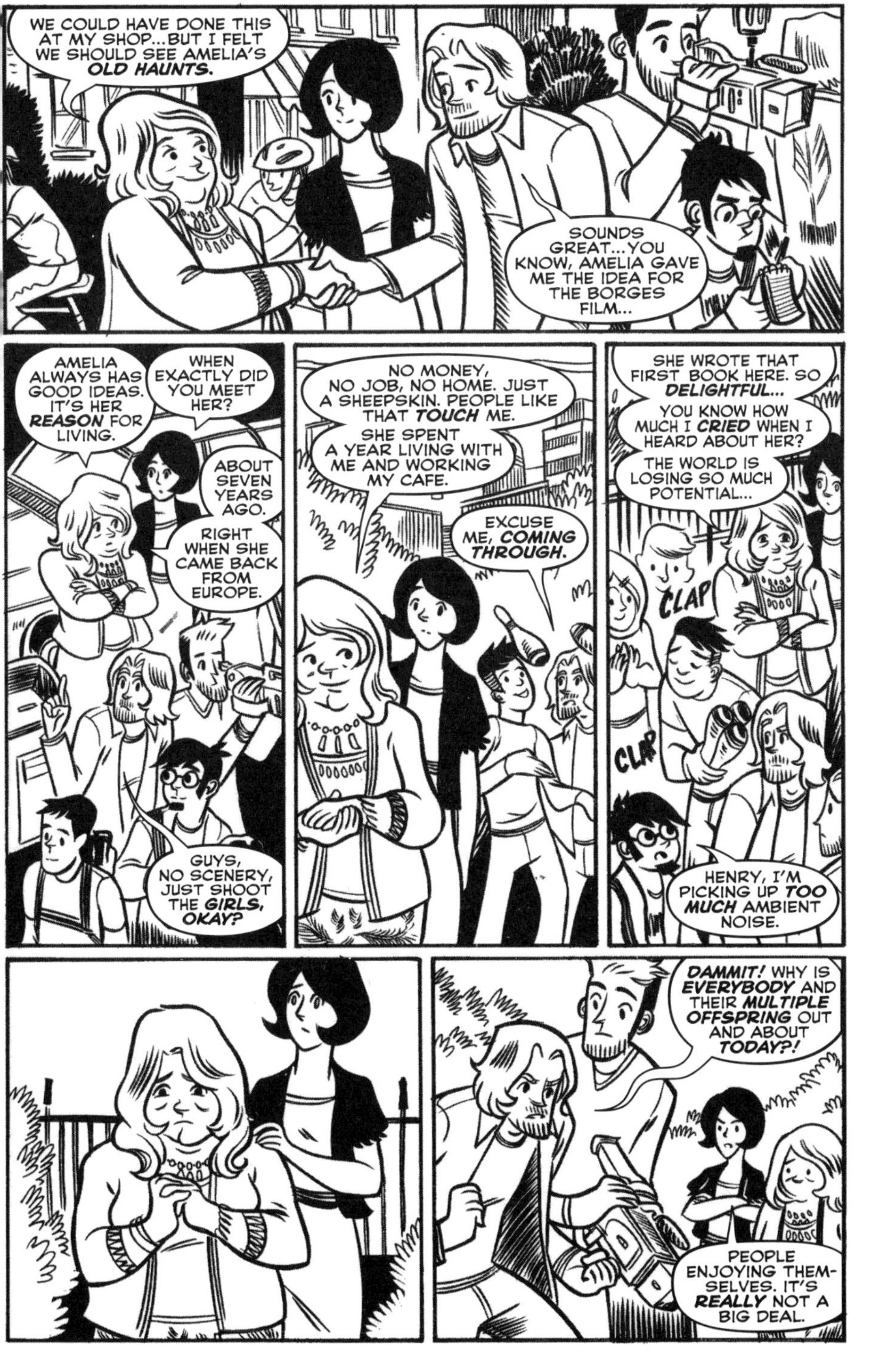
WE COULD HAVE DONE THIS AT MY SHOP...BUT I FELT WE SHOULD SEE AMELIA'S **OLD HAUNTS.**
SOUNDS GREAT...YOU KNOW, AMELIA GAVE ME THE IDEA FOR THE BORGES FILM...
AMELIA ALWAYS HAS GOOD IDEAS. IT'S HER **REASON** FOR LIVING.
WHEN EXACTLY DID YOU MEET HER?
ABOUT SEVEN YEARS AGO.
RIGHT WHEN SHE CAME BACK FROM EUROPE.
GUYS, NO SCENERY, JUST SHOOT THE **GIRLS, OKAY?**
NO MONEY, NO JOB, NO HOME. JUST A SHEEPSKIN. PEOPLE LIKE THAT **TOUCH** ME.
SHE SPENT A YEAR LIVING WITH ME AND WORKING MY CAFE.
EXCUSE ME, **COMING THROUGH.**
SHE WROTE THAT FIRST BOOK HERE. SO **DELIGHTFUL...**
YOU KNOW HOW MUCH I **CRIED** WHEN I HEARD ABOUT HER?
THE WORLD IS LOSING SO MUCH POTENTIAL...
CLAP
CLAP
HENRY, I'M PICKING UP **TOO MUCH** AMBIENT NOISE.
DAMMIT! WHY IS **EVERYBODY** AND THEIR **MULTIPLE OFFSPRING** OUT AND ABOUT **TODAY?!**
PEOPLE ENJOYING THEMSELVES. IT'S **REALLY** NOT A BIG DEAL.

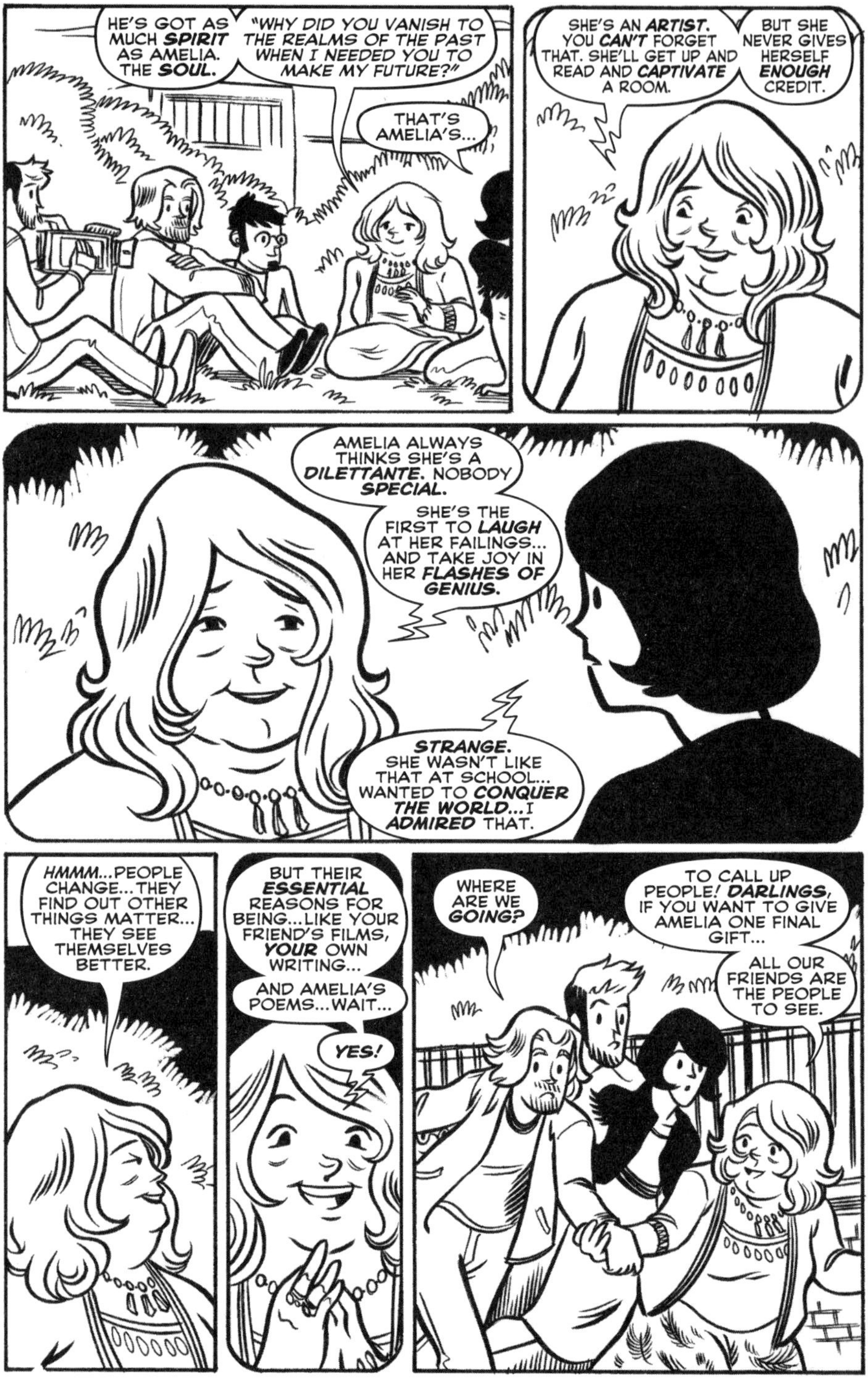
HE'S GOT AS MUCH SPIRIT AS AMELIA. THE SOUL.
"WHY DID YOU VANISH TO THE REALMS OF THE PAST WHEN I NEEDED YOU TO MAKE MY FUTURE?"
THAT'S AMELIA'S...
SHE'S AN ARTIST. YOU CAN'T FORGET THAT. SHE'LL GET UP AND READ AND CAPTIVATE A ROOM.
BUT SHE NEVER GIVES HERSELF ENOUGH CREDIT.
AMELIA ALWAYS THINKS SHE'S A DILETTANTE. NOBODY SPECIAL.
SHE'S THE FIRST TO LAUGH AT HER FAILINGS... AND TAKE JOY IN HER FLASHES OF GENIUS.
STRANGE. SHE WASN'T LIKE THAT AT SCHOOL... WANTED TO CONQUER THE WORLD... I ADMIRED THAT.
HMMM... PEOPLE CHANGE... THEY FIND OUT OTHER THINGS MATTER... THEY SEE THEMSELVES BETTER.
BUT THEIR ESSENTIAL REASONS FOR BEING... LIKE YOUR FRIEND'S FILMS, YOUR OWN WRITING...
AND AMELIA'S POEMS... WAIT...
YES!
WHERE ARE WE GOING?
TO CALL UP PEOPLE! DARLINGS, IF YOU WANT TO GIVE AMELIA ONE FINAL GIFT...
ALL OUR FRIENDS ARE THE PEOPLE TO SEE.

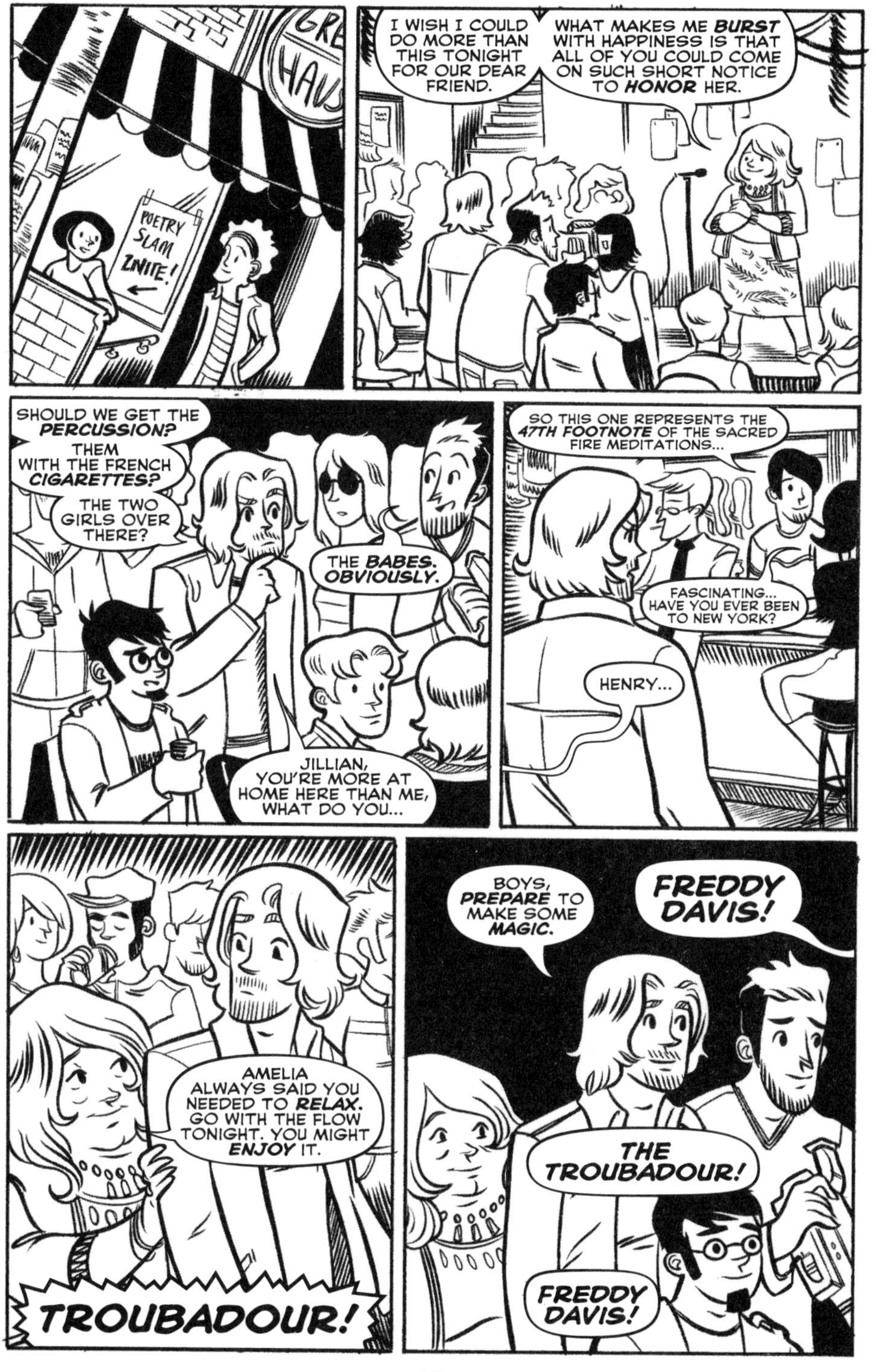

POETRY SLAM 2NITE!
I WISH I COULD DO MORE THAN THIS TONIGHT FOR OUR DEAR FRIEND.
WHAT MAKES ME BURST WITH HAPPINESS IS THAT ALL OF YOU COULD COME ON SUCH SHORT NOTICE TO HONOR HER.
SHOULD WE GET THE PERCUSSION?
THEM WITH THE FRENCH CIGARETTES?
THE TWO GIRLS OVER THERE?
THE BABES. OBVIOUSLY.
JILLIAN, YOU'RE MORE AT HOME HERE THAN ME, WHAT DO YOU...
SO THIS ONE REPRESENTS THE 47TH FOOTNOTE OF THE SACRED FIRE MEDITATIONS...
FASCINATING... HAVE YOU EVER BEEN TO NEW YORK?
HENRY...
AMELIA ALWAYS SAID YOU NEEDED TO RELAX. GO WITH THE FLOW TONIGHT. YOU MIGHT ENJOY IT.
TROUBADOUR!
BOYS, PREPARE TO MAKE SOME MAGIC.
FREDDY DAVIS!
THE TROUBADOUR!
FREDDY DAVIS!

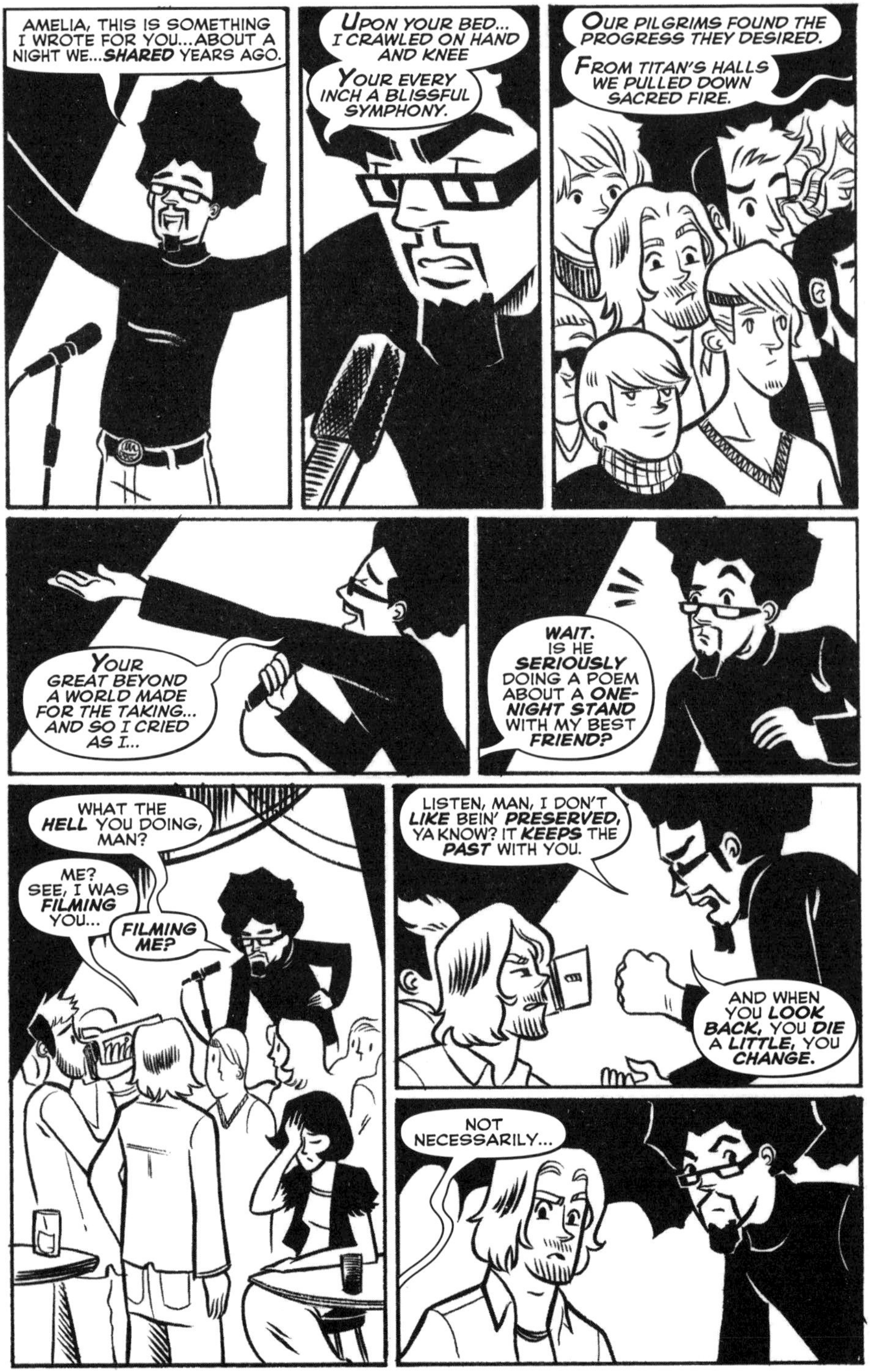
AMELIA, THIS IS SOMETHING I WROTE FOR YOU...ABOUT A NIGHT WE...SHARED YEARS AGO.
UPON YOUR BED... I CRAWLED ON HAND AND KNEE
YOUR EVERY INCH A BLISSFUL SYMPHONY.
OUR PILGRIMS FOUND THE PROGRESS THEY DESIRED.
FROM TITAN'S HALLS WE PULLED DOWN SACRED FIRE.
YOUR GREAT BEYOND A WORLD MADE FOR THE TAKING... AND SO I CRIED AS I...
WAIT. IS HE SERIOUSLY DOING A POEM ABOUT A ONE-NIGHT STAND WITH MY BEST FRIEND?
WHAT THE HELL YOU DOING, MAN?
ME? SEE, I WAS FILMING YOU...
FILMING ME?
LISTEN, MAN, I DON'T LIKE BEIN' PRESERVED, YA KNOW? IT KEEPS THE PAST WITH YOU.
AND WHEN YOU LOOK BACK, YOU DIE A LITTLE, YOU CHANGE.
NOT NECESSARILY...

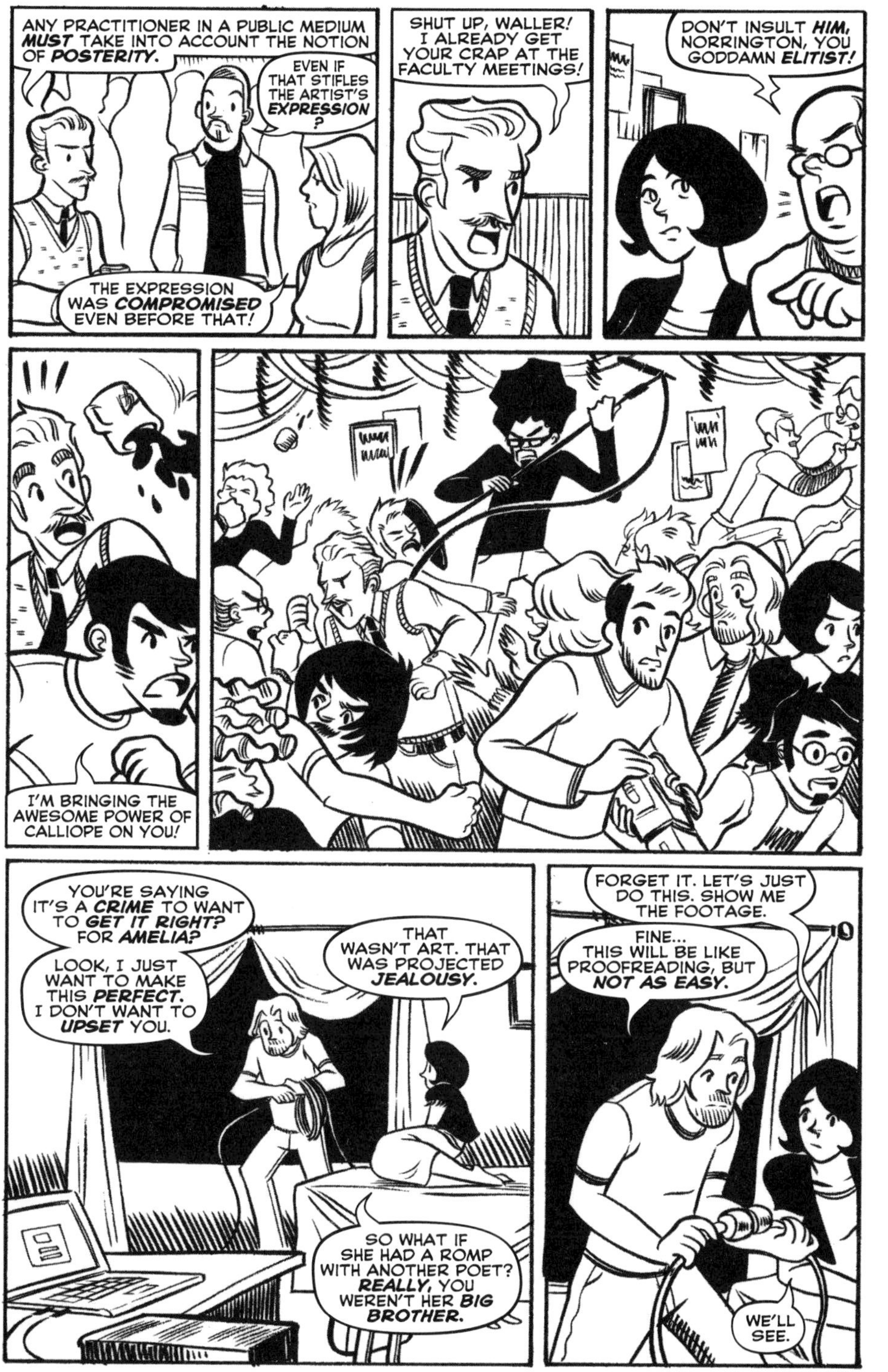
ANY PRACTITIONER IN A PUBLIC MEDIUM MUST TAKE INTO ACCOUNT THE NOTION OF POSTERITY.
EVEN IF THAT STIFLES THE ARTIST'S EXPRESSION?
THE EXPRESSION WAS COMPROMISED EVEN BEFORE THAT!
SHUT UP, WALLER! I ALREADY GET YOUR CRAP AT THE FACULTY MEETINGS!
DON'T INSULT HIM, NORRINGTON, YOU GODDAMN ELITIST!
I'M BRINGING THE AWESOME POWER OF CALLIOPE ON YOU!
YOU'RE SAYING IT'S A CRIME TO WANT TO GET IT RIGHT? FOR AMELIA?
LOOK, I JUST WANT TO MAKE THIS PERFECT. I DON'T WANT TO UPSET YOU.
THAT WASN'T ART. THAT WAS PROJECTED JEALOUSY.
SO WHAT IF SHE HAD A ROMP WITH ANOTHER POET? REALLY, YOU WEREN'T HER BIG BROTHER.
FORGET IT. LET'S JUST DO THIS. SHOW ME THE FOOTAGE.
FINE... THIS WILL BE LIKE PROOFREADING, BUT NOT AS EASY.
WE'LL SEE.

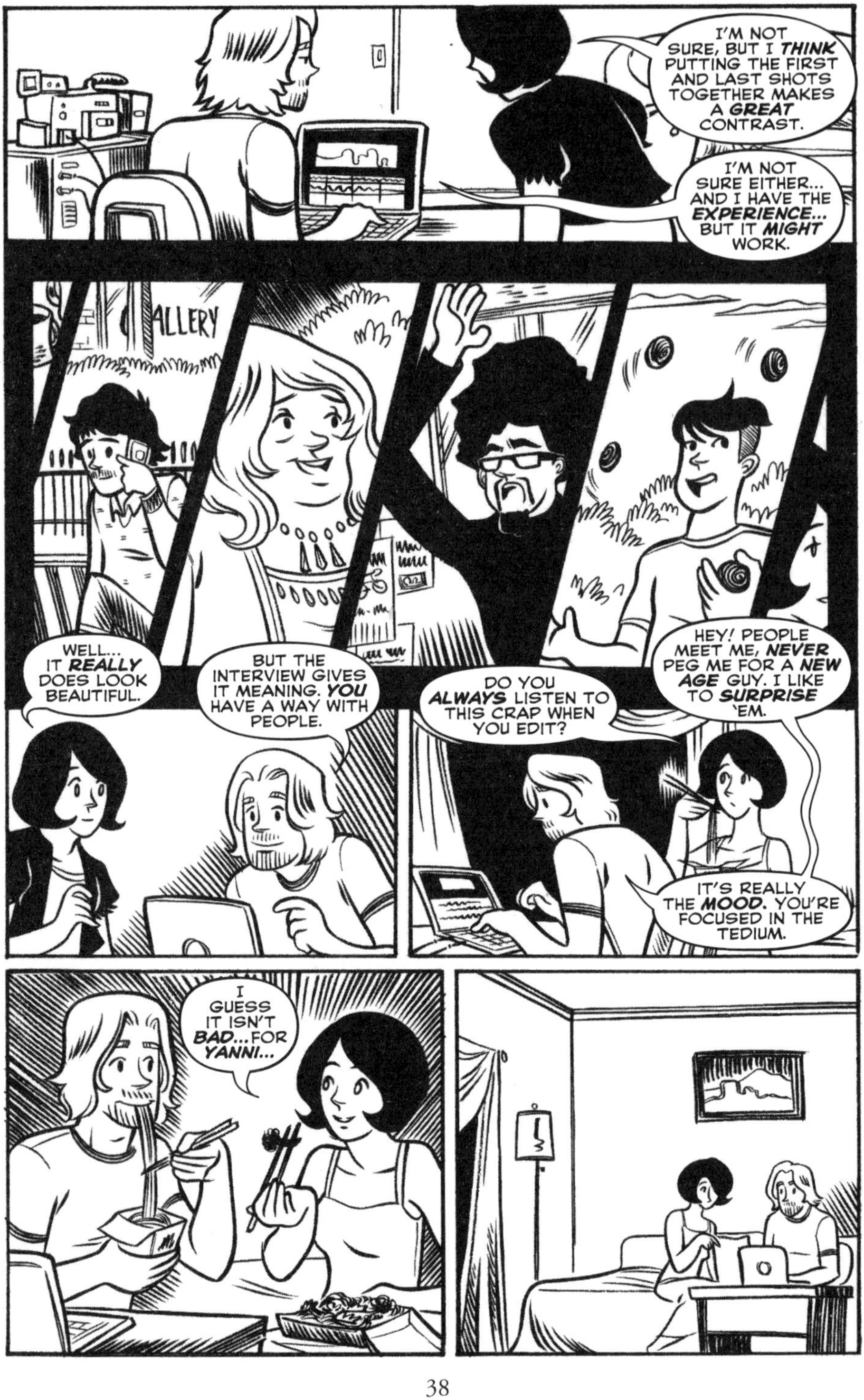
I'M NOT SURE, BUT I THINK PUTTING THE FIRST AND LAST SHOTS TOGETHER MAKES A GREAT CONTRAST.
I'M NOT SURE EITHER... AND I HAVE THE EXPERIENCE... BUT IT MIGHT WORK.
ALLERY
WELL... IT REALLY DOES LOOK BEAUTIFUL.
BUT THE INTERVIEW GIVES IT MEANING. YOU HAVE A WAY WITH PEOPLE.
DO YOU ALWAYS LISTEN TO THIS CRAP WHEN YOU EDIT?
HEY! PEOPLE MEET ME, NEVER PEG ME FOR A NEW AGE GUY. I LIKE TO SURPRISE 'EM.
IT'S REALLY THE MOOD. YOU'RE FOCUSED IN THE TEDIUM.
I GUESS IT ISN'T BAD...FOR YANNI...

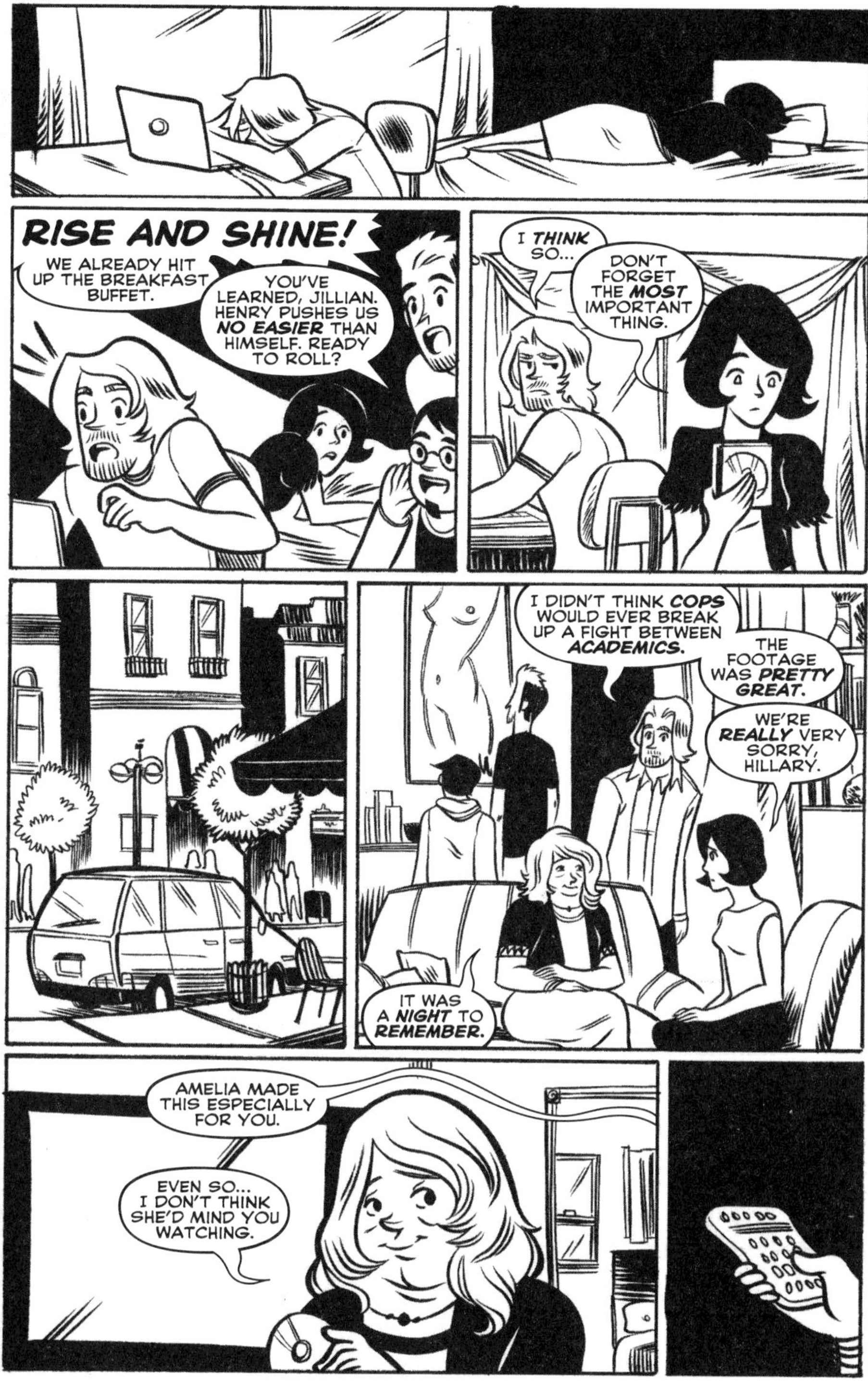
RISE AND SHINE!
WE ALREADY HIT UP THE BREAKFAST BUFFET.
YOU'VE LEARNED, JILLIAN. HENRY PUSHES US NO EASIER THAN HIMSELF. READY TO ROLL?
I THINK SO...
DON'T FORGET THE MOST IMPORTANT THING.
I DIDN'T THINK COPS WOULD EVER BREAK UP A FIGHT BETWEEN ACADEMICS.
THE FOOTAGE WAS PRETTY GREAT.
WE'RE REALLY VERY SORRY, HILLARY.
IT WAS A NIGHT TO REMEMBER.
AMELIA MADE THIS ESPECIALLY FOR YOU.
EVEN SO... I DON'T THINK SHE'D MIND YOU WATCHING.

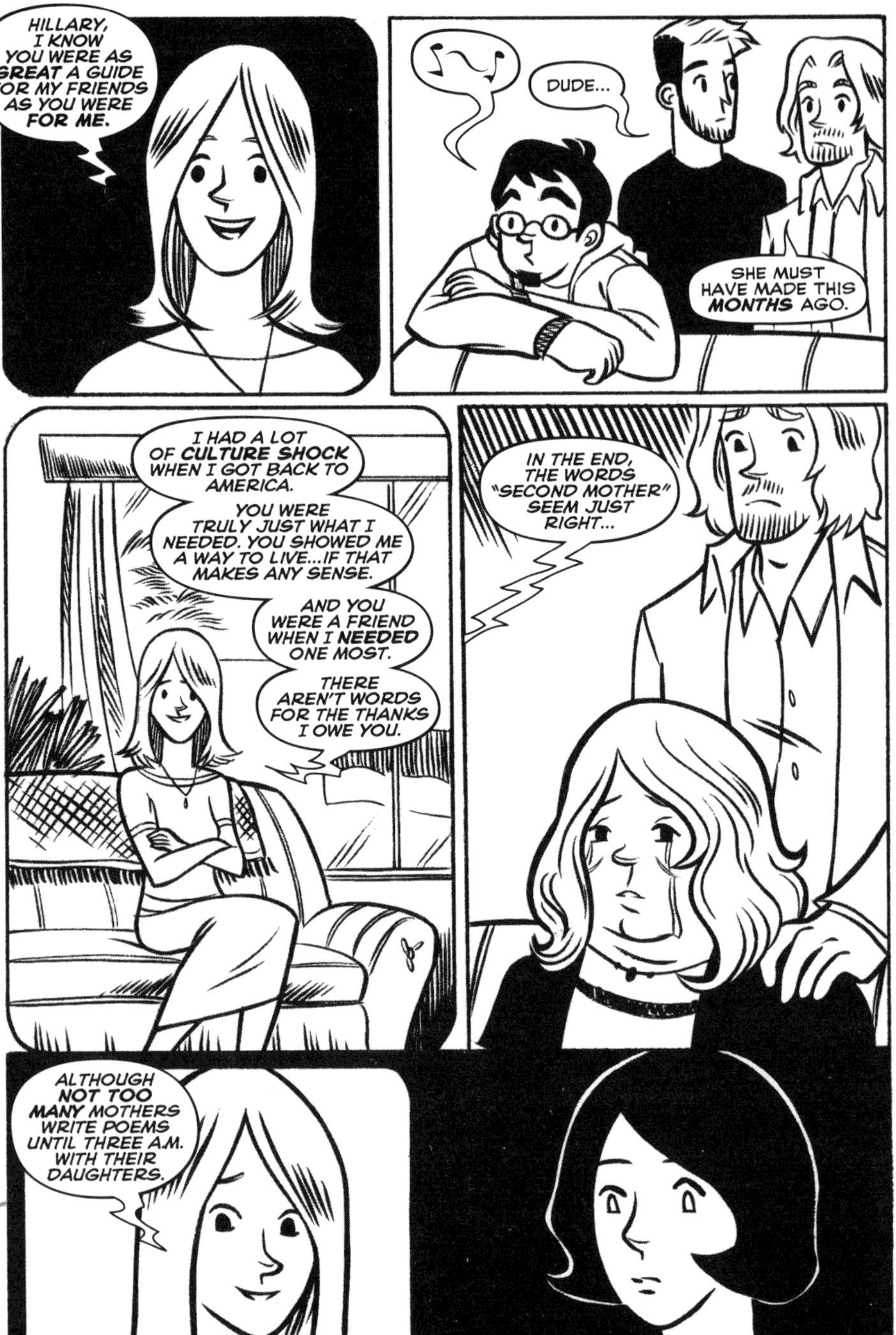
HILLARY, I KNOW YOU WERE AS GREAT A GUIDE FOR MY FRIENDS AS YOU WERE FOR ME.
DUDE...
SHE MUST HAVE MADE THIS MONTHS AGO.
I HAD A LOT OF CULTURE SHOCK WHEN I GOT BACK TO AMERICA.
YOU WERE TRULY JUST WHAT I NEEDED. YOU SHOWED ME A WAY TO LIVE...IF THAT MAKES ANY SENSE.
AND YOU WERE A FRIEND WHEN I NEEDED ONE MOST.
THERE AREN'T WORDS FOR THE THANKS I OWE YOU.
IN THE END, THE WORDS "SECOND MOTHER" SEEM JUST RIGHT...
ALTHOUGH NOT TOO MANY MOTHERS WRITE POEMS UNTIL THREE A.M. WITH THEIR DAUGHTERS.

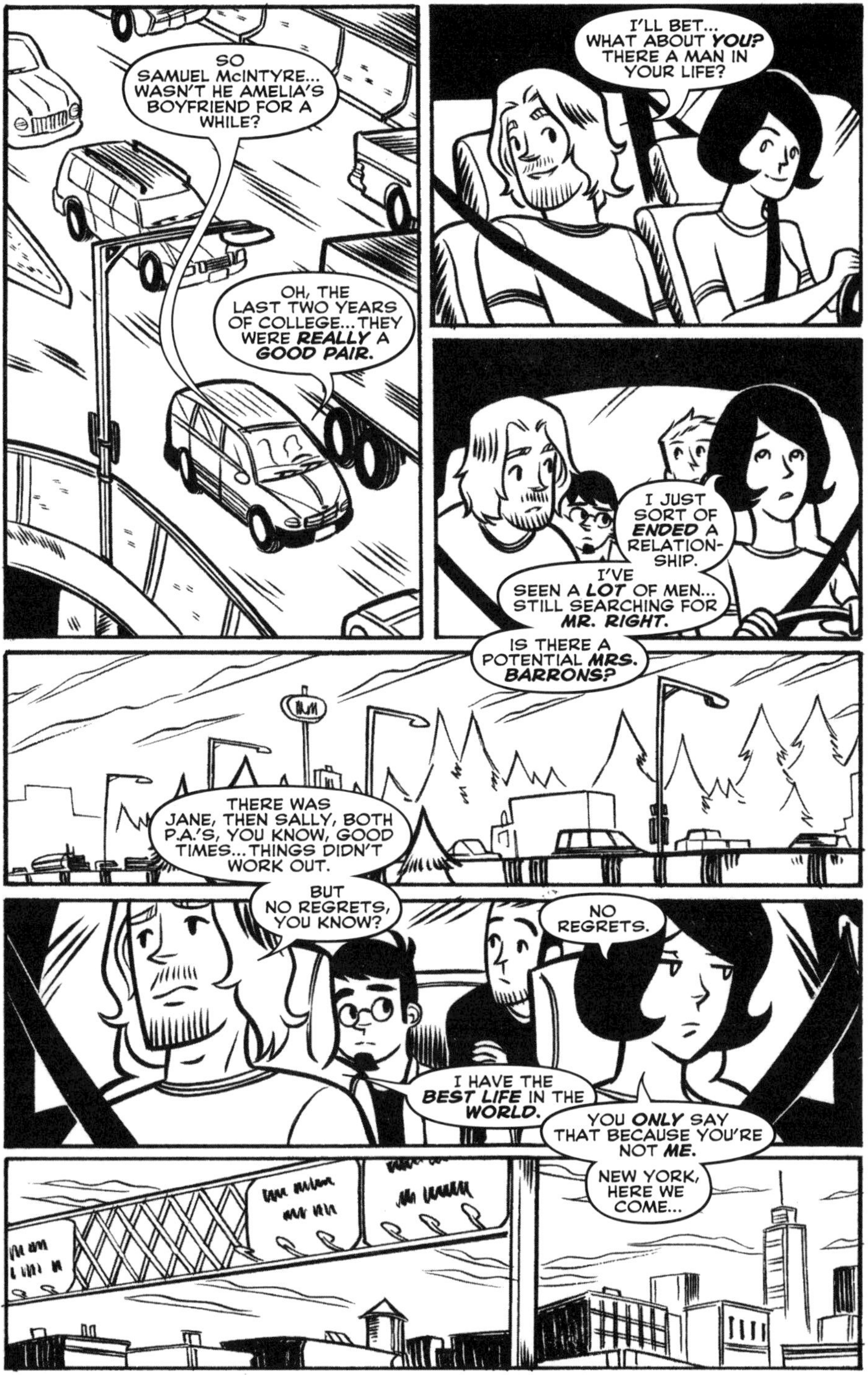
SO SAMUEL McINTYRE... WASN'T HE AMELIA'S BOYFRIEND FOR A WHILE?
OH, THE LAST TWO YEARS OF COLLEGE... THEY WERE REALLY A GOOD PAIR.
I'LL BET... WHAT ABOUT YOU? THERE A MAN IN YOUR LIFE?
I JUST SORT OF ENDED A RELATIONSHIP.
I'VE SEEN A LOT OF MEN... STILL SEARCHING FOR MR. RIGHT.
IS THERE A POTENTIAL MRS. BARRONS?
THERE WAS JANE, THEN SALLY, BOTH P.A.'S, YOU KNOW, GOOD TIMES... THINGS DIDN'T WORK OUT.
BUT NO REGRETS, YOU KNOW?
NO REGRETS.
I HAVE THE BEST LIFE IN THE WORLD.
YOU ONLY SAY THAT BECAUSE YOU'RE NOT ME.
NEW YORK, HERE WE COME...

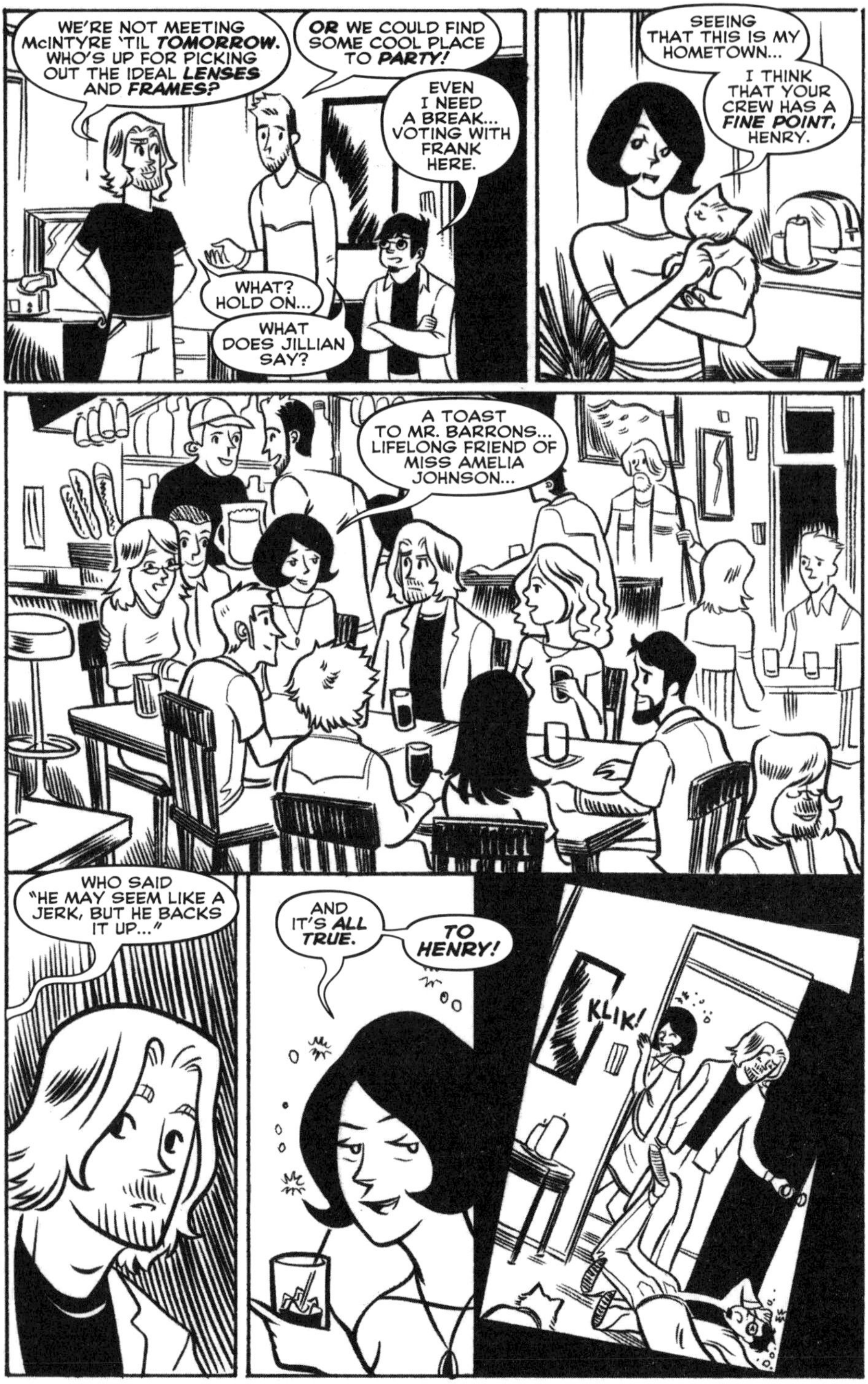
WE'RE NOT MEETING McINTYRE 'TIL **TOMORROW.** WHO'S UP FOR PICKING OUT THE IDEAL **LENSES** AND **FRAMES?**
OR WE COULD FIND SOME COOL PLACE TO **PARTY!**
EVEN I NEED A BREAK... VOTING WITH FRANK HERE.
WHAT? HOLD ON...
WHAT DOES JILLIAN SAY?
SEEING THAT THIS IS MY HOMETOWN...
I THINK THAT YOUR CREW HAS A **FINE POINT,** HENRY.
A TOAST TO MR. BARRONS... LIFELONG FRIEND OF MISS AMELIA JOHNSON...
WHO SAID "HE MAY SEEM LIKE A JERK, BUT HE BACKS IT UP..."
AND IT'S **ALL TRUE.**
TO HENRY!
KLIK!

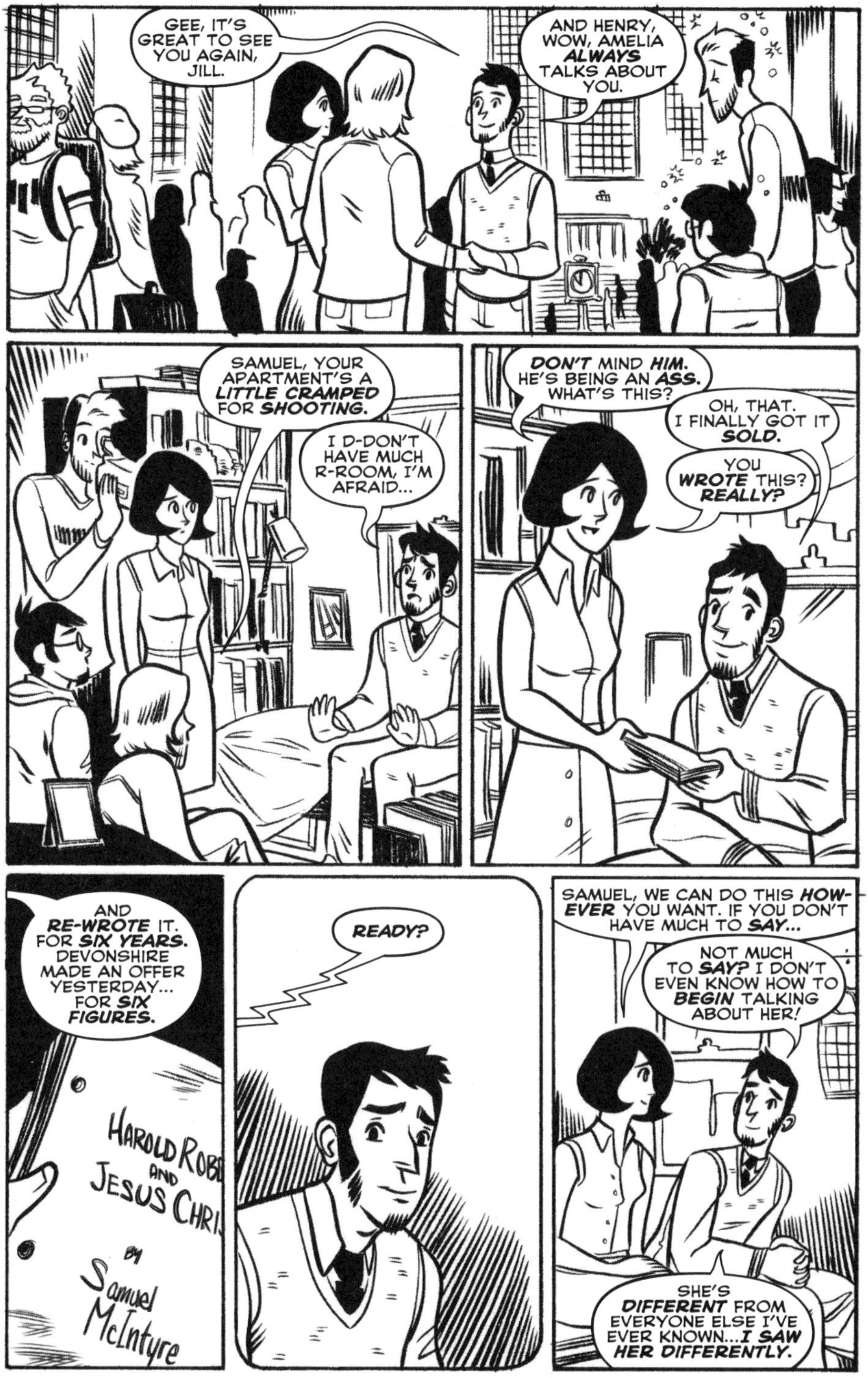
GEE, IT'S GREAT TO SEE YOU AGAIN, JILL.
AND HENRY, WOW, AMELIA ALWAYS TALKS ABOUT YOU.
SAMUEL, YOUR APARTMENT'S A LITTLE CRAMPED FOR SHOOTING.
I D-DON'T HAVE MUCH R-ROOM, I'M AFRAID...
DON'T MIND HIM. HE'S BEING AN ASS. WHAT'S THIS?
OH, THAT. I FINALLY GOT IT SOLD.
YOU WROTE THIS? REALLY?
AND RE-WROTE IT. FOR SIX YEARS. DEVONSHIRE MADE AN OFFER YESTERDAY... FOR SIX FIGURES.
HAROLD ROB AND JESUS CHRI
BY
Samuel McIntyre
READY?
SAMUEL, WE CAN DO THIS HOW-EVER YOU WANT. IF YOU DON'T HAVE MUCH TO SAY...
NOT MUCH TO SAY? I DON'T EVEN KNOW HOW TO BEGIN TALKING ABOUT HER!
SHE'S DIFFERENT FROM EVERYONE ELSE I'VE EVER KNOWN...I SAW HER DIFFERENTLY.

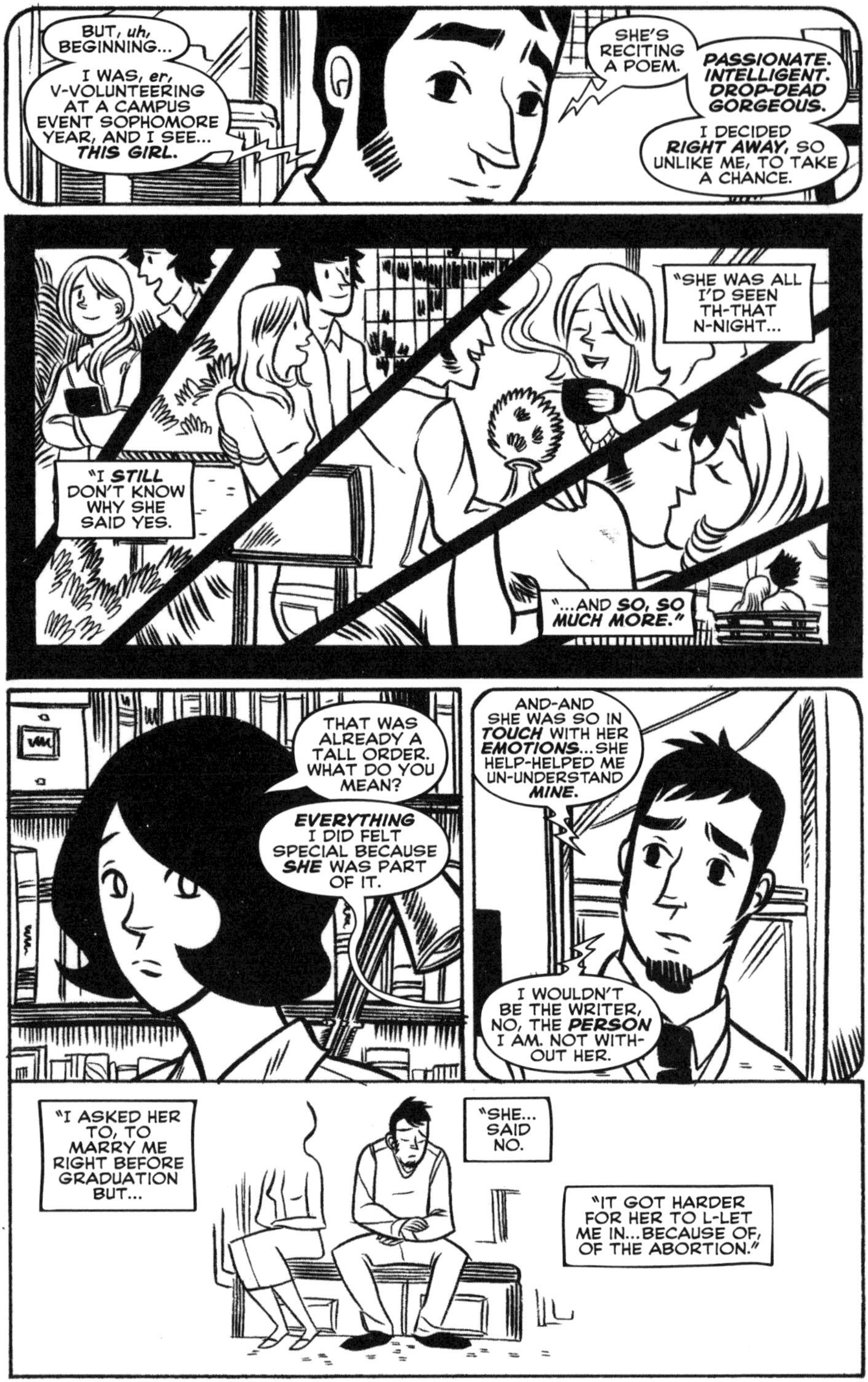
BUT, uh, BEGINNING...
I WAS, er, V-VOLUNTEERING AT A CAMPUS EVENT SOPHOMORE YEAR, AND I SEE... THIS GIRL.
SHE'S RECITING A POEM.
PASSIONATE. INTELLIGENT. DROP-DEAD GORGEOUS.
I DECIDED RIGHT AWAY, SO UNLIKE ME, TO TAKE A CHANCE.
"I STILL DON'T KNOW WHY SHE SAID YES.
"SHE WAS ALL I'D SEEN TH-THAT N-NIGHT...
"...AND SO, SO MUCH MORE."
THAT WAS ALREADY A TALL ORDER. WHAT DO YOU MEAN?
EVERYTHING I DID FELT SPECIAL BECAUSE SHE WAS PART OF IT.
AND-AND SHE WAS SO IN TOUCH WITH HER EMOTIONS... SHE HELP-HELPED ME UN-UNDERSTAND MINE.
I WOULDN'T BE THE WRITER, NO, THE PERSON I AM. NOT WITH-OUT HER.
"I ASKED HER TO, TO MARRY ME RIGHT BEFORE GRADUATION BUT...
"SHE... SAID NO.
"IT GOT HARDER FOR HER TO L-LET ME IN... BECAUSE OF, OF THE ABORTION."

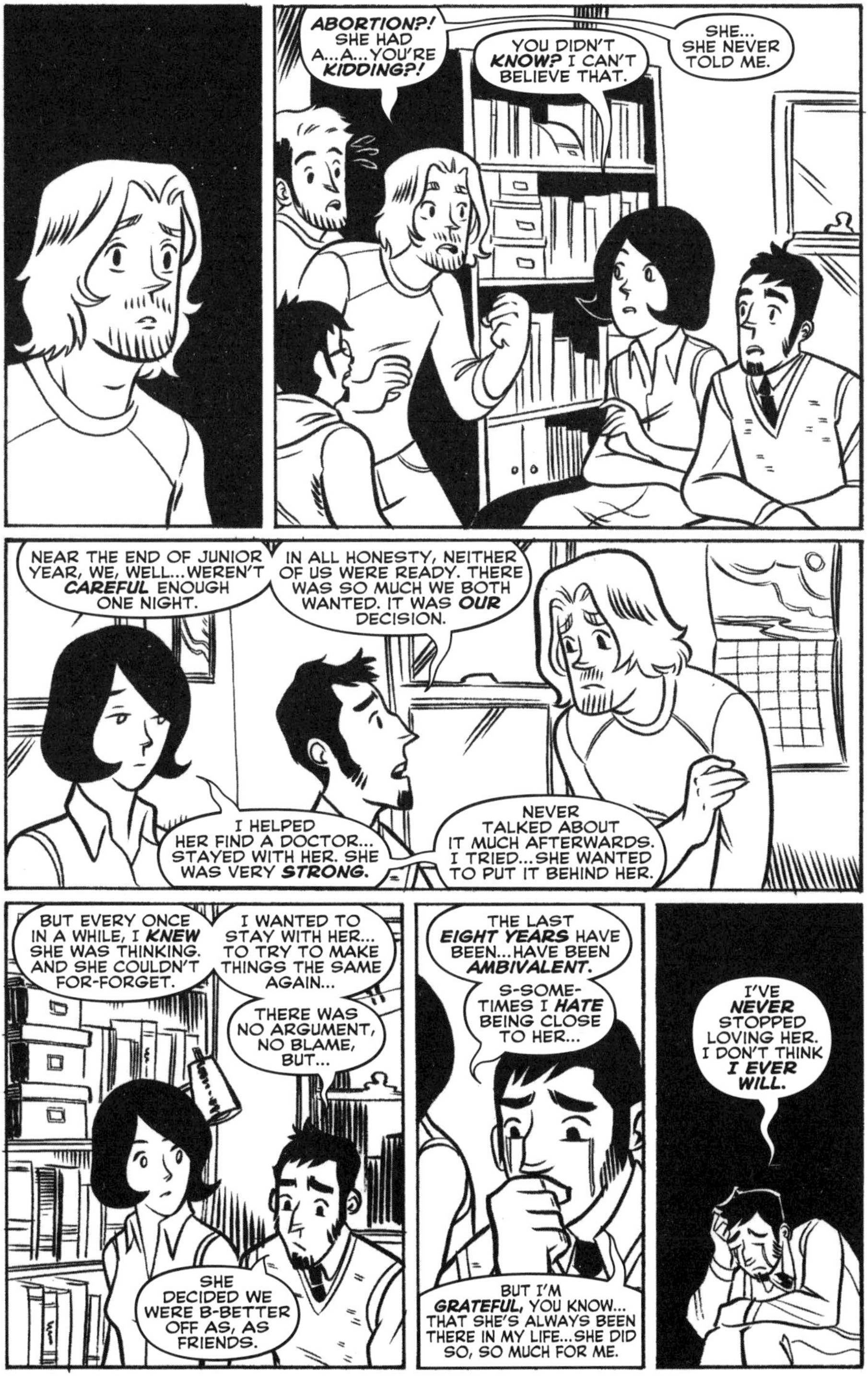
ABORTION?! SHE HAD A...A...YOU'RE KIDDING?!
YOU DIDN'T KNOW? I CAN'T BELIEVE THAT.
SHE... SHE NEVER TOLD ME.
NEAR THE END OF JUNIOR YEAR, WE, WELL...WEREN'T CAREFUL ENOUGH ONE NIGHT.
IN ALL HONESTY, NEITHER OF US WERE READY. THERE WAS SO MUCH WE BOTH WANTED. IT WAS OUR DECISION.
I HELPED HER FIND A DOCTOR... STAYED WITH HER. SHE WAS VERY STRONG.
NEVER TALKED ABOUT IT MUCH AFTERWARDS. I TRIED...SHE WANTED TO PUT IT BEHIND HER.
BUT EVERY ONCE IN A WHILE, I KNEW SHE WAS THINKING. AND SHE COULDN'T FOR-FORGET.
I WANTED TO STAY WITH HER... TO TRY TO MAKE THINGS THE SAME AGAIN...
THERE WAS NO ARGUMENT, NO BLAME, BUT...
SHE DECIDED WE WERE B-BETTER OFF AS, AS FRIENDS.
THE LAST EIGHT YEARS HAVE BEEN...HAVE BEEN AMBIVALENT.
S-SOME-TIMES I HATE BEING CLOSE TO HER...
BUT I'M GRATEFUL, YOU KNOW... THAT SHE'S ALWAYS BEEN THERE IN MY LIFE...SHE DID SO, SO MUCH FOR ME.
I'VE NEVER STOPPED LOVING HER. I DON'T THINK I EVER WILL.

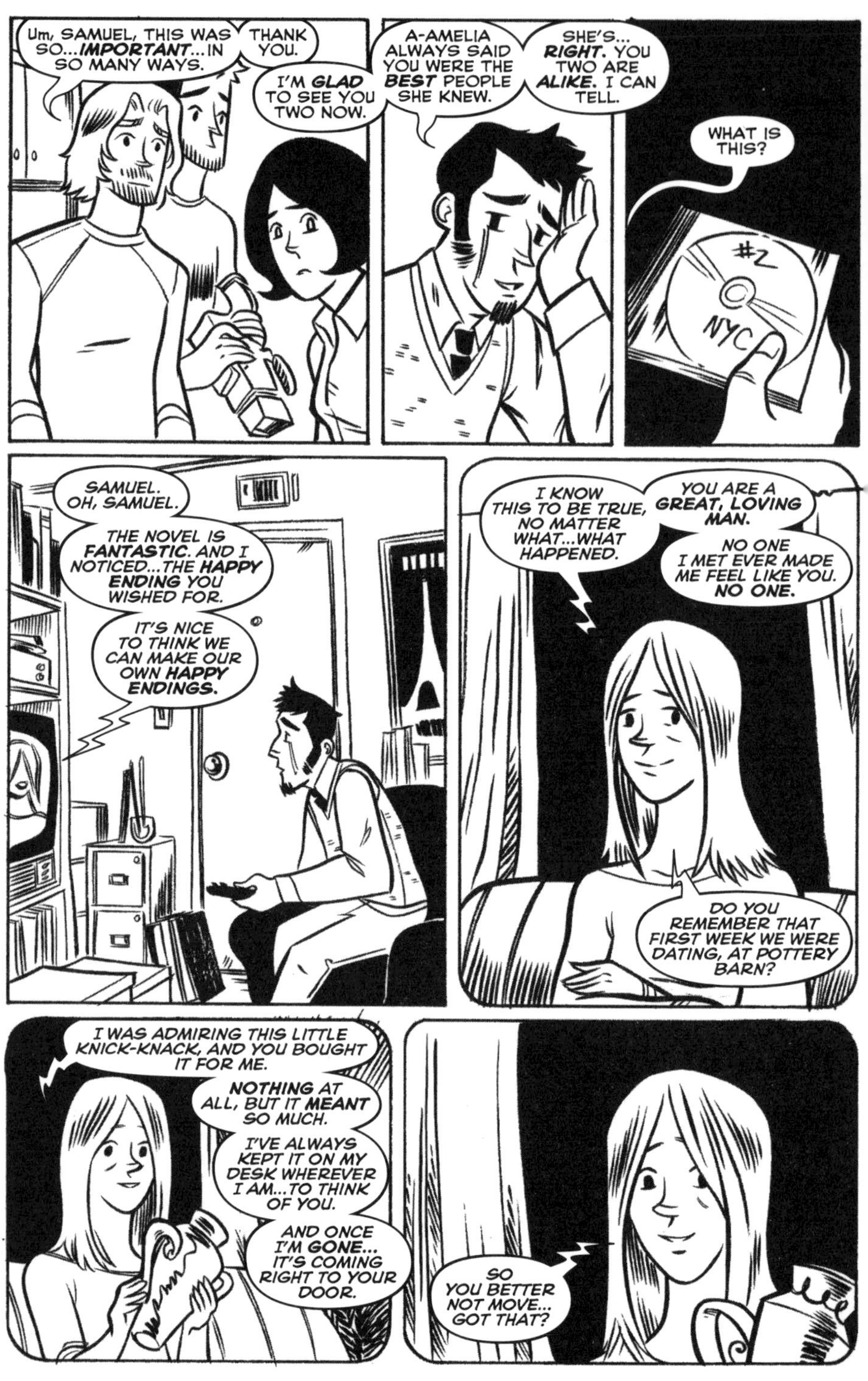
Um, SAMUEL, THIS WAS SO...IMPORTANT...IN SO MANY WAYS.
THANK YOU.
I'M GLAD TO SEE YOU TWO NOW.
A-AMELIA ALWAYS SAID YOU WERE THE BEST PEOPLE SHE KNEW.
SHE'S... RIGHT. YOU TWO ARE ALIKE. I CAN TELL.
WHAT IS THIS?
#2
NYC
SAMUEL. OH, SAMUEL.
THE NOVEL IS FANTASTIC. AND I NOTICED...THE HAPPY ENDING YOU WISHED FOR.
IT'S NICE TO THINK WE CAN MAKE OUR OWN HAPPY ENDINGS.
I KNOW THIS TO BE TRUE, NO MATTER WHAT...WHAT HAPPENED.
YOU ARE A GREAT, LOVING MAN.
NO ONE I MET EVER MADE ME FEEL LIKE YOU. NO ONE.
DO YOU REMEMBER THAT FIRST WEEK WE WERE DATING, AT POTTERY BARN?
I WAS ADMIRING THIS LITTLE KNICK-KNACK, AND YOU BOUGHT IT FOR ME.
NOTHING AT ALL, BUT IT MEANT SO MUCH.
I'VE ALWAYS KEPT IT ON MY DESK WHEREVER I AM...TO THINK OF YOU.
AND ONCE I'M GONE... IT'S COMING RIGHT TO YOUR DOOR.
SO YOU BETTER NOT MOVE... GOT THAT?

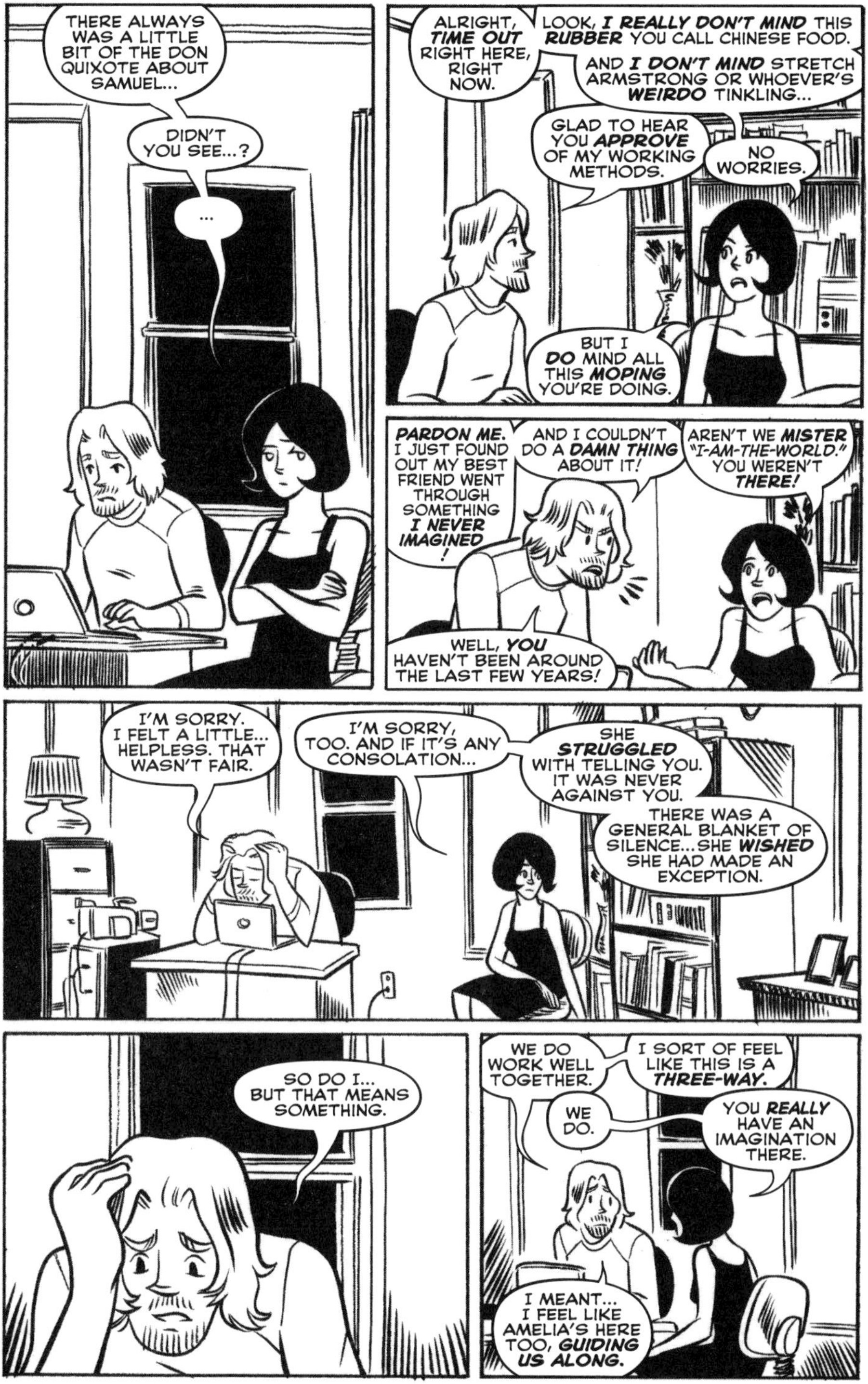

THERE ALWAYS WAS A LITTLE BIT OF THE DON QUIXOTE ABOUT SAMUEL...
DIDN'T YOU SEE...?
...
ALRIGHT, TIME OUT RIGHT HERE, RIGHT NOW.
LOOK, I REALLY DON'T MIND THIS RUBBER YOU CALL CHINESE FOOD.
AND I DON'T MIND STRETCH ARMSTRONG OR WHOEVER'S WEIRDO TINKLING...
GLAD TO HEAR YOU APPROVE OF MY WORKING METHODS.
NO WORRIES.
BUT I DO MIND ALL THIS MOPING YOU'RE DOING.
PARDON ME. I JUST FOUND OUT MY BEST FRIEND WENT THROUGH SOMETHING I NEVER IMAGINED!
AND I COULDN'T DO A DAMN THING ABOUT IT!
AREN'T WE MISTER "I-AM-THE-WORLD." YOU WEREN'T THERE!
WELL, YOU HAVEN'T BEEN AROUND THE LAST FEW YEARS!
I'M SORRY. I FELT A LITTLE... HELPLESS. THAT WASN'T FAIR.
I'M SORRY, TOO. AND IF IT'S ANY CONSOLATION...
SHE STRUGGLED WITH TELLING YOU. IT WAS NEVER AGAINST YOU.
THERE WAS A GENERAL BLANKET OF SILENCE...SHE WISHED SHE HAD MADE AN EXCEPTION.
SO DO I... BUT THAT MEANS SOMETHING.
WE DO WORK WELL TOGETHER.
I SORT OF FEEL LIKE THIS IS A THREE-WAY.
WE DO.
YOU REALLY HAVE AN IMAGINATION THERE.
I MEANT... I FEEL LIKE AMELIA'S HERE TOO, GUIDING US ALONG.

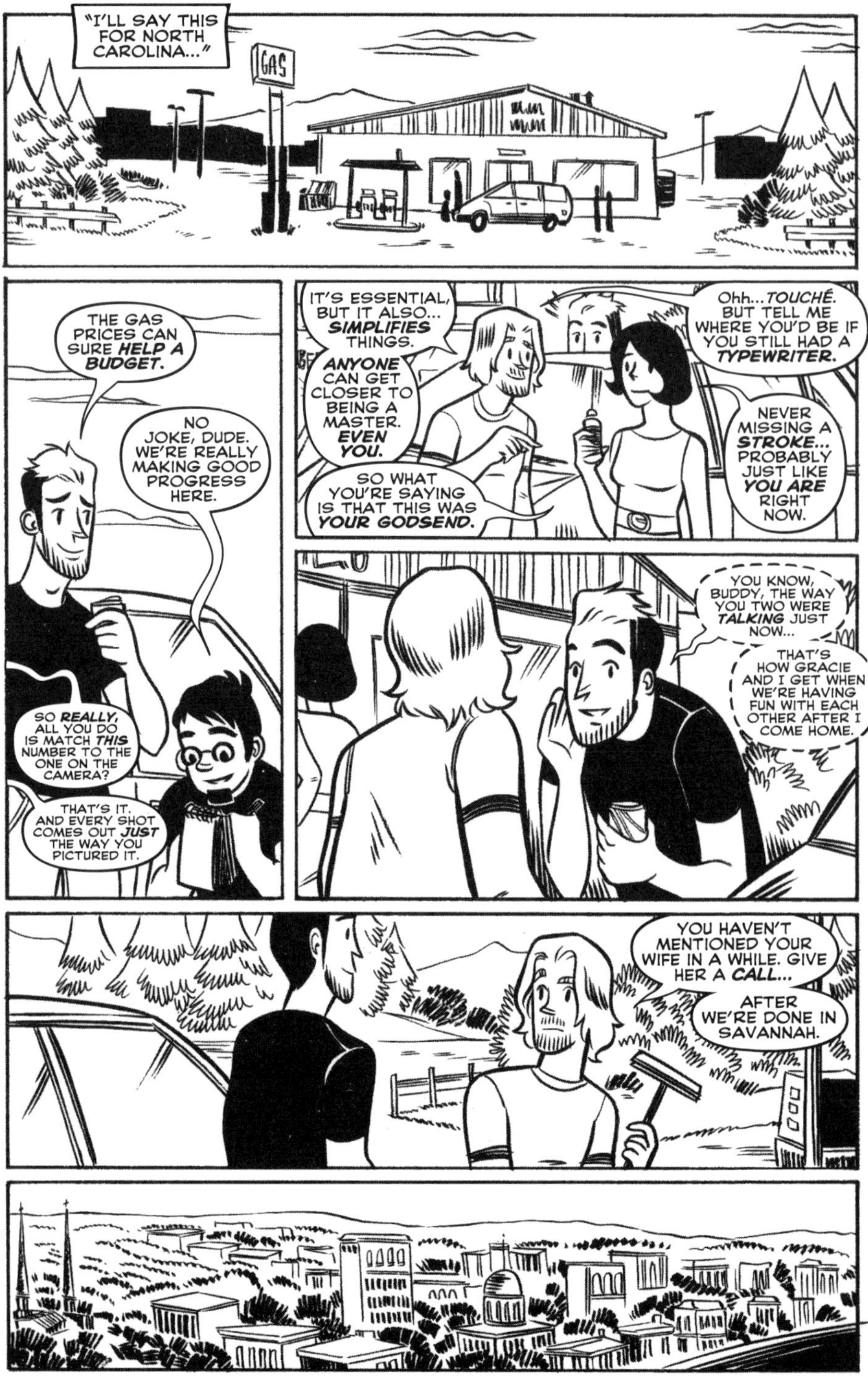
"I'LL SAY THIS FOR NORTH CAROLINA..."
GAS
THE GAS PRICES CAN SURE HELP A BUDGET.
NO JOKE, DUDE. WE'RE REALLY MAKING GOOD PROGRESS HERE.
SO REALLY, ALL YOU DO IS MATCH THIS NUMBER TO THE ONE ON THE CAMERA?
THAT'S IT. AND EVERY SHOT COMES OUT JUST THE WAY YOU PICTURED IT.
IT'S ESSENTIAL, BUT IT ALSO... SIMPLIFIES THINGS.
ANYONE CAN GET CLOSER TO BEING A MASTER. EVEN YOU.
SO WHAT YOU'RE SAYING IS THAT THIS WAS YOUR GODSEND.
Ohh...TOUCHÉ. BUT TELL ME WHERE YOU'D BE IF YOU STILL HAD A TYPEWRITER.
NEVER MISSING A STROKE... PROBABLY JUST LIKE YOU ARE RIGHT NOW.
YOU KNOW, BUDDY, THE WAY YOU TWO WERE TALKING JUST NOW...
THAT'S HOW GRACIE AND I GET WHEN WE'RE HAVING FUN WITH EACH OTHER AFTER I COME HOME.
YOU HAVEN'T MENTIONED YOUR WIFE IN A WHILE. GIVE HER A CALL...
AFTER WE'RE DONE IN SAVANNAH.

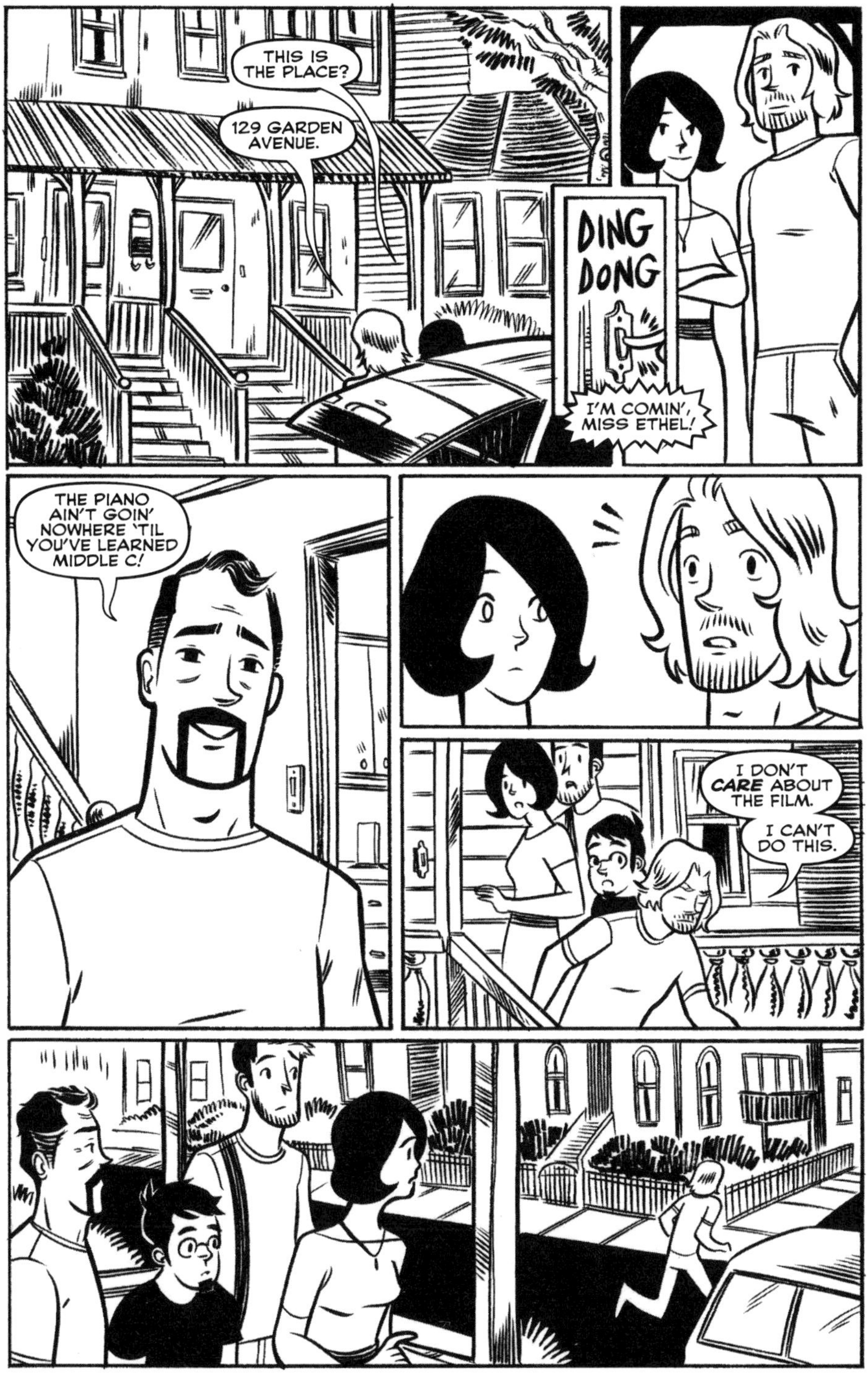
THIS IS THE PLACE?
129 GARDEN AVENUE.
DING DONG
I'M COMIN', MISS ETHEL!
THE PIANO AIN'T GOIN' NOWHERE 'TIL YOU'VE LEARNED MIDDLE C!
I DON'T CARE ABOUT THE FILM.
I CAN'T DO THIS.

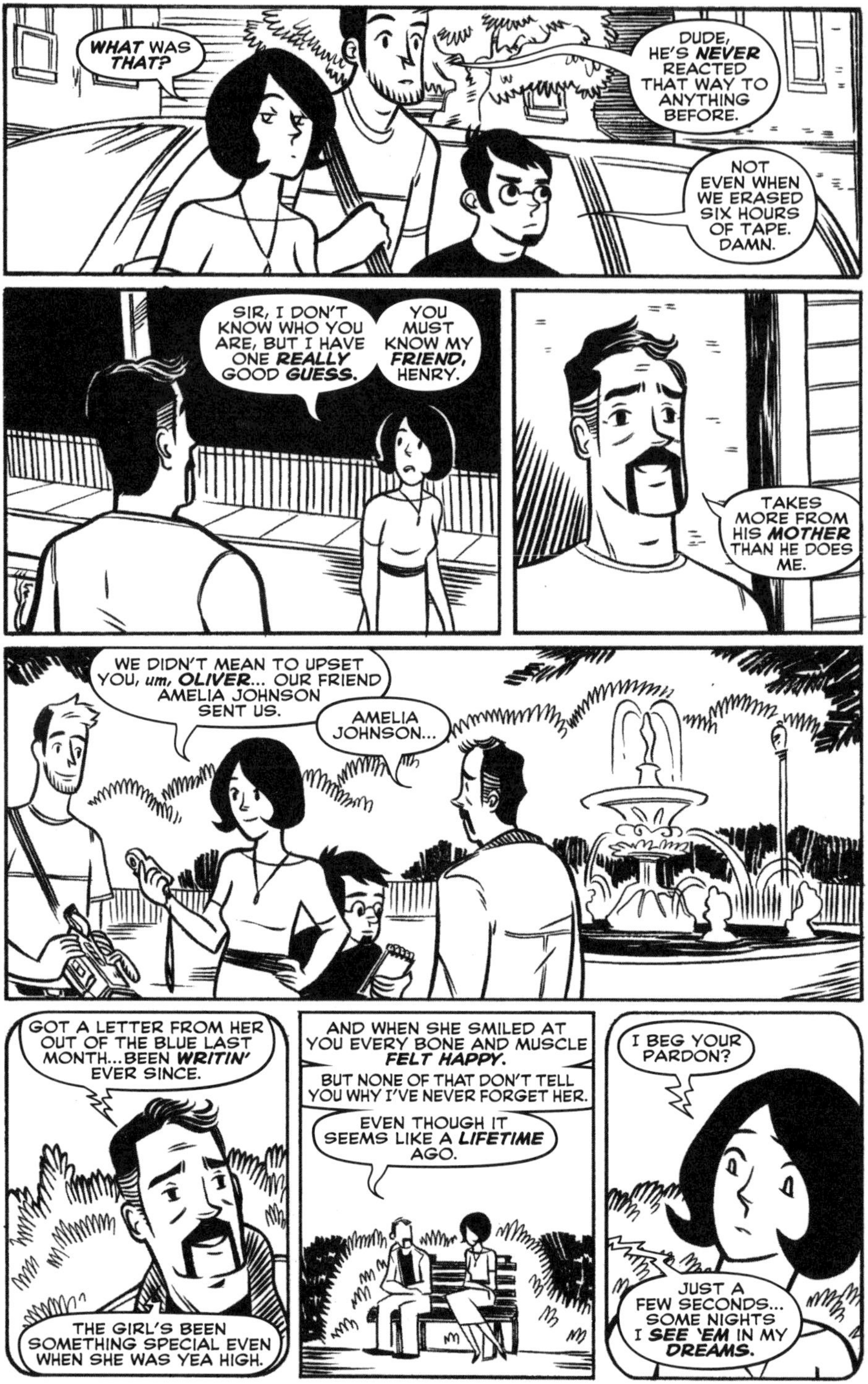
WHAT WAS THAT?
DUDE, HE'S NEVER REACTED THAT WAY TO ANYTHING BEFORE.
NOT EVEN WHEN WE ERASED SIX HOURS OF TAPE. DAMN.
SIR, I DON'T KNOW WHO YOU ARE, BUT I HAVE ONE REALLY GOOD GUESS.
YOU MUST KNOW MY FRIEND, HENRY.
TAKES MORE FROM HIS MOTHER THAN HE DOES ME.
WE DIDN'T MEAN TO UPSET YOU, um, OLIVER... OUR FRIEND AMELIA JOHNSON SENT US.
AMELIA JOHNSON...
GOT A LETTER FROM HER OUT OF THE BLUE LAST MONTH...BEEN WRITIN' EVER SINCE.
THE GIRL'S BEEN SOMETHING SPECIAL EVEN WHEN SHE WAS YEA HIGH.
AND WHEN SHE SMILED AT YOU EVERY BONE AND MUSCLE FELT HAPPY.
BUT NONE OF THAT DON'T TELL YOU WHY I'VE NEVER FORGET HER.
EVEN THOUGH IT SEEMS LIKE A LIFETIME AGO.
I BEG YOUR PARDON?
JUST A FEW SECONDS... SOME NIGHTS I SEE 'EM IN MY DREAMS.

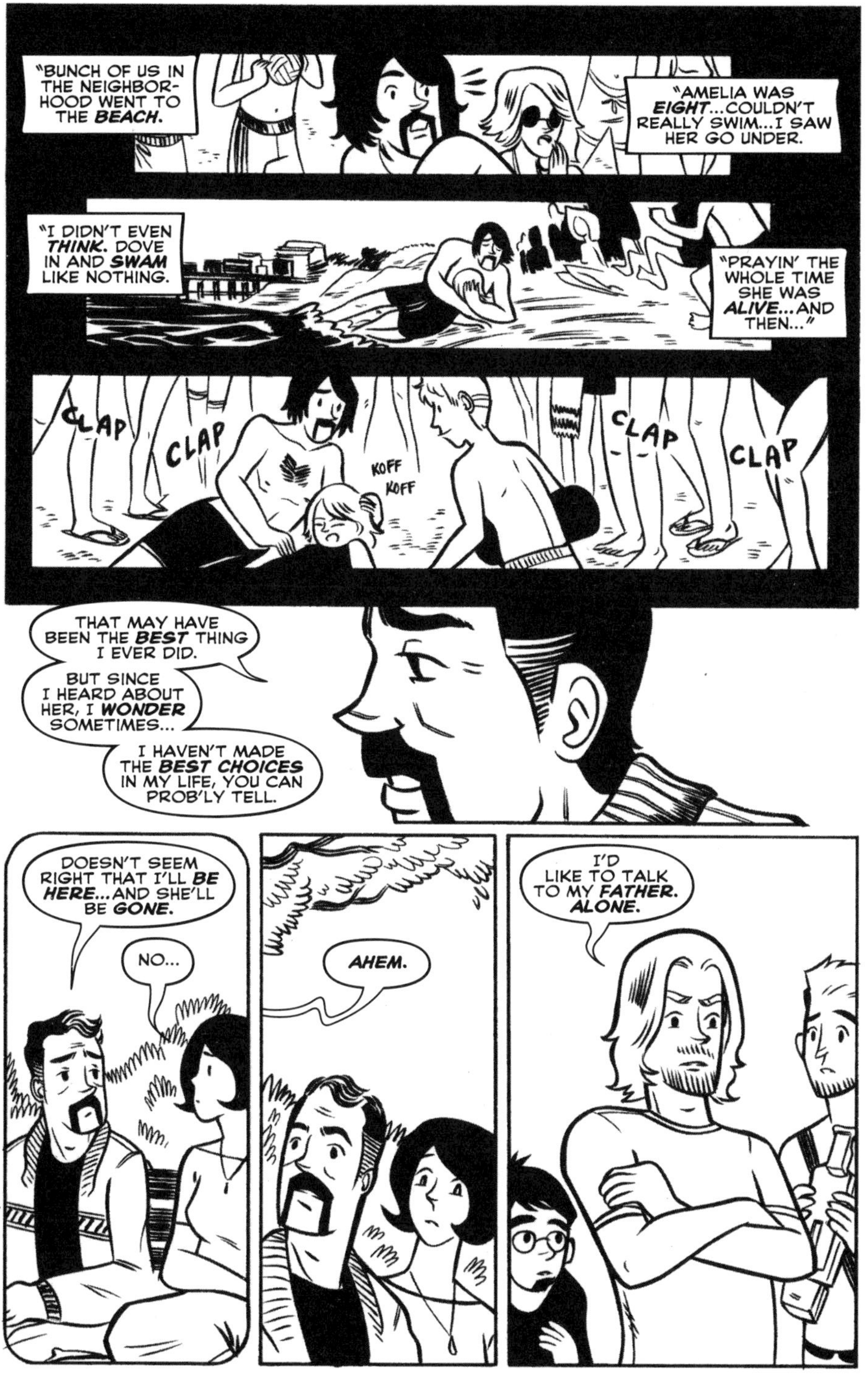

"BUNCH OF US IN THE NEIGHBOR-HOOD WENT TO THE BEACH.
"AMELIA WAS EIGHT...COULDN'T REALLY SWIM...I SAW HER GO UNDER.
"I DIDN'T EVEN THINK. DOVE IN AND SWAM LIKE NOTHING.
"PRAYIN' THE WHOLE TIME SHE WAS ALIVE...AND THEN..."
CLAP
CLAP
KOFF
KOFF
CLAP
CLAP
THAT MAY HAVE BEEN THE BEST THING I EVER DID.
BUT SINCE I HEARD ABOUT HER, I WONDER SOMETIMES...
I HAVEN'T MADE THE BEST CHOICES IN MY LIFE, YOU CAN PROB'LY TELL.
DOESN'T SEEM RIGHT THAT I'LL BE HERE...AND SHE'LL BE GONE.
NO...
AHEM.
I'D LIKE TO TALK TO MY FATHER. ALONE.

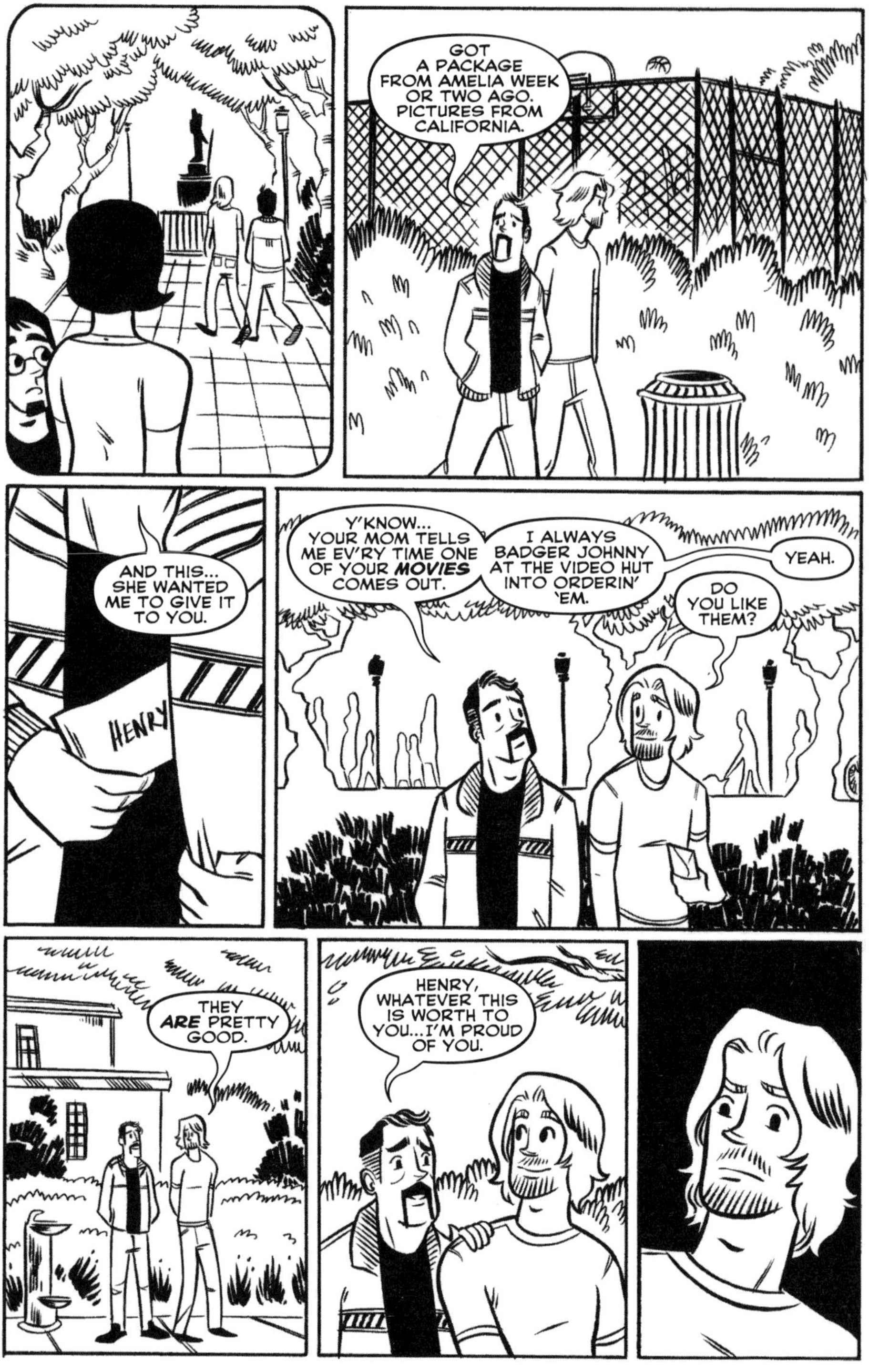
GOT A PACKAGE FROM AMELIA WEEK OR TWO AGO. PICTURES FROM CALIFORNIA.
AND THIS... SHE WANTED ME TO GIVE IT TO YOU.
HENRY
Y'KNOW... YOUR MOM TELLS ME EV'RY TIME ONE OF YOUR **MOVIES** COMES OUT.
I ALWAYS BADGER JOHNNY AT THE VIDEO HUT INTO ORDERIN' 'EM.
YEAH.
DO YOU LIKE THEM?
THEY **ARE** PRETTY GOOD.
HENRY, WHATEVER THIS IS WORTH TO YOU...I'M PROUD OF YOU.

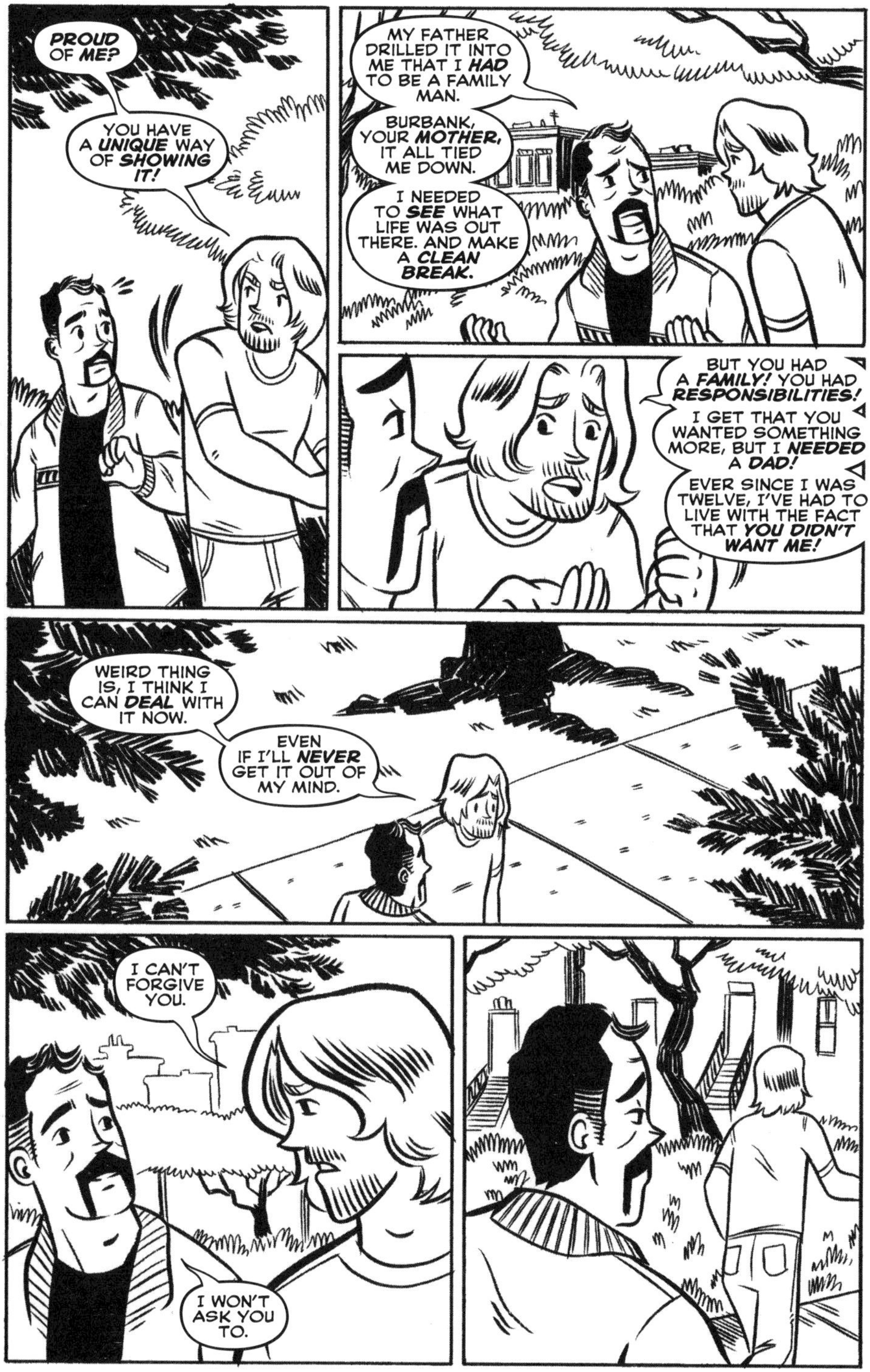
PROUD OF ME?
YOU HAVE A UNIQUE WAY OF SHOWING IT!
MY FATHER DRILLED IT INTO ME THAT I HAD TO BE A FAMILY MAN.
BURBANK, YOUR MOTHER, IT ALL TIED ME DOWN.
I NEEDED TO SEE WHAT LIFE WAS OUT THERE. AND MAKE A CLEAN BREAK.
BUT YOU HAD A FAMILY! YOU HAD RESPONSIBILITIES!
I GET THAT YOU WANTED SOMETHING MORE, BUT I NEEDED A DAD!
EVER SINCE I WAS TWELVE, I'VE HAD TO LIVE WITH THE FACT THAT YOU DIDN'T WANT ME!
WEIRD THING IS, I THINK I CAN DEAL WITH IT NOW.
EVEN IF I'LL NEVER GET IT OUT OF MY MIND.
I CAN'T FORGIVE YOU.
I WON'T ASK YOU TO.

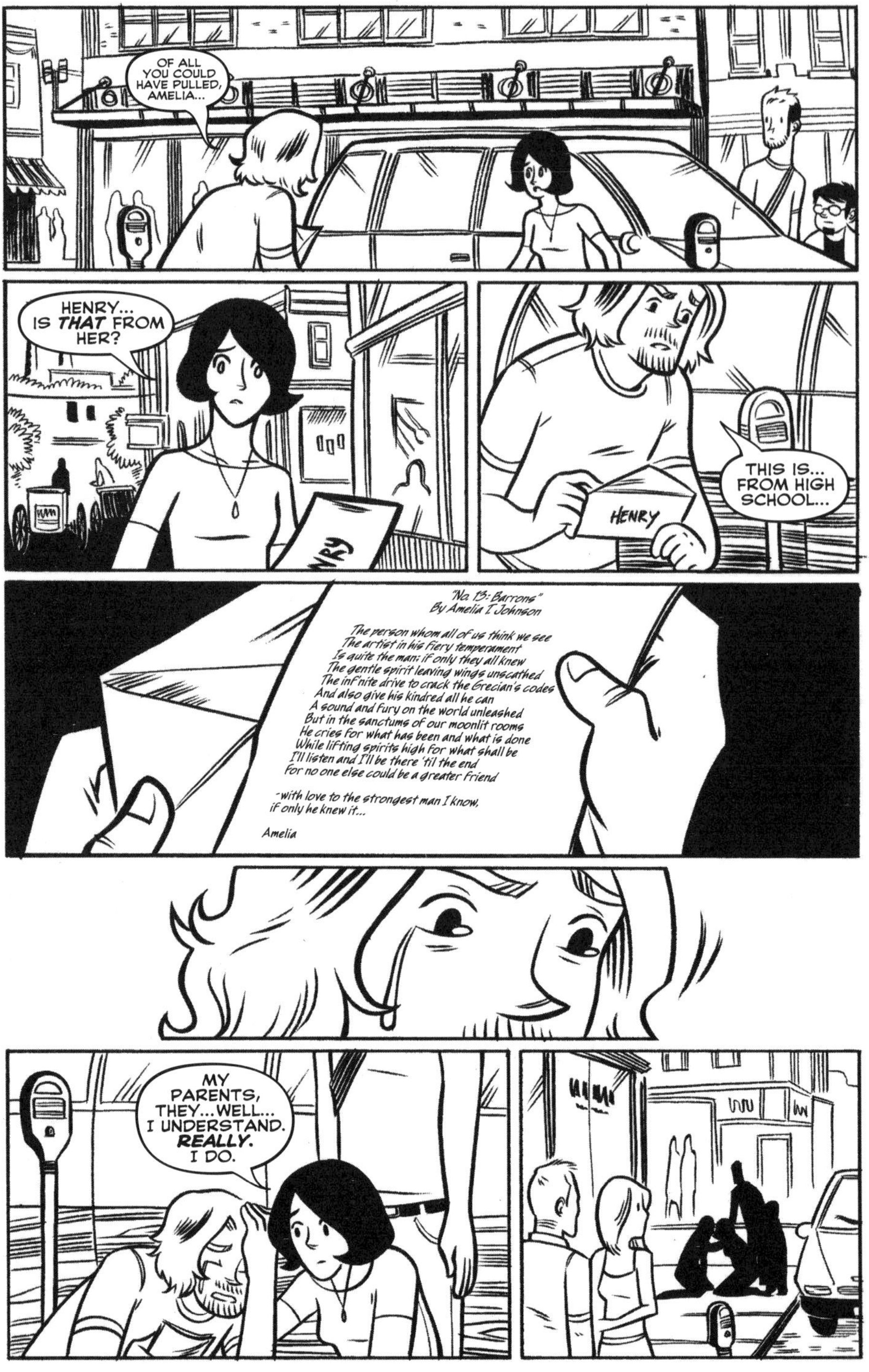
OF ALL YOU COULD HAVE PULLED, AMELIA...
HENRY... IS THAT FROM HER?
HENRY
HENRY
THIS IS... FROM HIGH SCHOOL...
"No. 13: Barrons"
By Amelia I. Johnson
The person whom all of us think we see
The artist in his fiery temperament
Is quite the man; if only they all knew
The gentle spirit leaving wings unscathed
The inf'nite drive to crack the Grecian's codes
And also give his kindred all he can
A sound and fury on the world unleashed
But in the sanctums of our moonlit rooms
He cries for what has been and what is done
While lifting spirits high for what shall be
I'll listen and I'll be there 'til the end
For no one else could be a greater friend
-with love to the strongest man I know,
if only he knew it...
Amelia
MY PARENTS, THEY...WELL... I UNDERSTAND. REALLY. I DO.

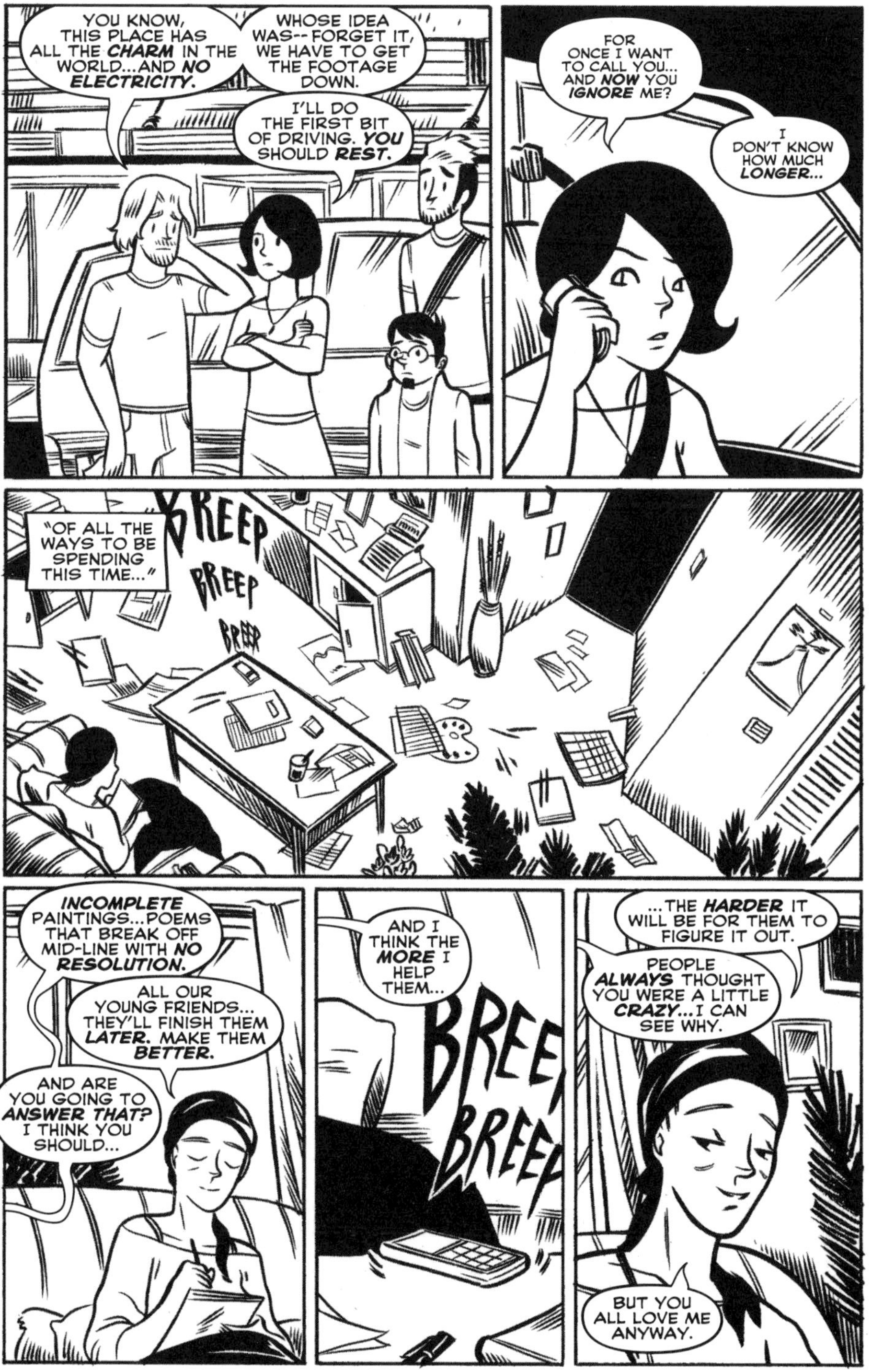
YOU KNOW, THIS PLACE HAS ALL THE CHARM IN THE WORLD...AND NO ELECTRICITY.
WHOSE IDEA WAS-- FORGET IT, WE HAVE TO GET THE FOOTAGE DOWN.
I'LL DO THE FIRST BIT OF DRIVING. YOU SHOULD REST.
FOR ONCE I WANT TO CALL YOU... AND NOW YOU IGNORE ME?
I DON'T KNOW HOW MUCH LONGER...
"OF ALL THE WAYS TO BE SPENDING THIS TIME..."
BREEP
BREEP
BREEP
INCOMPLETE PAINTINGS...POEMS THAT BREAK OFF MID-LINE WITH NO RESOLUTION.
ALL OUR YOUNG FRIENDS... THEY'LL FINISH THEM LATER. MAKE THEM BETTER.
AND ARE YOU GOING TO ANSWER THAT? I THINK YOU SHOULD...
AND I THINK THE MORE I HELP THEM...
...THE HARDER IT WILL BE FOR THEM TO FIGURE IT OUT.
PEOPLE ALWAYS THOUGHT YOU WERE A LITTLE CRAZY...I CAN SEE WHY.
BUT YOU ALL LOVE ME ANYWAY.

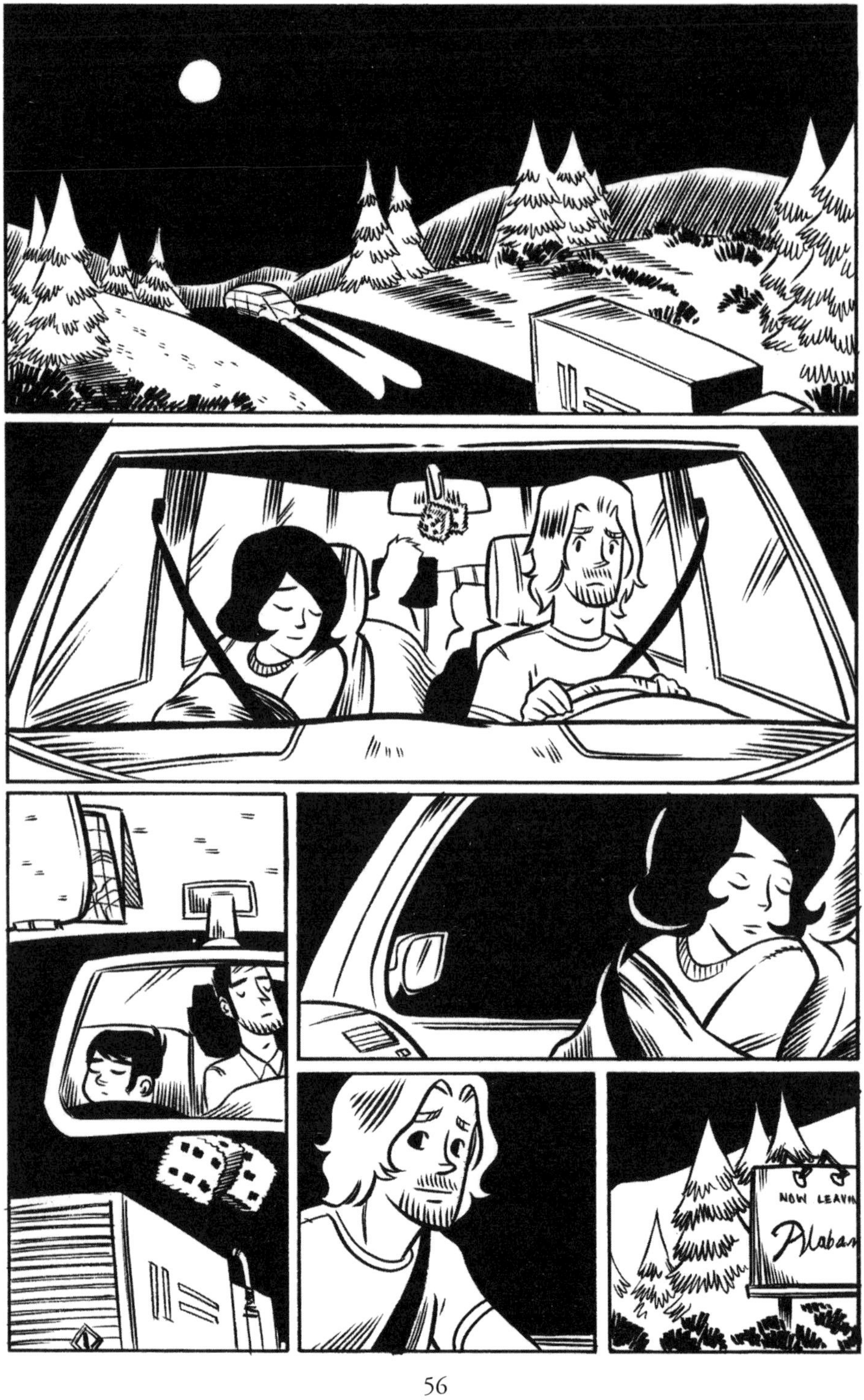
NOW LEAVIN
Alaban

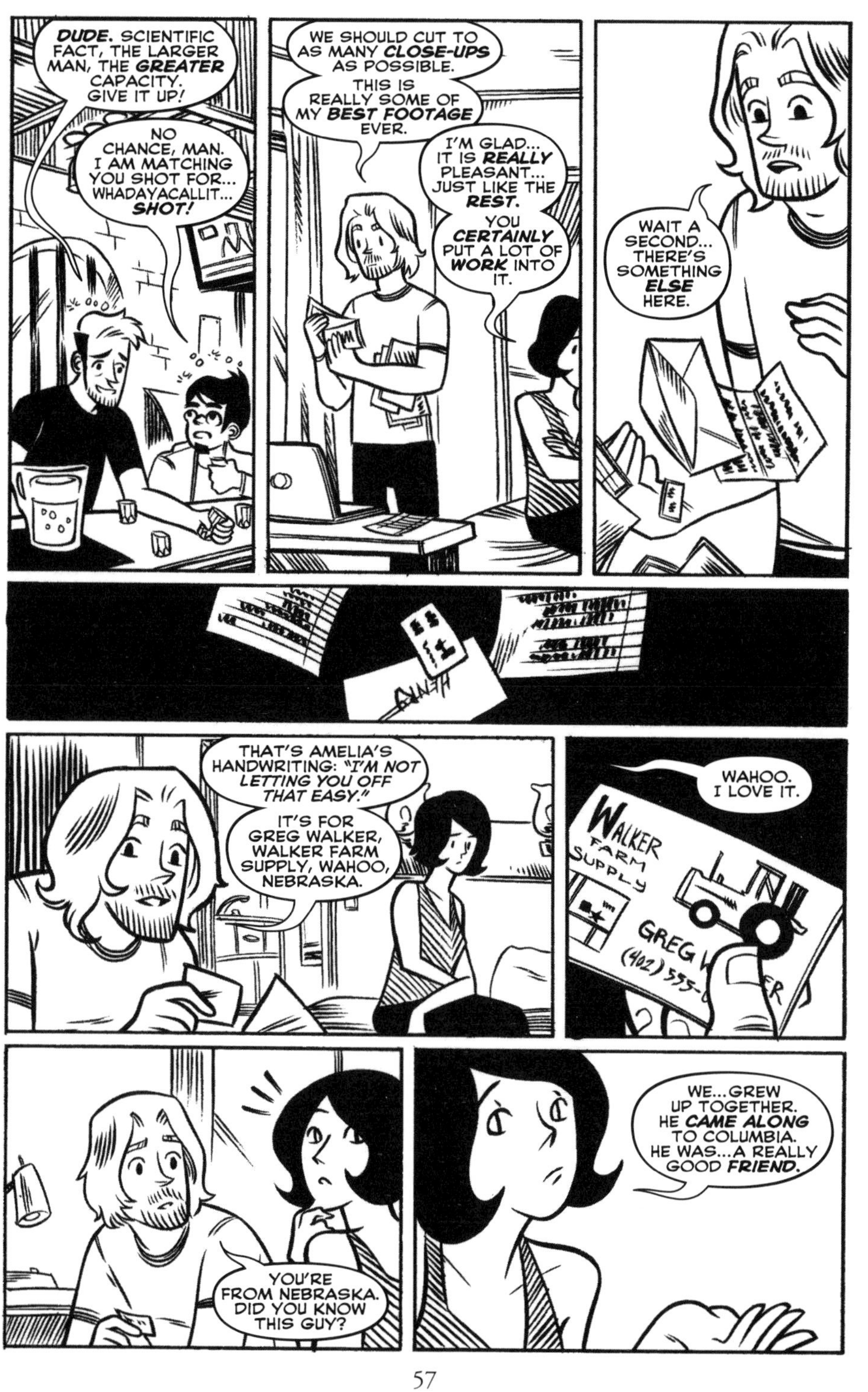
DUDE. SCIENTIFIC FACT, THE LARGER MAN, THE GREATER CAPACITY. GIVE IT UP!
NO CHANCE, MAN. I AM MATCHING YOU SHOT FOR... WHADAYACALLIT... SHOT!
WE SHOULD CUT TO AS MANY CLOSE-UPS AS POSSIBLE.
THIS IS REALLY SOME OF MY BEST FOOTAGE EVER.
I'M GLAD... IT IS REALLY PLEASANT... JUST LIKE THE REST.
YOU CERTAINLY PUT A LOT OF WORK INTO IT.
WAIT A SECOND... THERE'S SOMETHING ELSE HERE.
THAT'S AMELIA'S HANDWRITING: "I'M NOT LETTING YOU OFF THAT EASY."
IT'S FOR GREG WALKER, WALKER FARM SUPPLY, WAHOO, NEBRASKA.
WALKER FARM SUPPLY
GREG
WAHOO. I LOVE IT.
YOU'RE FROM NEBRASKA. DID YOU KNOW THIS GUY?
WE...GREW UP TOGETHER. HE CAME ALONG TO COLUMBIA. HE WAS...A REALLY GOOD FRIEND.

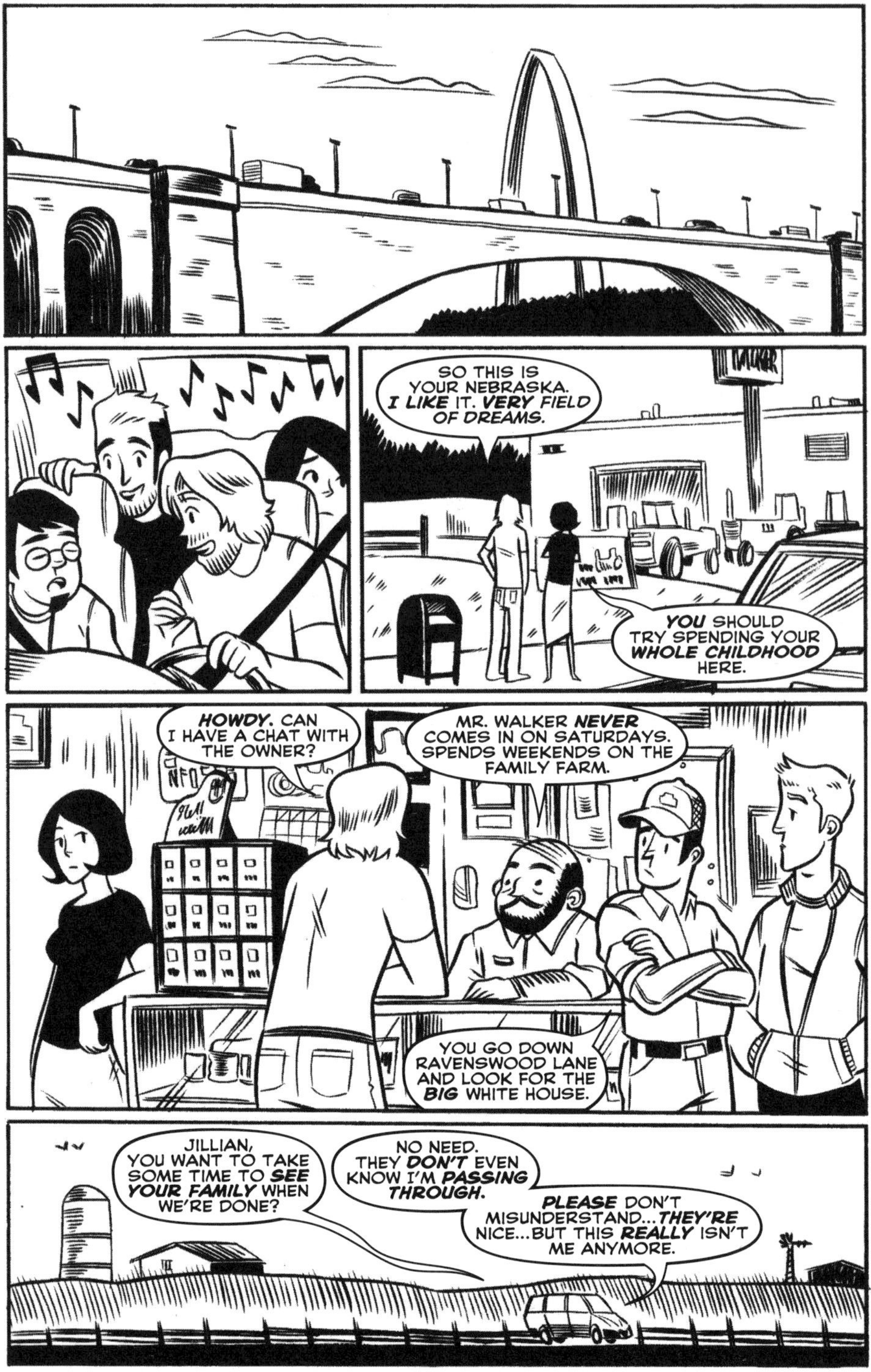
SO THIS IS YOUR NEBRASKA. I LIKE IT. VERY FIELD OF DREAMS.
YOU SHOULD TRY SPENDING YOUR WHOLE CHILDHOOD HERE.
HOWDY. CAN I HAVE A CHAT WITH THE OWNER?
MR. WALKER NEVER COMES IN ON SATURDAYS. SPENDS WEEKENDS ON THE FAMILY FARM.
YOU GO DOWN RAVENSWOOD LANE AND LOOK FOR THE BIG WHITE HOUSE.
JILLIAN, YOU WANT TO TAKE SOME TIME TO SEE YOUR FAMILY WHEN WE'RE DONE?
NO NEED. THEY DON'T EVEN KNOW I'M PASSING THROUGH.
PLEASE DON'T MISUNDERSTAND...THEY'RE NICE...BUT THIS REALLY ISN'T ME ANYMORE.

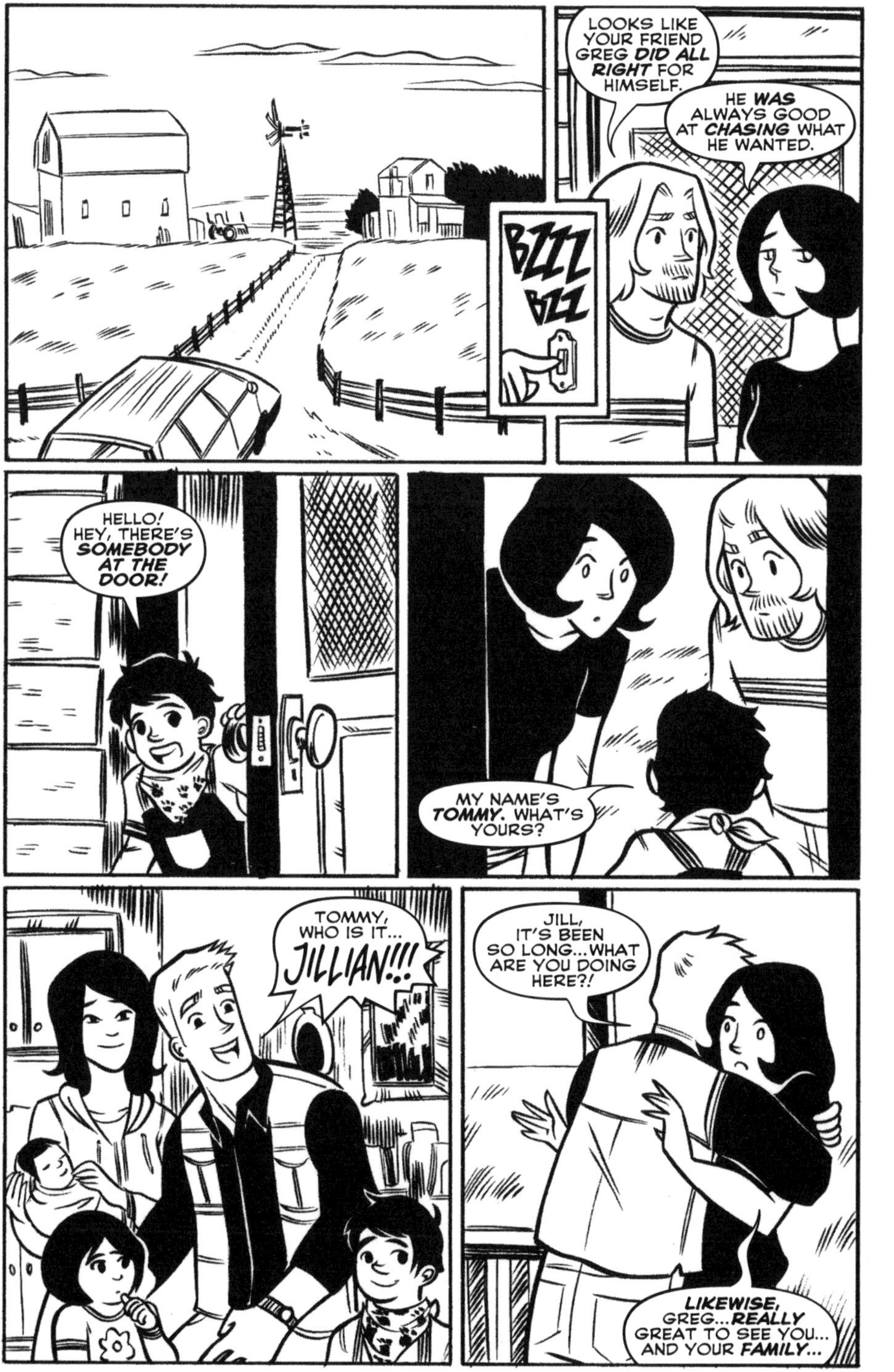

LOOKS LIKE YOUR FRIEND GREG DID ALL RIGHT FOR HIMSELF.
HE WAS ALWAYS GOOD AT CHASING WHAT HE WANTED.
BZZZ BZZ
HELLO! HEY, THERE'S SOMEBODY AT THE DOOR!
MY NAME'S TOMMY. WHAT'S YOURS?
TOMMY, WHO IS IT... JILLIAN!!!
JILL, IT'S BEEN SO LONG...WHAT ARE YOU DOING HERE?!
LIKEWISE, GREG...REALLY GREAT TO SEE YOU... AND YOUR FAMILY...

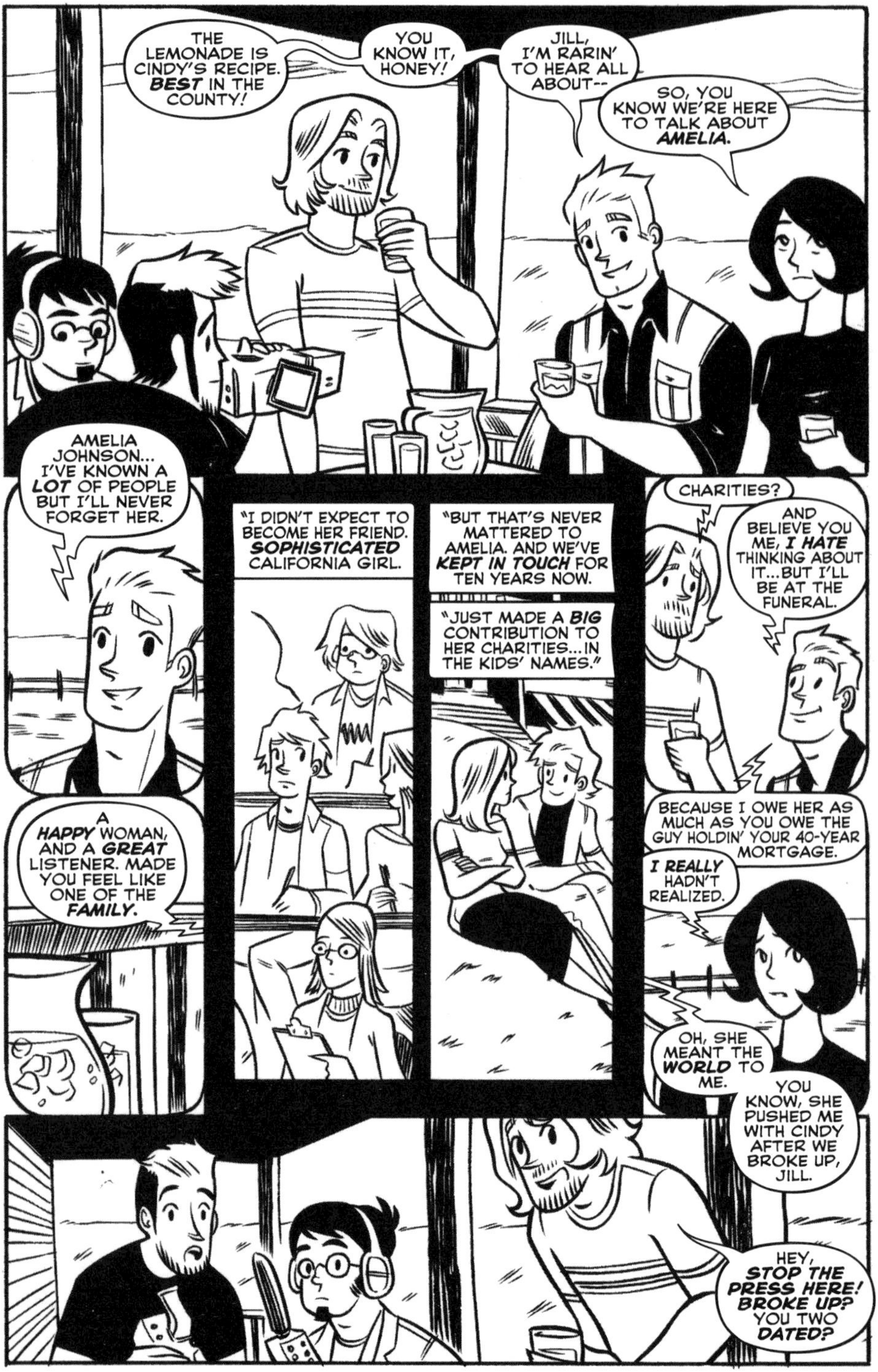
THE LEMONADE IS CINDY'S RECIPE. BEST IN THE COUNTY!
YOU KNOW IT, HONEY!
JILL, I'M RARIN' TO HEAR ALL ABOUT--
SO, YOU KNOW WE'RE HERE TO TALK ABOUT AMELIA.
AMELIA JOHNSON... I'VE KNOWN A LOT OF PEOPLE BUT I'LL NEVER FORGET HER.
A HAPPY WOMAN, AND A GREAT LISTENER. MADE YOU FEEL LIKE ONE OF THE FAMILY.
"I DIDN'T EXPECT TO BECOME HER FRIEND. SOPHISTICATED CALIFORNIA GIRL.
"BUT THAT'S NEVER MATTERED TO AMELIA. AND WE'VE KEPT IN TOUCH FOR TEN YEARS NOW.
"JUST MADE A BIG CONTRIBUTION TO HER CHARITIES...IN THE KIDS' NAMES."
CHARITIES?
AND BELIEVE YOU ME, I HATE THINKING ABOUT IT...BUT I'LL BE AT THE FUNERAL.
BECAUSE I OWE HER AS MUCH AS YOU OWE THE GUY HOLDIN' YOUR 40-YEAR MORTGAGE.
I REALLY HADN'T REALIZED.
OH, SHE MEANT THE WORLD TO ME.
YOU KNOW, SHE PUSHED ME WITH CINDY AFTER WE BROKE UP, JILL.
HEY, STOP THE PRESS HERE! BROKE UP? YOU TWO DATED?

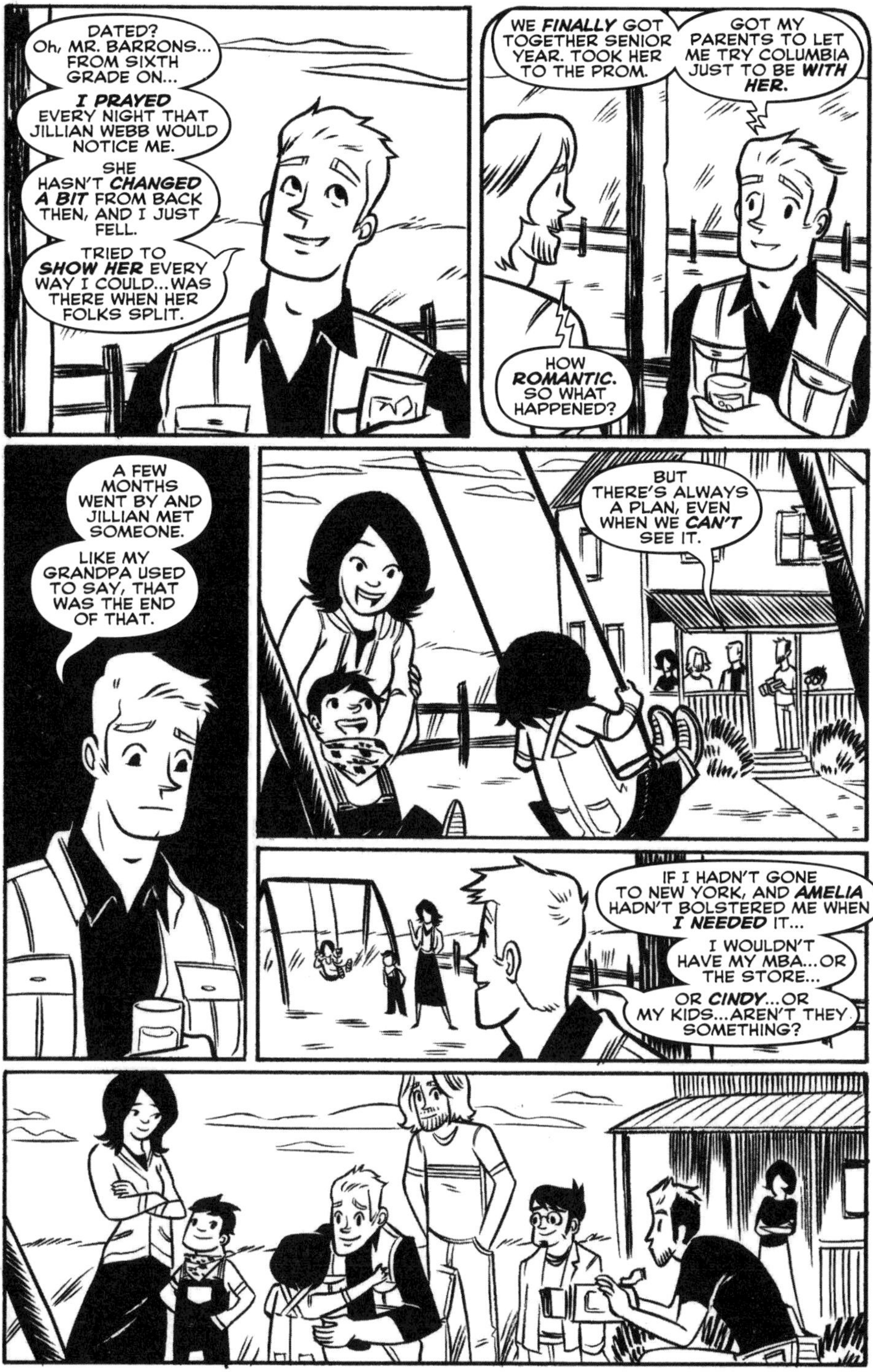
DATED? Oh, MR. BARRONS... FROM SIXTH GRADE ON...
I PRAYED EVERY NIGHT THAT JILLIAN WEBB WOULD NOTICE ME.
SHE HASN'T CHANGED A BIT FROM BACK THEN, AND I JUST FELL.
TRIED TO SHOW HER EVERY WAY I COULD...WAS THERE WHEN HER FOLKS SPLIT.
WE FINALLY GOT TOGETHER SENIOR YEAR. TOOK HER TO THE PROM.
GOT MY PARENTS TO LET ME TRY COLUMBIA JUST TO BE WITH HER.
HOW ROMANTIC. SO WHAT HAPPENED?
A FEW MONTHS WENT BY AND JILLIAN MET SOMEONE.
LIKE MY GRANDPA USED TO SAY, THAT WAS THE END OF THAT.
BUT THERE'S ALWAYS A PLAN, EVEN WHEN WE CAN'T SEE IT.
IF I HADN'T GONE TO NEW YORK, AND AMELIA HADN'T BOLSTERED ME WHEN I NEEDED IT...
I WOULDN'T HAVE MY MBA...OR THE STORE...
OR CINDY...OR MY KIDS...AREN'T THEY SOMETHING?

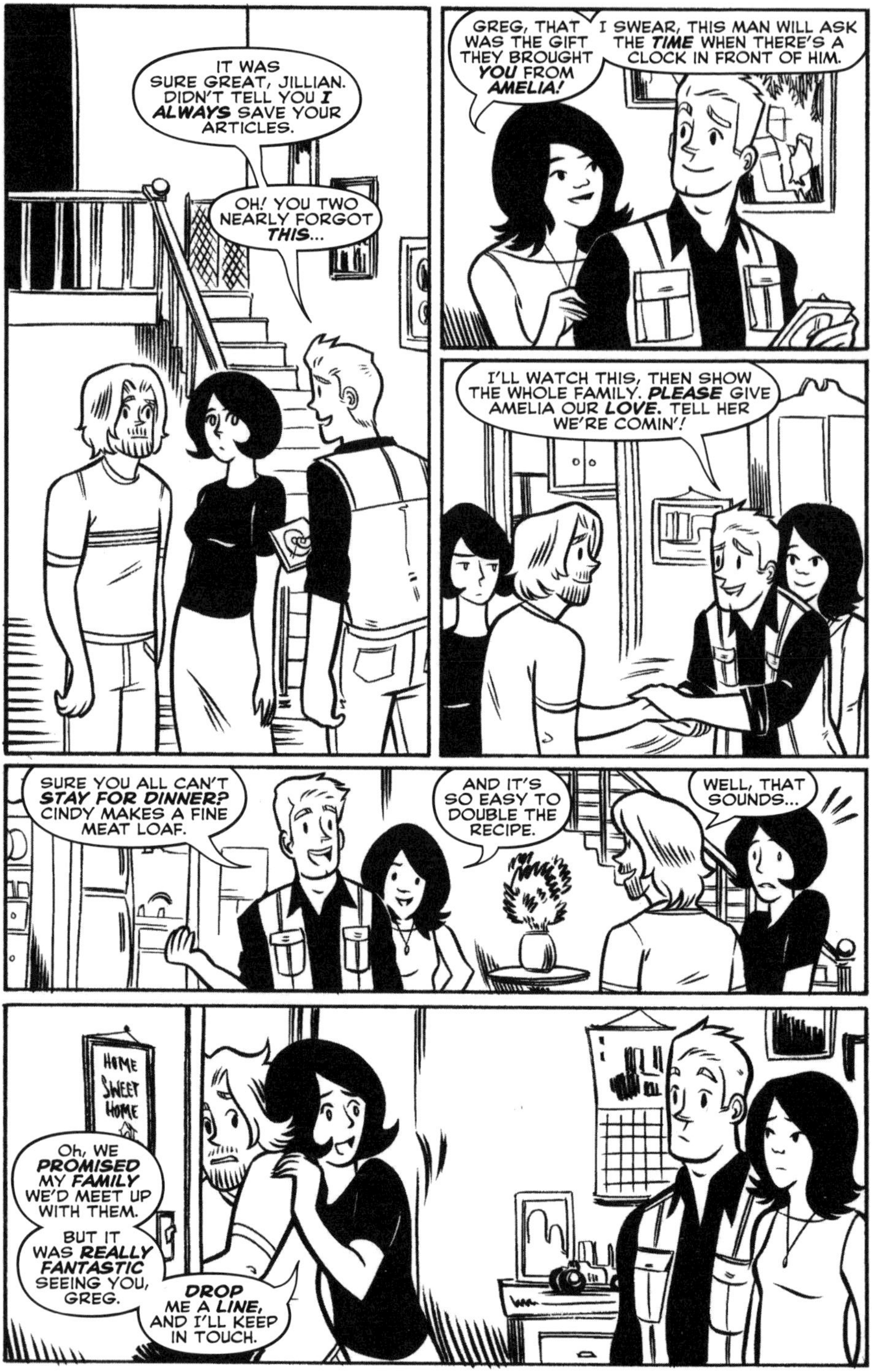
IT WAS SURE GREAT, JILLIAN. DIDN'T TELL YOU I ALWAYS SAVE YOUR ARTICLES.
OH! YOU TWO NEARLY FORGOT THIS...
GREG, THAT WAS THE GIFT THEY BROUGHT YOU FROM AMELIA!
I SWEAR, THIS MAN WILL ASK THE TIME WHEN THERE'S A CLOCK IN FRONT OF HIM.
I'LL WATCH THIS, THEN SHOW THE WHOLE FAMILY. PLEASE GIVE AMELIA OUR LOVE. TELL HER WE'RE COMIN'!
SURE YOU ALL CAN'T STAY FOR DINNER? CINDY MAKES A FINE MEAT LOAF.
AND IT'S SO EASY TO DOUBLE THE RECIPE.
WELL, THAT SOUNDS...
HOME SWEET HOME
Oh, WE PROMISED MY FAMILY WE'D MEET UP WITH THEM.
BUT IT WAS REALLY FANTASTIC SEEING YOU, GREG.
DROP ME A LINE, AND I'LL KEEP IN TOUCH.

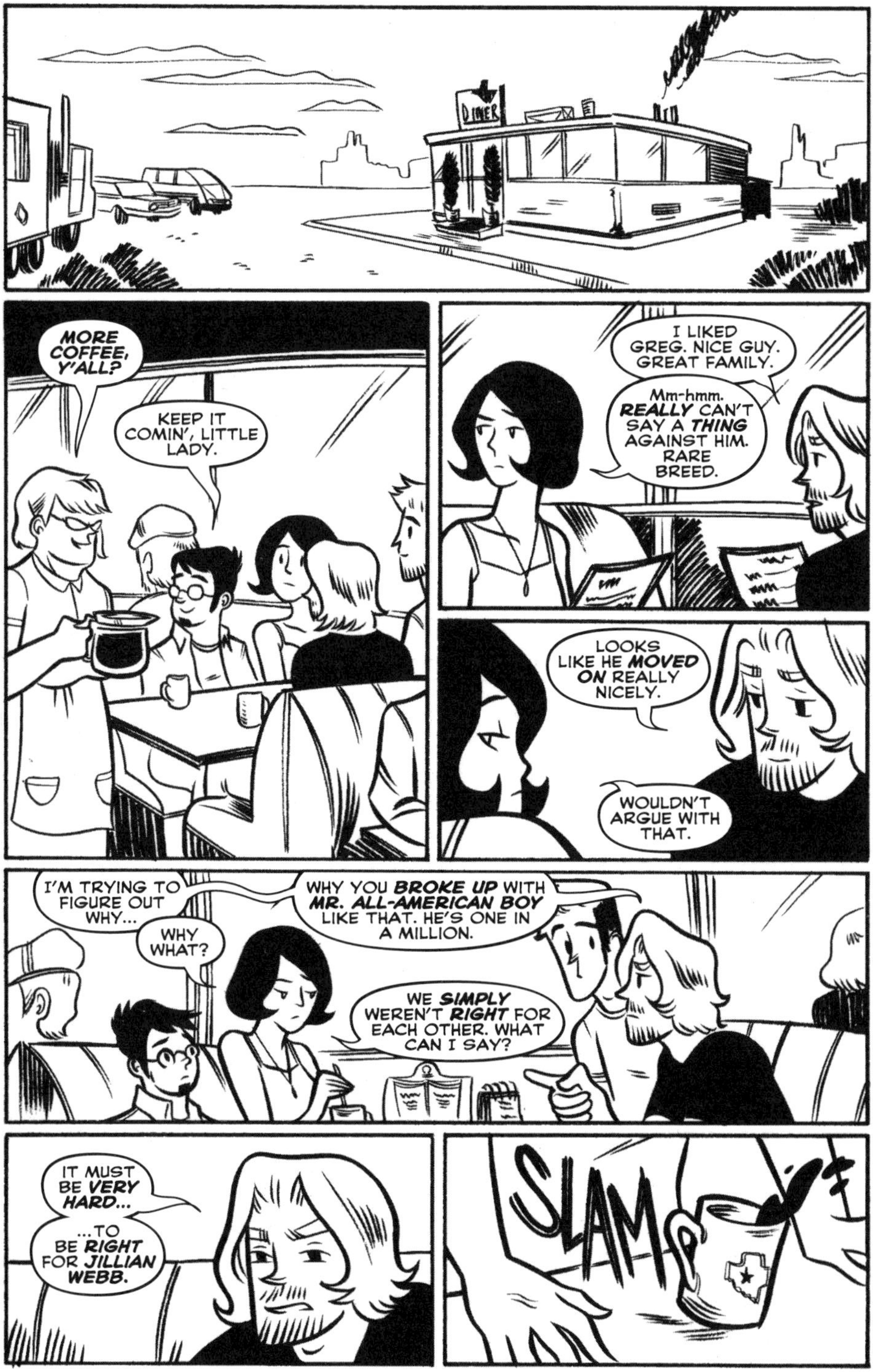

DINER
MORE COFFEE, Y'ALL?
KEEP IT COMIN', LITTLE LADY.
I LIKED GREG. NICE GUY. GREAT FAMILY.
Mm-hmm. REALLY CAN'T SAY A THING AGAINST HIM. RARE BREED.
LOOKS LIKE HE MOVED ON REALLY NICELY.
WOULDN'T ARGUE WITH THAT.
I'M TRYING TO FIGURE OUT WHY...
WHY WHAT?
WHY YOU BROKE UP WITH MR. ALL-AMERICAN BOY LIKE THAT. HE'S ONE IN A MILLION.
WE SIMPLY WEREN'T RIGHT FOR EACH OTHER. WHAT CAN I SAY?
IT MUST BE VERY HARD...
...TO BE RIGHT FOR JILLIAN WEBB.
SLAM

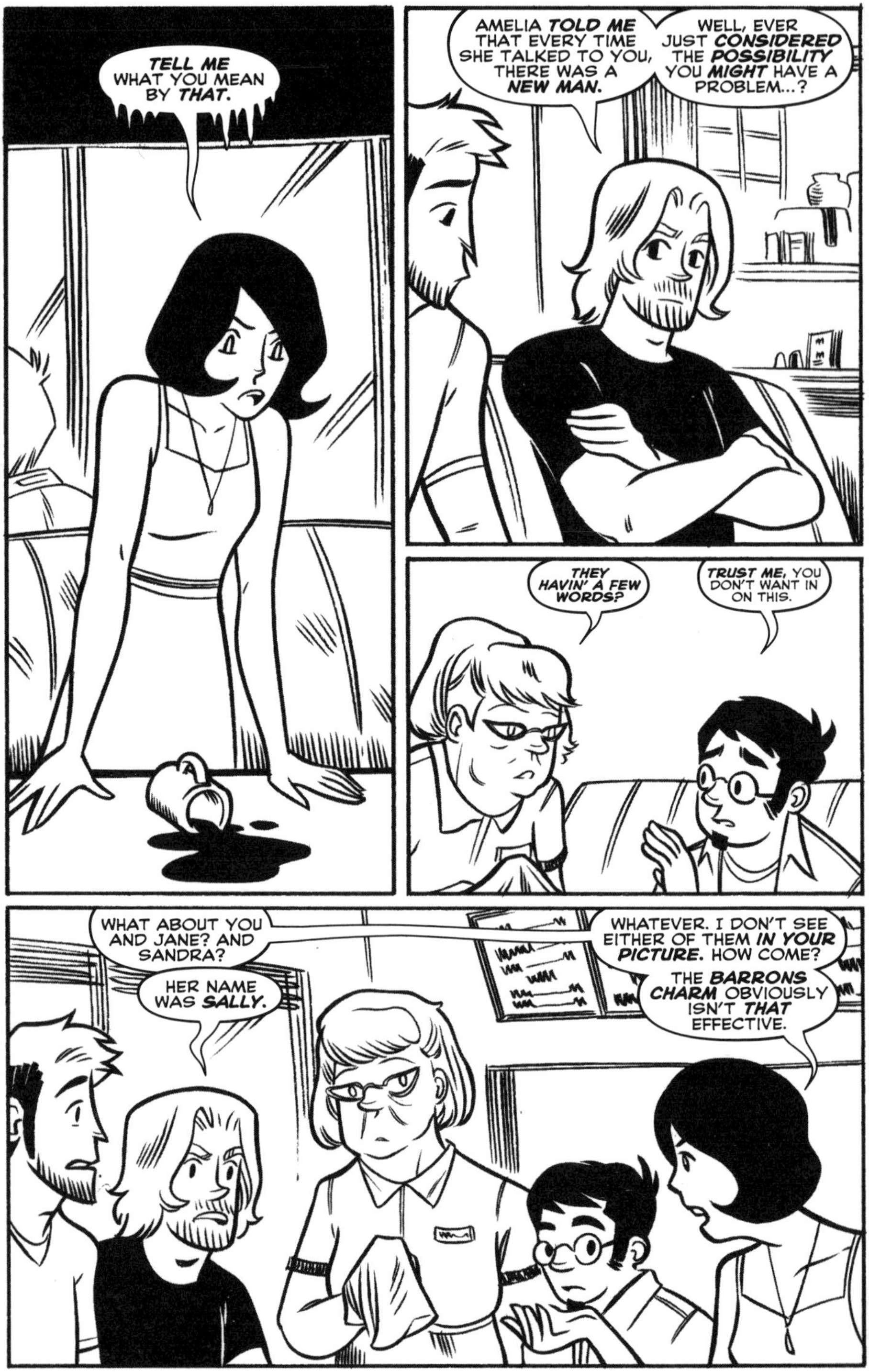
TELL ME WHAT YOU MEAN BY THAT.
AMELIA TOLD ME THAT EVERY TIME SHE TALKED TO YOU, THERE WAS A NEW MAN.
WELL, EVER JUST CONSIDERED THE POSSIBILITY YOU MIGHT HAVE A PROBLEM...?
THEY HAVIN' A FEW WORDS?
TRUST ME, YOU DON'T WANT IN ON THIS.
WHAT ABOUT YOU AND JANE? AND SANDRA?
HER NAME WAS SALLY.
WHATEVER. I DON'T SEE EITHER OF THEM IN YOUR PICTURE. HOW COME?
THE BARRONS CHARM OBVIOUSLY ISN'T THAT EFFECTIVE.

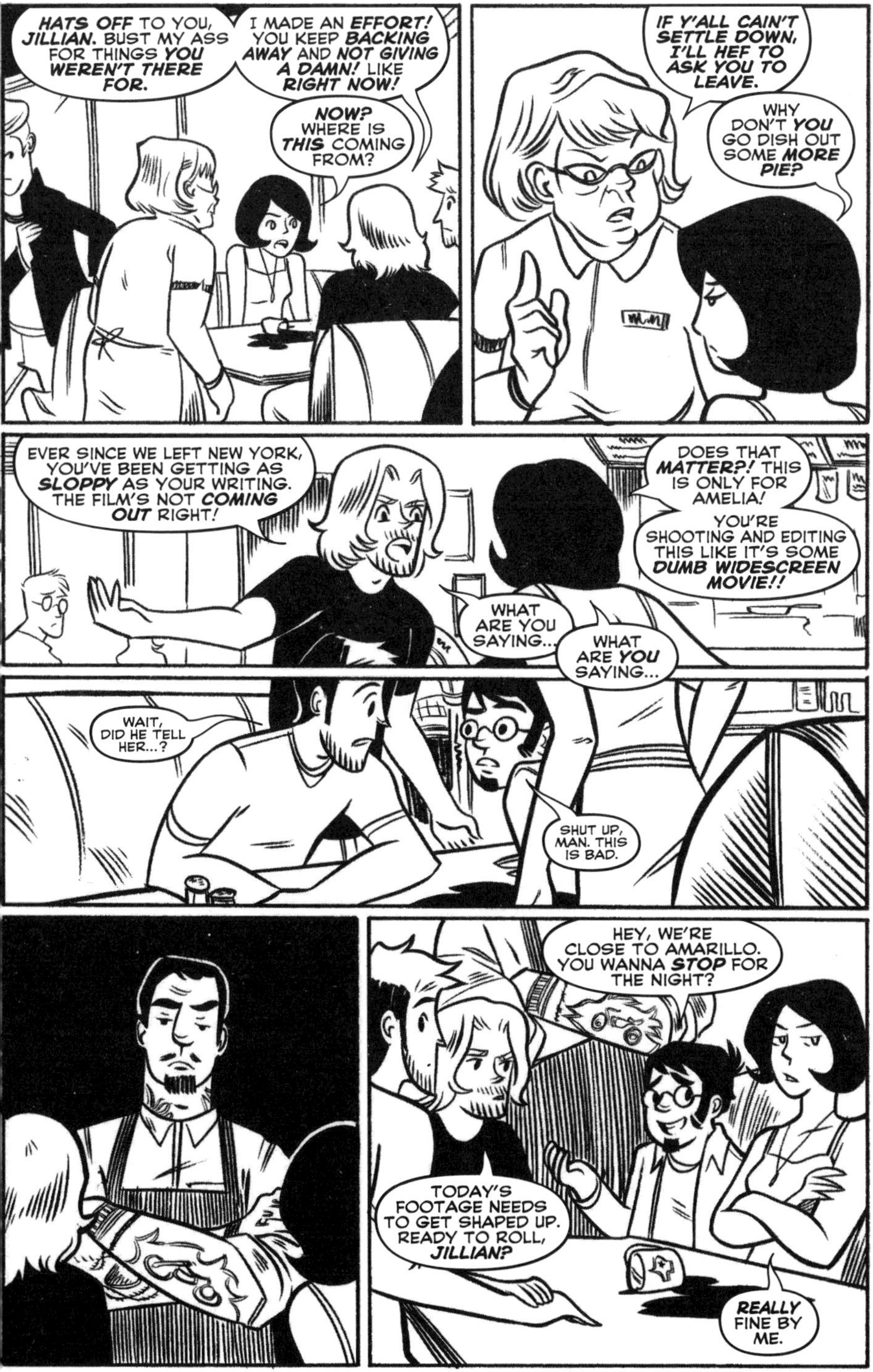
HATS OFF TO YOU, JILLIAN. BUST MY ASS FOR THINGS YOU WEREN'T THERE FOR.
I MADE AN EFFORT! YOU KEEP BACKING AWAY AND NOT GIVING A DAMN! LIKE RIGHT NOW!
NOW? WHERE IS THIS COMING FROM?
IF Y'ALL CAIN'T SETTLE DOWN, I'LL HEF TO ASK YOU TO LEAVE.
WHY DON'T YOU GO DISH OUT SOME MORE PIE?
EVER SINCE WE LEFT NEW YORK, YOU'VE BEEN GETTING AS SLOPPY AS YOUR WRITING. THE FILM'S NOT COMING OUT RIGHT!
DOES THAT MATTER?! THIS IS ONLY FOR AMELIA!
YOU'RE SHOOTING AND EDITING THIS LIKE IT'S SOME DUMB WIDESCREEN MOVIE!!
WHAT ARE YOU SAYING...
WHAT ARE YOU SAYING...
WAIT, DID HE TELL HER...?
SHUT UP, MAN. THIS IS BAD.
HEY, WE'RE CLOSE TO AMARILLO. YOU WANNA STOP FOR THE NIGHT?
TODAY'S FOOTAGE NEEDS TO GET SHAPED UP. READY TO ROLL, JILLIAN?
REALLY FINE BY ME.

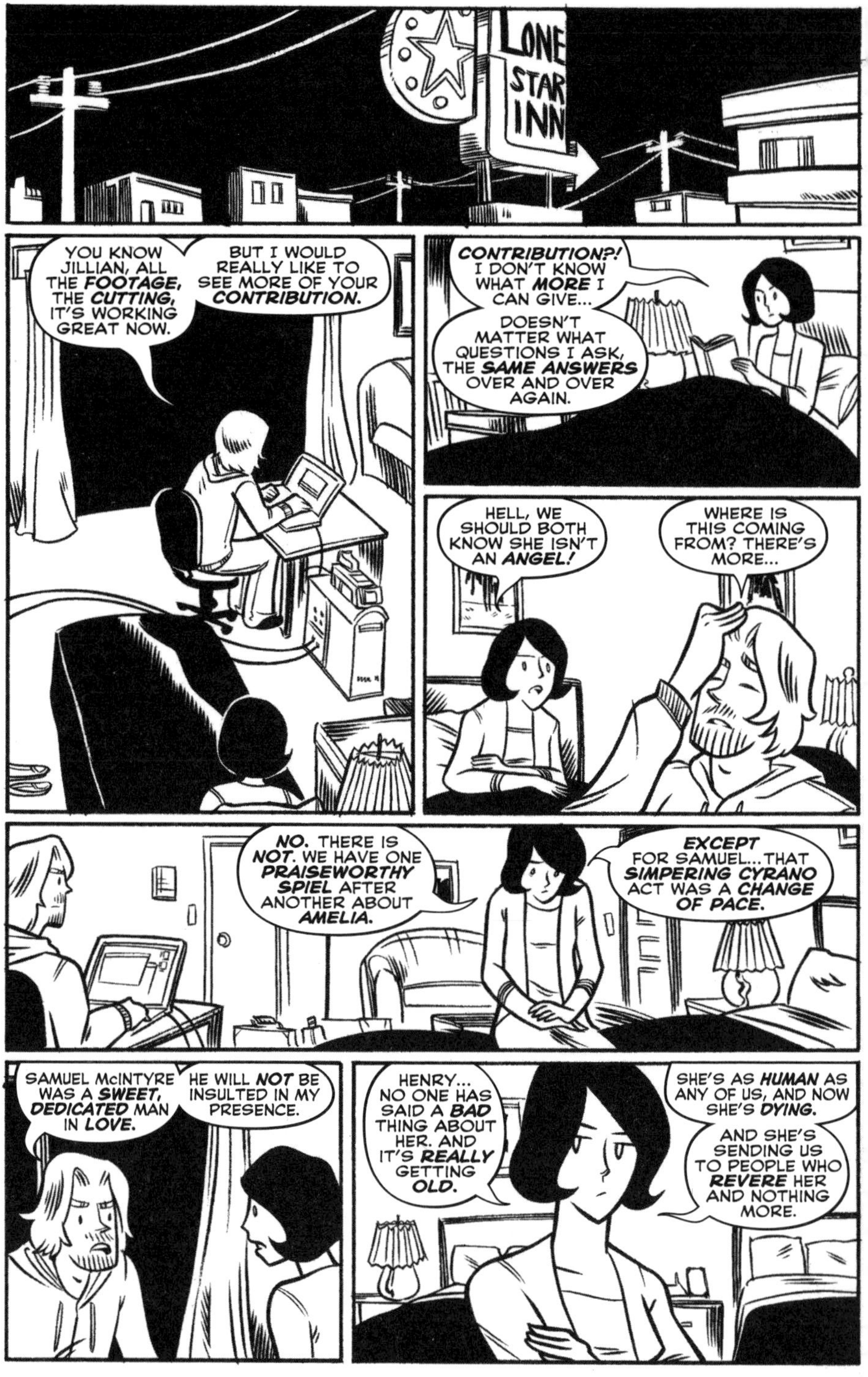
LONE STAR INN
YOU KNOW JILLIAN, ALL THE FOOTAGE, THE CUTTING, IT'S WORKING GREAT NOW.
BUT I WOULD REALLY LIKE TO SEE MORE OF YOUR CONTRIBUTION.
CONTRIBUTION?! I DON'T KNOW WHAT MORE I CAN GIVE...
DOESN'T MATTER WHAT QUESTIONS I ASK, THE SAME ANSWERS OVER AND OVER AGAIN.
HELL, WE SHOULD BOTH KNOW SHE ISN'T AN ANGEL!
WHERE IS THIS COMING FROM? THERE'S MORE...
NO. THERE IS NOT. WE HAVE ONE PRAISEWORTHY SPIEL AFTER ANOTHER ABOUT AMELIA.
EXCEPT FOR SAMUEL...THAT SIMPERING CYRANO ACT WAS A CHANGE OF PACE.
SAMUEL McINTYRE WAS A SWEET, DEDICATED MAN IN LOVE.
HE WILL NOT BE INSULTED IN MY PRESENCE.
HENRY... NO ONE HAS SAID A BAD THING ABOUT HER. AND IT'S REALLY GETTING OLD.
SHE'S AS HUMAN AS ANY OF US, AND NOW SHE'S DYING.
AND SHE'S SENDING US TO PEOPLE WHO REVERE HER AND NOTHING MORE.

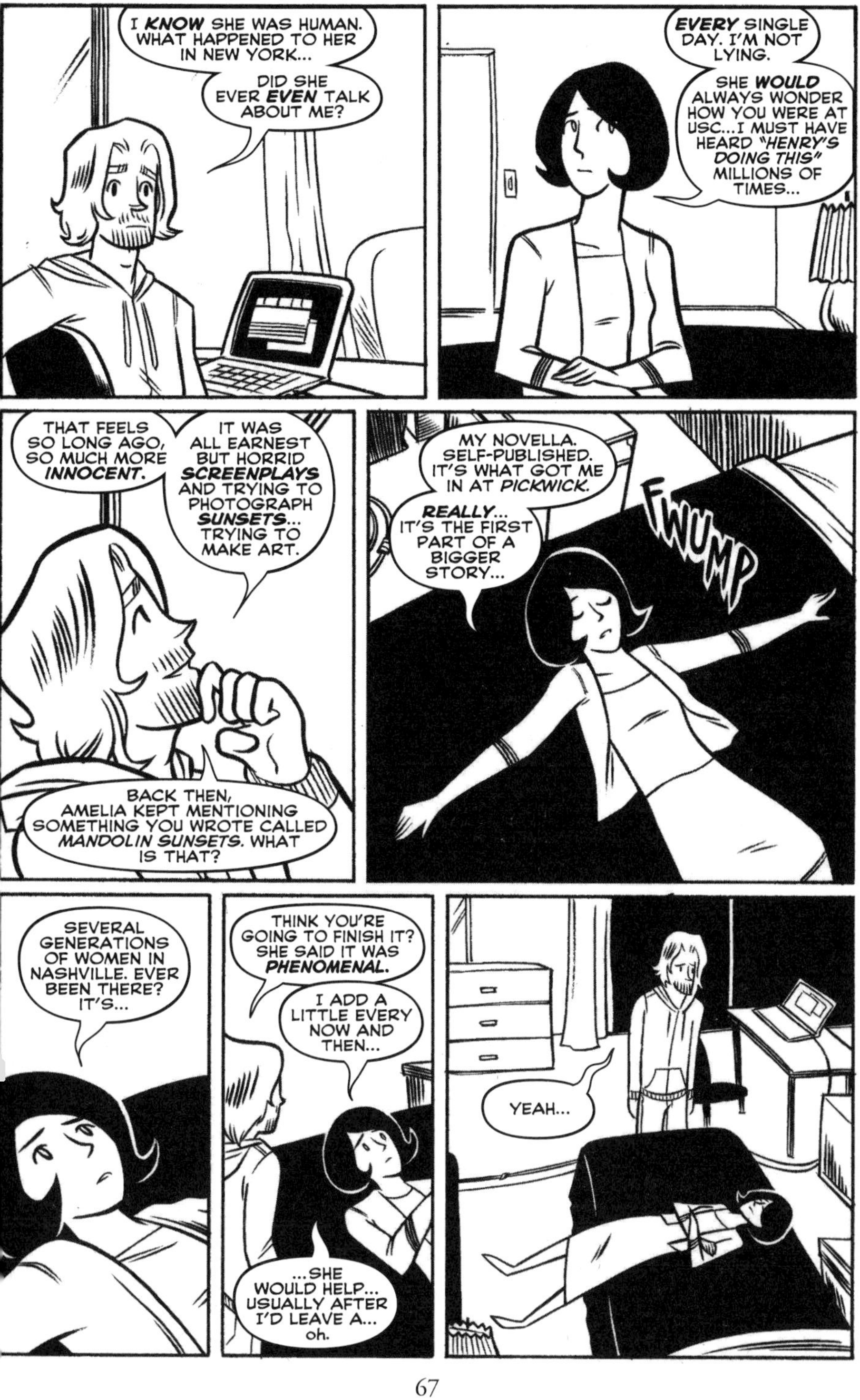
I KNOW SHE WAS HUMAN. WHAT HAPPENED TO HER IN NEW YORK...
DID SHE EVER EVEN TALK ABOUT ME?
EVERY SINGLE DAY. I'M NOT LYING.
SHE WOULD ALWAYS WONDER HOW YOU WERE AT USC...I MUST HAVE HEARD "HENRY'S DOING THIS" MILLIONS OF TIMES...
THAT FEELS SO LONG AGO, SO MUCH MORE INNOCENT.
IT WAS ALL EARNEST BUT HORRID SCREENPLAYS AND TRYING TO PHOTOGRAPH SUNSETS... TRYING TO MAKE ART.
BACK THEN, AMELIA KEPT MENTIONING SOMETHING YOU WROTE CALLED MANDOLIN SUNSETS. WHAT IS THAT?
MY NOVELLA. SELF-PUBLISHED. IT'S WHAT GOT ME IN AT PICKWICK.
REALLY... IT'S THE FIRST PART OF A BIGGER STORY...
FWUMP
SEVERAL GENERATIONS OF WOMEN IN NASHVILLE. EVER BEEN THERE? IT'S...
THINK YOU'RE GOING TO FINISH IT? SHE SAID IT WAS PHENOMENAL.
I ADD A LITTLE EVERY NOW AND THEN...
...SHE WOULD HELP... USUALLY AFTER I'D LEAVE A... oh.
YEAH...

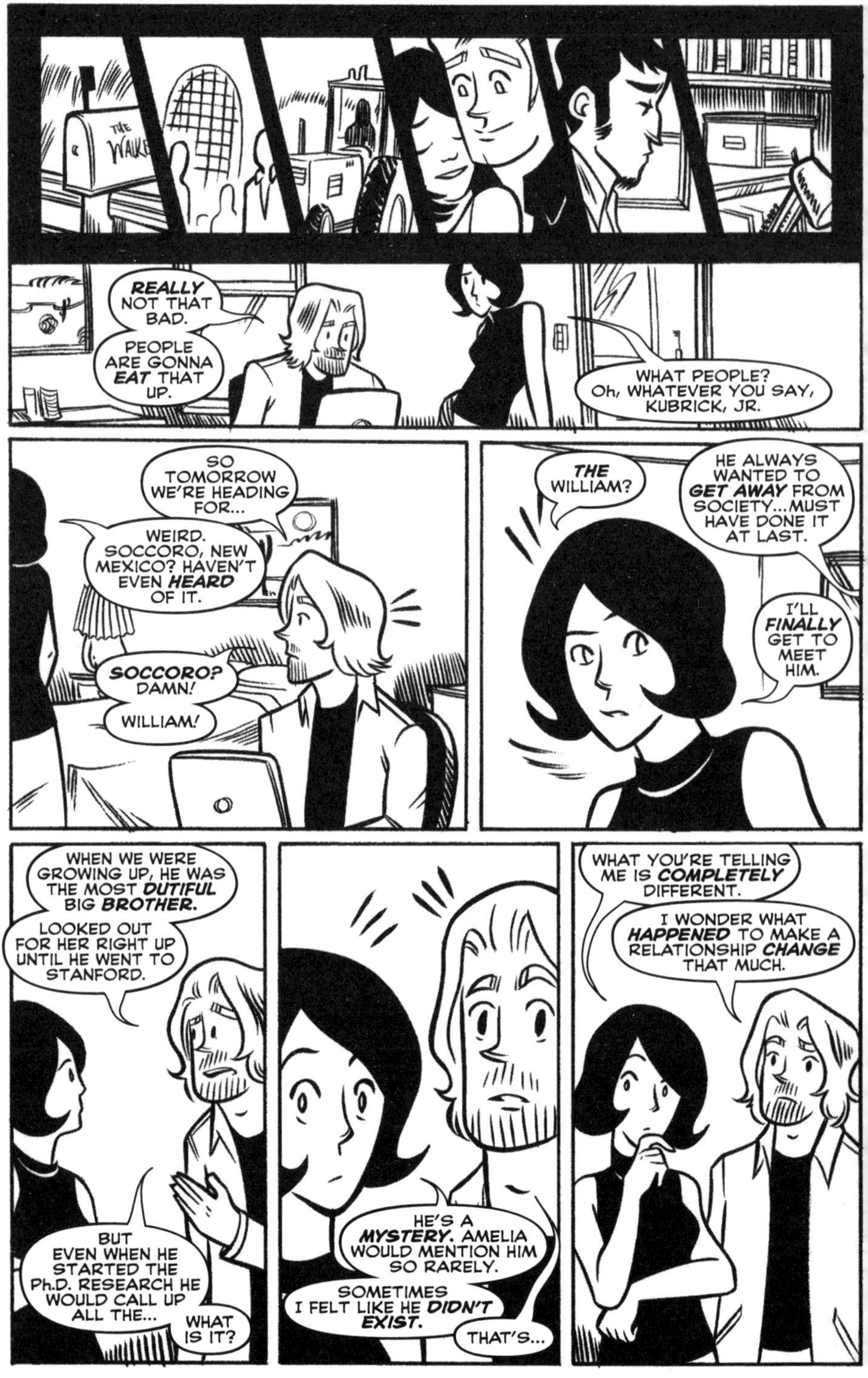
THE WALKE
REALLY NOT THAT BAD.
PEOPLE ARE GONNA EAT THAT UP.
WHAT PEOPLE? Oh, WHATEVER YOU SAY, KUBRICK, JR.
SO TOMORROW WE'RE HEADING FOR...
WEIRD. SOCCORO, NEW MEXICO? HAVEN'T EVEN HEARD OF IT.
SOCCORO? DAMN!
WILLIAM!
THE WILLIAM?
HE ALWAYS WANTED TO GET AWAY FROM SOCIETY...MUST HAVE DONE IT AT LAST.
I'LL FINALLY GET TO MEET HIM.
WHEN WE WERE GROWING UP, HE WAS THE MOST DUTIFUL BIG BROTHER.
LOOKED OUT FOR HER RIGHT UP UNTIL HE WENT TO STANFORD.
BUT EVEN WHEN HE STARTED THE Ph.D. RESEARCH HE WOULD CALL UP ALL THE...
WHAT IS IT?
HE'S A MYSTERY. AMELIA WOULD MENTION HIM SO RARELY.
SOMETIMES I FELT LIKE HE DIDN'T EXIST.
THAT'S...
WHAT YOU'RE TELLING ME IS COMPLETELY DIFFERENT.
I WONDER WHAT HAPPENED TO MAKE A RELATIONSHIP CHANGE THAT MUCH.

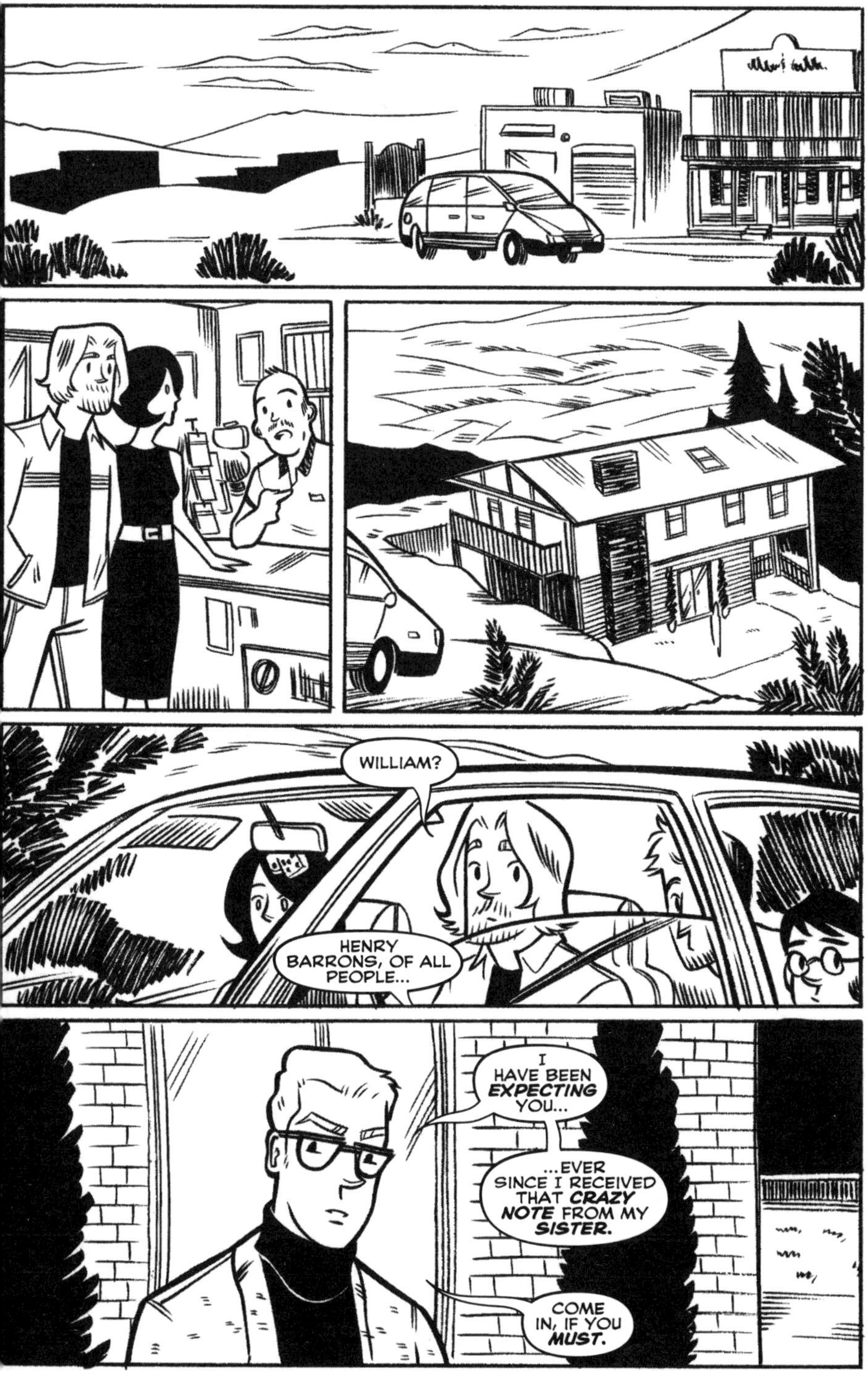
WILLIAM?
HENRY BARRONS, OF ALL PEOPLE...
I HAVE BEEN EXPECTING YOU...
...EVER SINCE I RECEIVED THAT CRAZY NOTE FROM MY SISTER.
COME IN, IF YOU MUST.

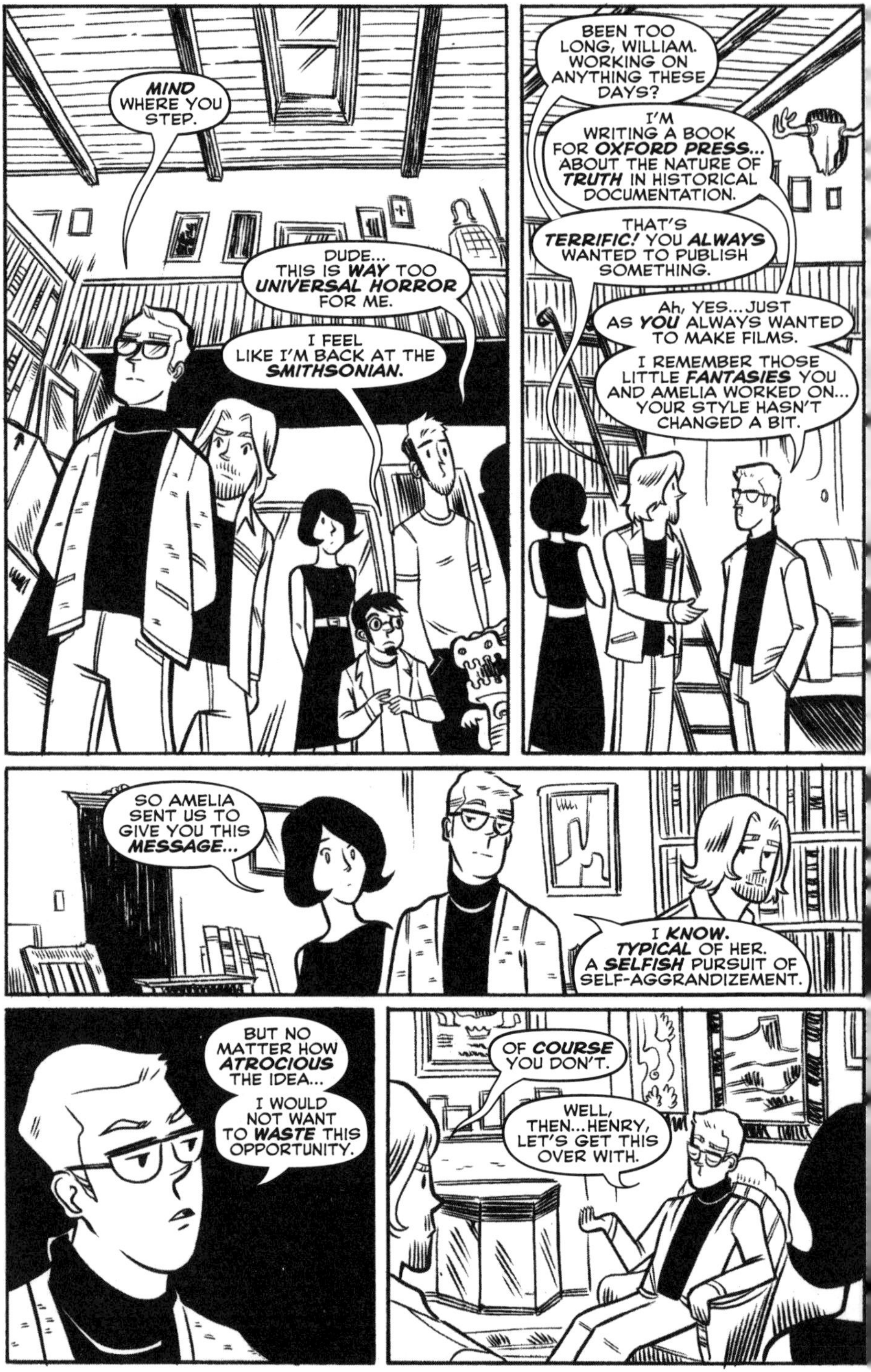
MIND WHERE YOU STEP.
DUDE... THIS IS WAY TOO UNIVERSAL HORROR FOR ME.
I FEEL LIKE I'M BACK AT THE SMITHSONIAN.
BEEN TOO LONG, WILLIAM. WORKING ON ANYTHING THESE DAYS?
I'M WRITING A BOOK FOR OXFORD PRESS... ABOUT THE NATURE OF TRUTH IN HISTORICAL DOCUMENTATION.
THAT'S TERRIFIC! YOU ALWAYS WANTED TO PUBLISH SOMETHING.
Ah, YES... JUST AS YOU ALWAYS WANTED TO MAKE FILMS.
I REMEMBER THOSE LITTLE FANTASIES YOU AND AMELIA WORKED ON... YOUR STYLE HASN'T CHANGED A BIT.
SO AMELIA SENT US TO GIVE YOU THIS MESSAGE...
I KNOW. TYPICAL OF HER. A SELFISH PURSUIT OF SELF-AGGRANDIZEMENT.
BUT NO MATTER HOW ATROCIOUS THE IDEA...
I WOULD NOT WANT TO WASTE THIS OPPORTUNITY.
OF COURSE YOU DON'T.
WELL, THEN... HENRY, LET'S GET THIS OVER WITH.

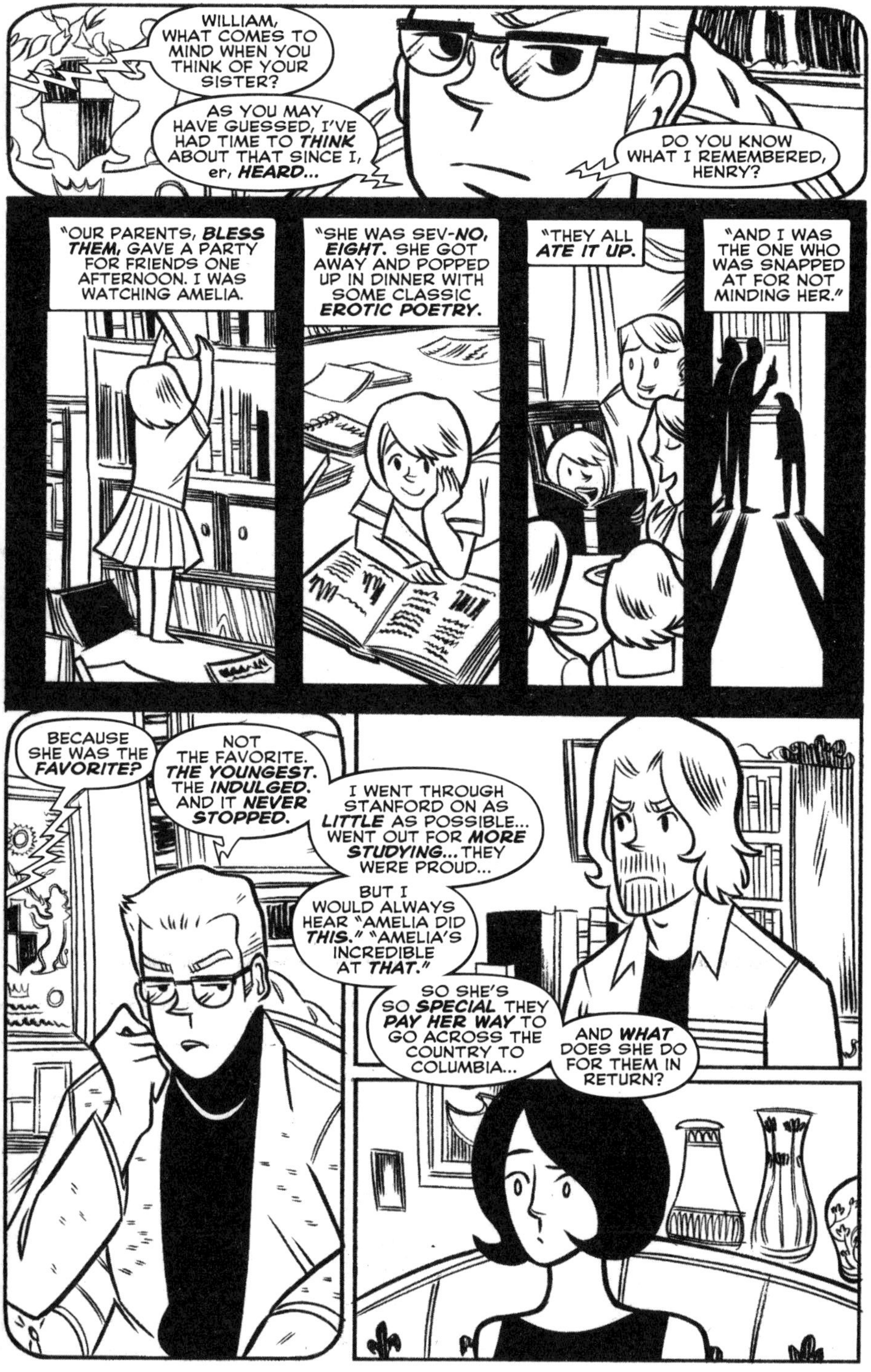
WILLIAM, WHAT COMES TO MIND WHEN YOU THINK OF YOUR SISTER?
AS YOU MAY HAVE GUESSED, I'VE HAD TIME TO THINK ABOUT THAT SINCE I, er, HEARD...
DO YOU KNOW WHAT I REMEMBERED, HENRY?
"OUR PARENTS, BLESS THEM, GAVE A PARTY FOR FRIENDS ONE AFTERNOON. I WAS WATCHING AMELIA.
"SHE WAS SEV-NO, EIGHT. SHE GOT AWAY AND POPPED UP IN DINNER WITH SOME CLASSIC EROTIC POETRY.
"THEY ALL ATE IT UP.
"AND I WAS THE ONE WHO WAS SNAPPED AT FOR NOT MINDING HER."
BECAUSE SHE WAS THE FAVORITE?
NOT THE FAVORITE. THE YOUNGEST. THE INDULGED. AND IT NEVER STOPPED.
I WENT THROUGH STANFORD ON AS LITTLE AS POSSIBLE... WENT OUT FOR MORE STUDYING... THEY WERE PROUD...
BUT I WOULD ALWAYS HEAR "AMELIA DID THIS." "AMELIA'S INCREDIBLE AT THAT."
SO SHE'S SO SPECIAL THEY PAY HER WAY TO GO ACROSS THE COUNTRY TO COLUMBIA...
AND WHAT DOES SHE DO FOR THEM IN RETURN?

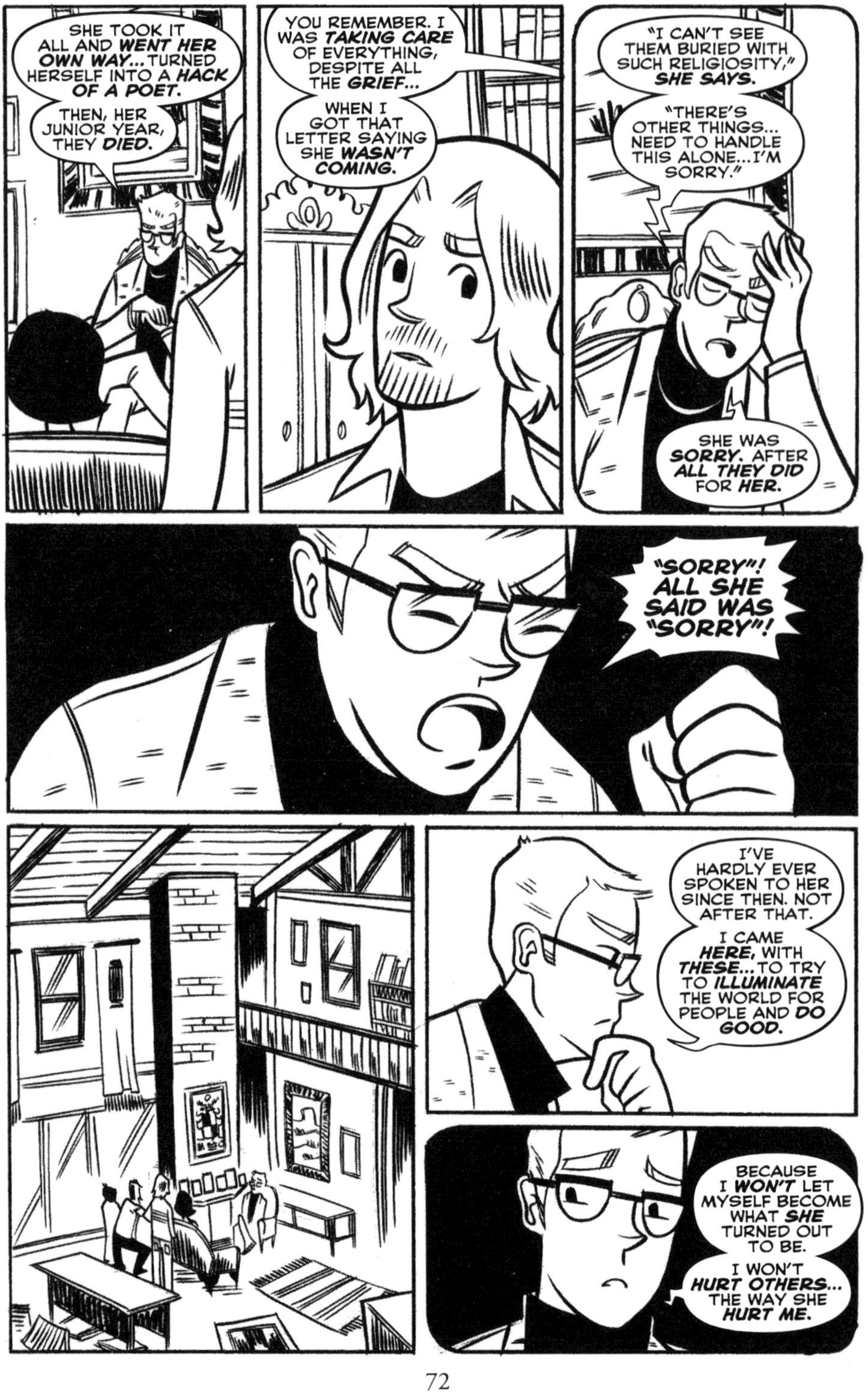
SHE TOOK IT ALL AND WENT HER OWN WAY...TURNED HERSELF INTO A HACK OF A POET.
THEN, HER JUNIOR YEAR, THEY DIED.
YOU REMEMBER. I WAS TAKING CARE OF EVERYTHING, DESPITE ALL THE GRIEF...
WHEN I GOT THAT LETTER SAYING SHE WASN'T COMING.
"I CAN'T SEE THEM BURIED WITH SUCH RELIGIOSITY," SHE SAYS.
"THERE'S OTHER THINGS... NEED TO HANDLE THIS ALONE...I'M SORRY."
SHE WAS SORRY. AFTER ALL THEY DID FOR HER.
"SORRY"! ALL SHE SAID WAS "SORRY"!
I'VE HARDLY EVER SPOKEN TO HER SINCE THEN. NOT AFTER THAT.
I CAME HERE, WITH THESE...TO TRY TO ILLUMINATE THE WORLD FOR PEOPLE AND DO GOOD.
BECAUSE I WON'T LET MYSELF BECOME WHAT SHE TURNED OUT TO BE.
I WON'T HURT OTHERS... THE WAY SHE HURT ME.

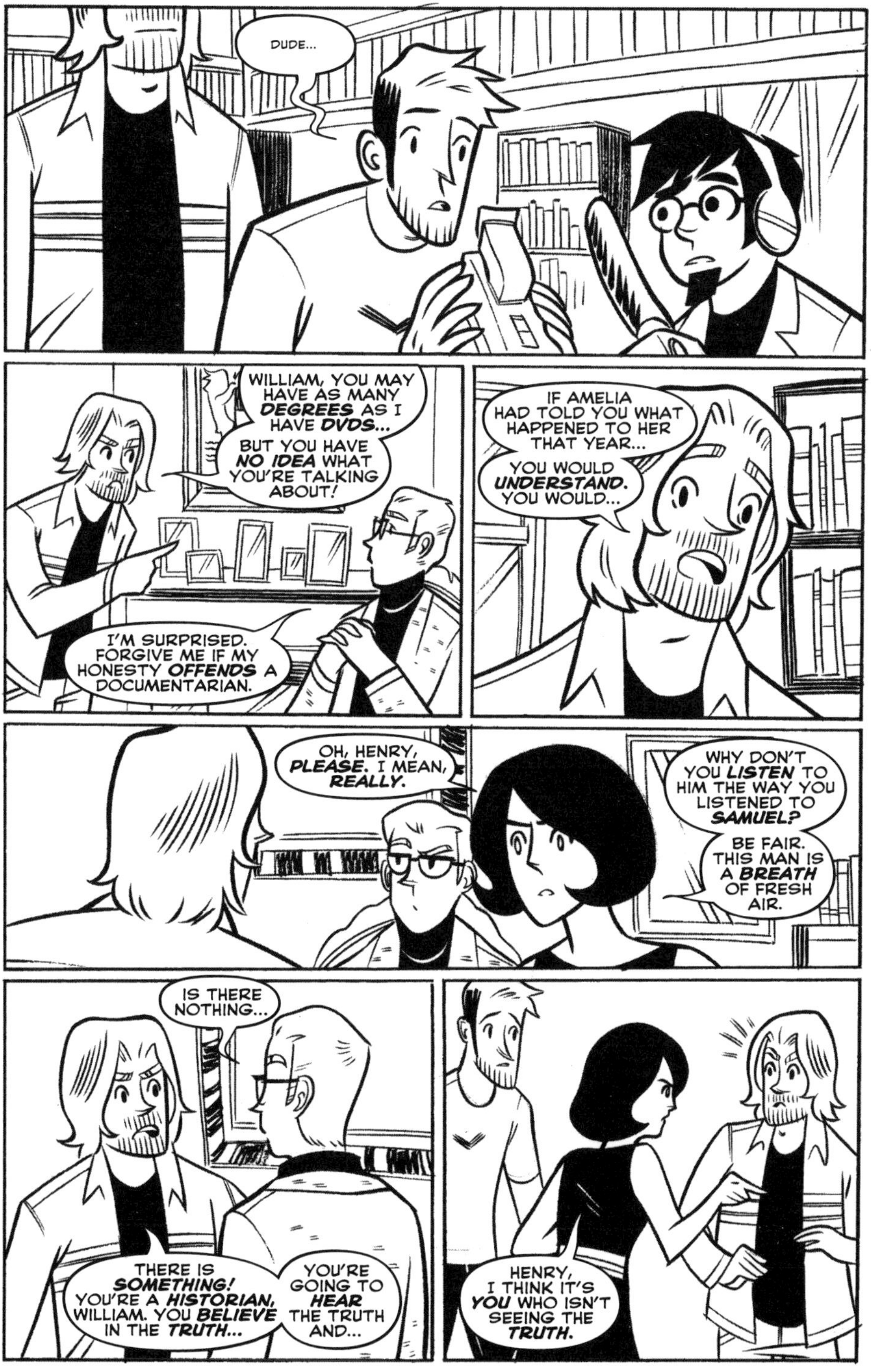
DUDE...
WILLIAM, YOU MAY HAVE AS MANY DEGREES AS I HAVE DVDS...
BUT YOU HAVE NO IDEA WHAT YOU'RE TALKING ABOUT!
I'M SURPRISED. FORGIVE ME IF MY HONESTY OFFENDS A DOCUMENTARIAN.
IF AMELIA HAD TOLD YOU WHAT HAPPENED TO HER THAT YEAR...
YOU WOULD UNDERSTAND. YOU WOULD...
OH, HENRY, PLEASE. I MEAN, REALLY.
WHY DON'T YOU LISTEN TO HIM THE WAY YOU LISTENED TO SAMUEL?
BE FAIR. THIS MAN IS A BREATH OF FRESH AIR.
IS THERE NOTHING...
THERE IS SOMETHING! YOU'RE A HISTORIAN, WILLIAM. YOU BELIEVE IN THE TRUTH...
YOU'RE GOING TO HEAR THE TRUTH AND...
HENRY, I THINK IT'S YOU WHO ISN'T SEEING THE TRUTH.

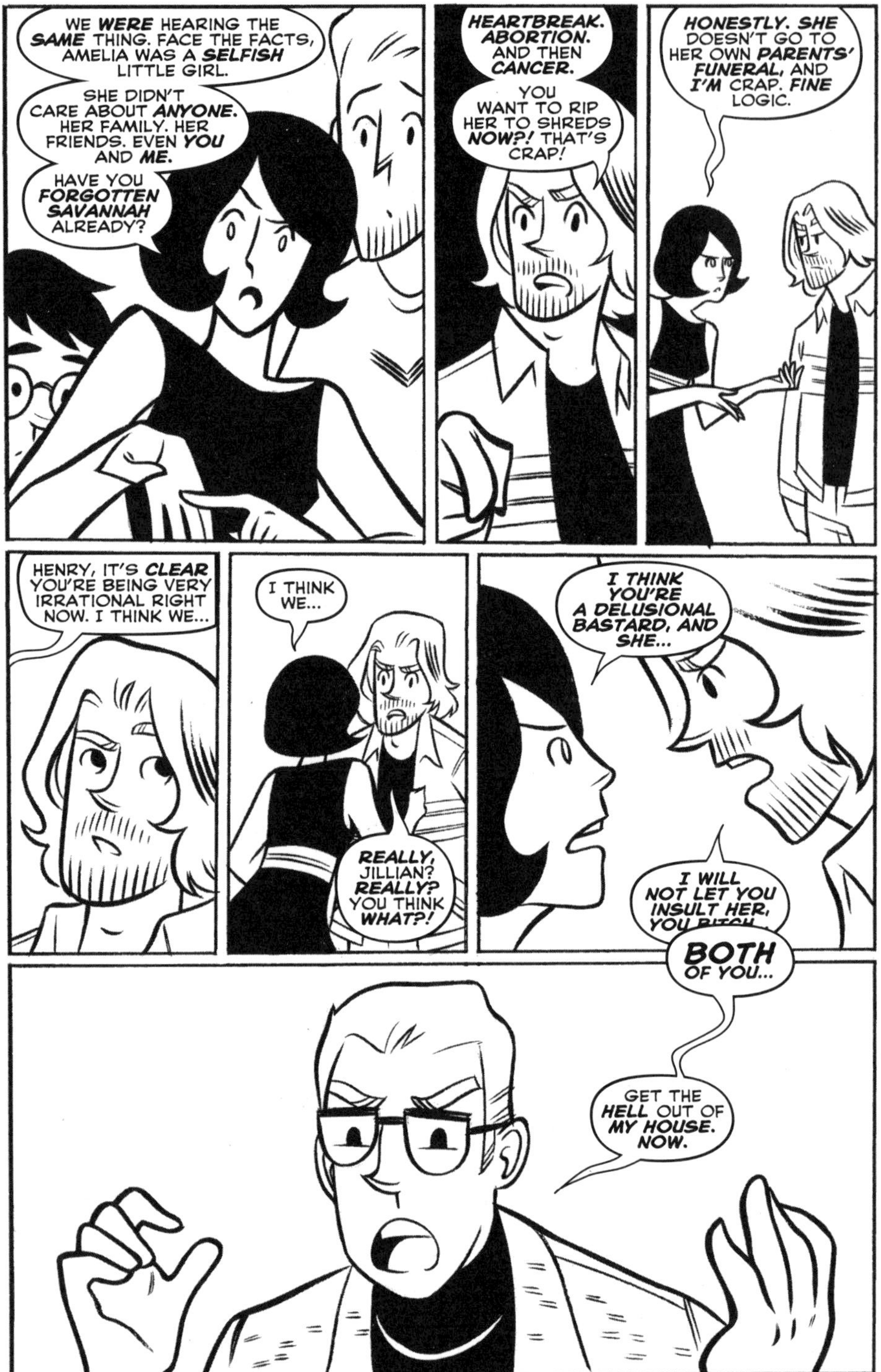
WE WERE HEARING THE SAME THING. FACE THE FACTS, AMELIA WAS A SELFISH LITTLE GIRL.
SHE DIDN'T CARE ABOUT ANYONE. HER FAMILY. HER FRIENDS. EVEN YOU AND ME.
HAVE YOU FORGOTTEN SAVANNAH ALREADY?
HEARTBREAK. ABORTION. AND THEN CANCER.
YOU WANT TO RIP HER TO SHREDS NOW?! THAT'S CRAP!
HONESTLY. SHE DOESN'T GO TO HER OWN PARENTS' FUNERAL, AND I'M CRAP. FINE LOGIC.
HENRY, IT'S CLEAR YOU'RE BEING VERY IRRATIONAL RIGHT NOW. I THINK WE...
I THINK WE...
REALLY, JILLIAN? REALLY? YOU THINK WHAT?!
I THINK YOU'RE A DELUSIONAL BASTARD, AND SHE...
I WILL NOT LET YOU INSULT HER,
BOTH OF YOU...
GET THE HELL OUT OF MY HOUSE. NOW.

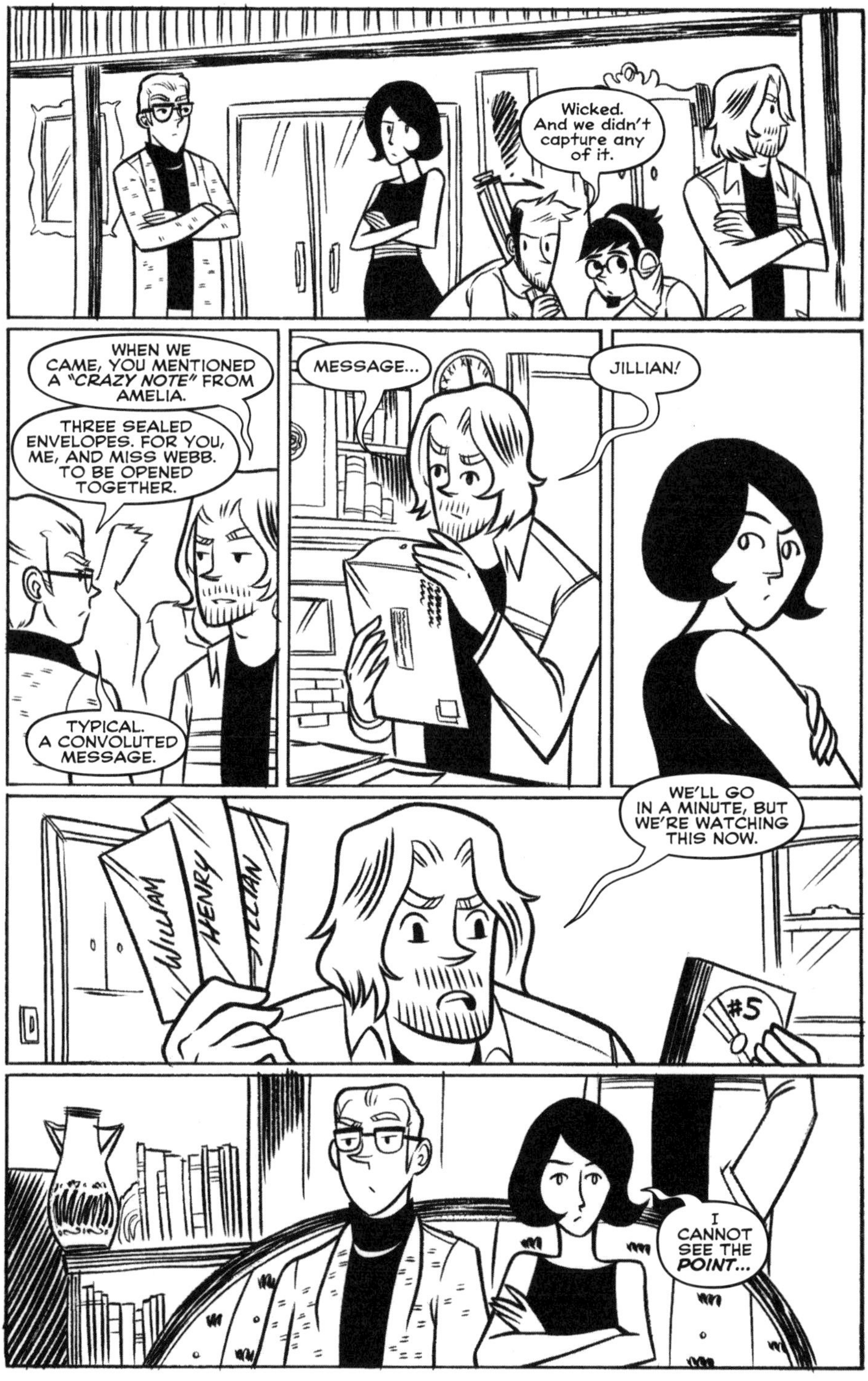

Wicked. And we didn't capture any of it.
WHEN WE CAME, YOU MENTIONED A "CRAZY NOTE" FROM AMELIA.
THREE SEALED ENVELOPES. FOR YOU, ME, AND MISS WEBB. TO BE OPENED TOGETHER.
TYPICAL. A CONVOLUTED MESSAGE.
MESSAGE...
JILLIAN!
WILLIAM
HENRY
JILLIAN
WE'LL GO IN A MINUTE, BUT WE'RE WATCHING THIS NOW.
#5
I CANNOT SEE THE POINT...

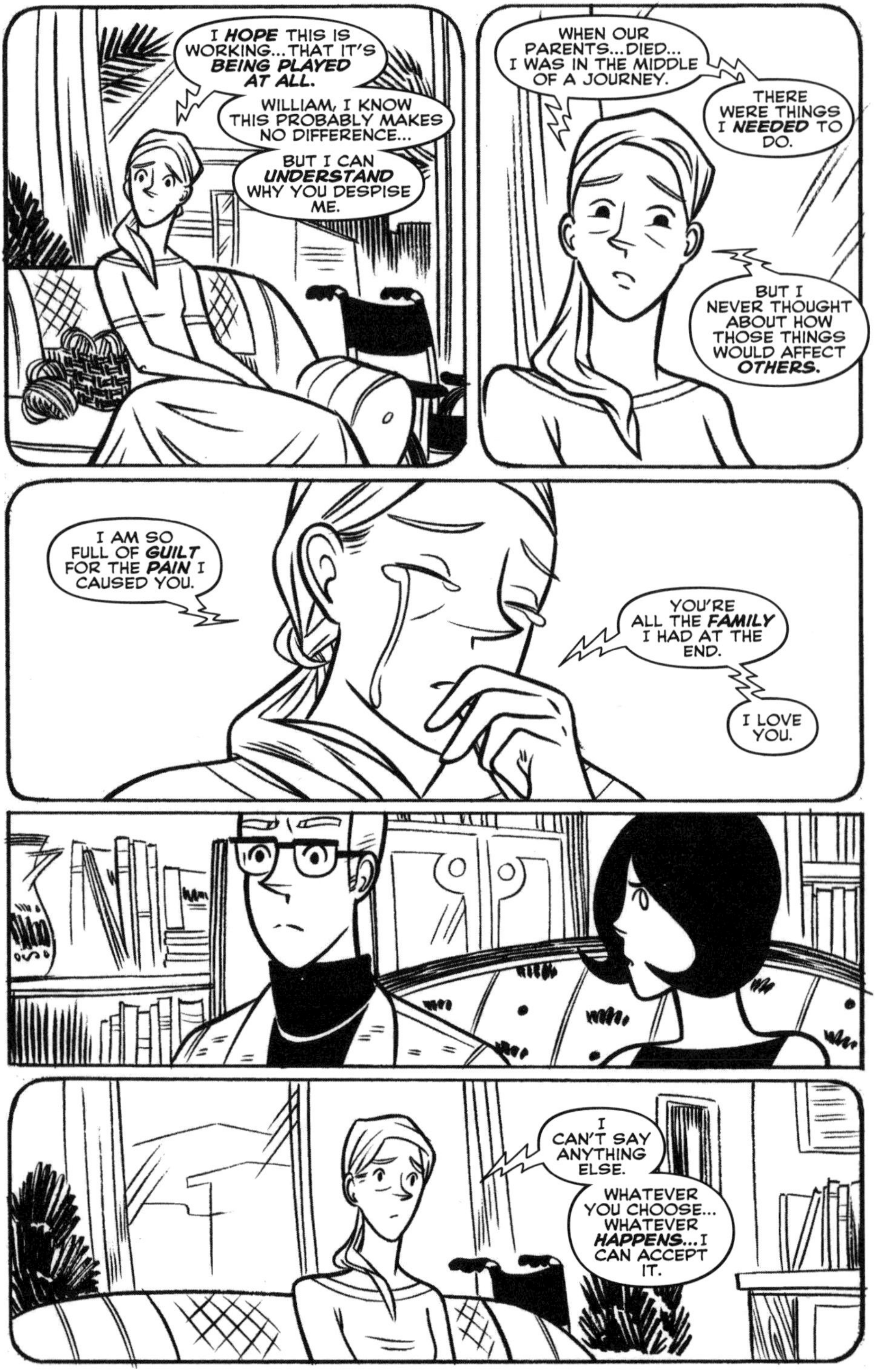

I HOPE THIS IS WORKING...THAT IT'S BEING PLAYED AT ALL.
WILLIAM, I KNOW THIS PROBABLY MAKES NO DIFFERENCE...
BUT I CAN UNDERSTAND WHY YOU DESPISE ME.
WHEN OUR PARENTS...DIED... I WAS IN THE MIDDLE OF A JOURNEY.
THERE WERE THINGS I NEEDED TO DO.
BUT I NEVER THOUGHT ABOUT HOW THOSE THINGS WOULD AFFECT OTHERS.
I AM SO FULL OF GUILT FOR THE PAIN I CAUSED YOU.
YOU'RE ALL THE FAMILY I HAD AT THE END.
I LOVE YOU.
I CAN'T SAY ANYTHING ELSE.
WHATEVER YOU CHOOSE... WHATEVER HAPPENS...I CAN ACCEPT IT.

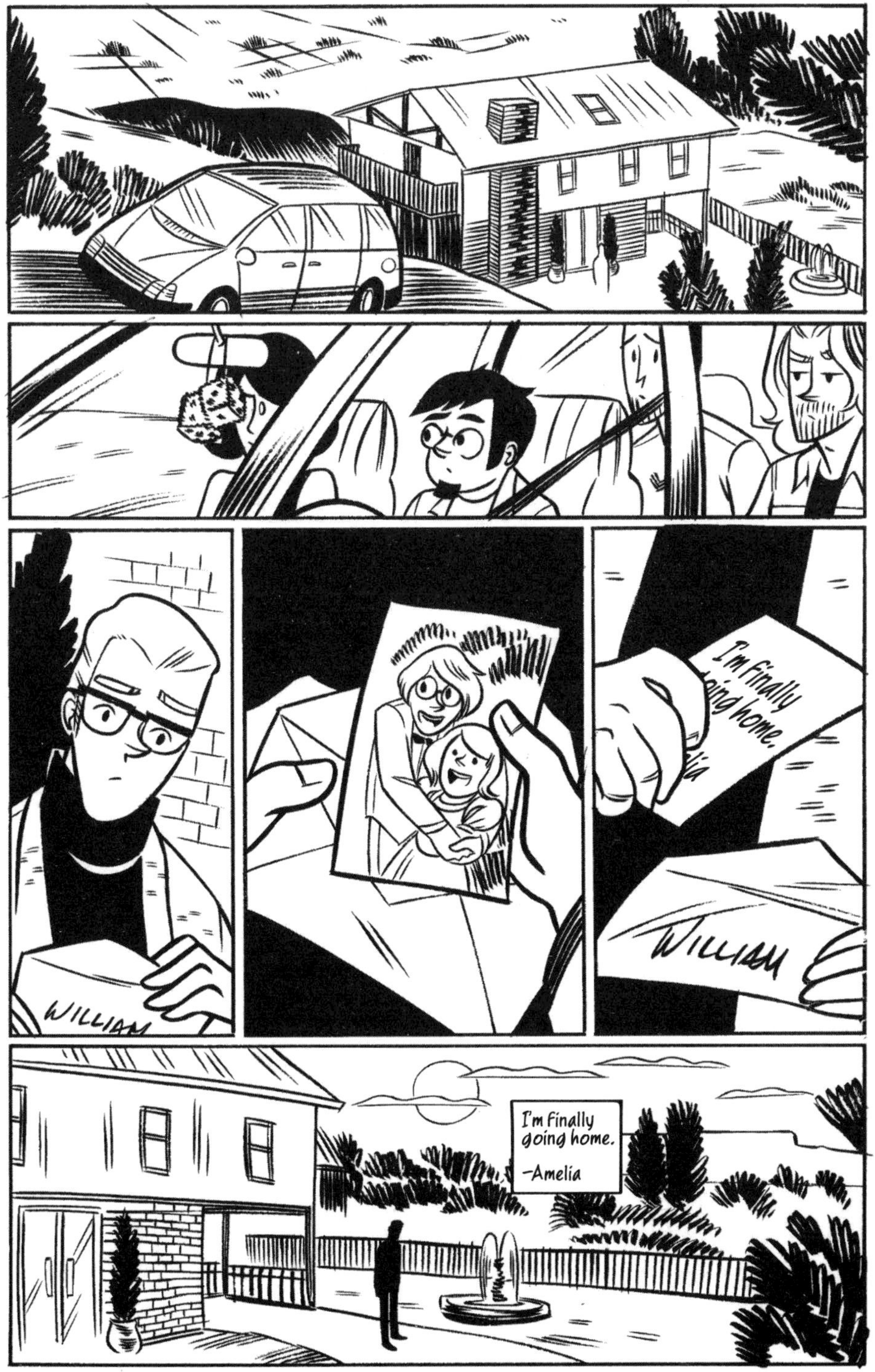

WILLIAM
I'm finally going home.
WILLIAM
I'm finally going home.
-Amelia

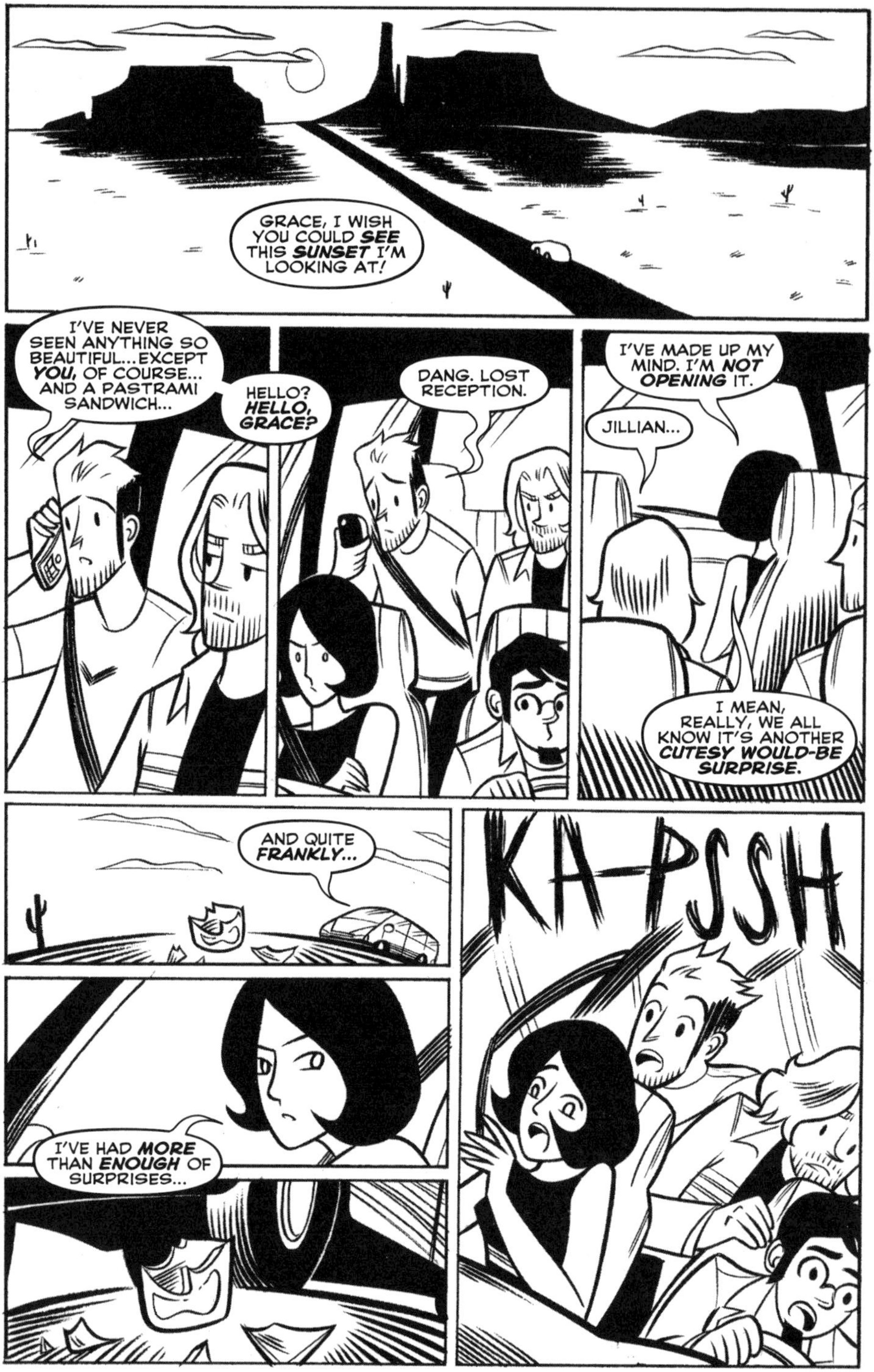

GRACE, I WISH YOU COULD SEE THIS SUNSET I'M LOOKING AT!
I'VE NEVER SEEN ANYTHING SO BEAUTIFUL...EXCEPT YOU, OF COURSE... AND A PASTRAMI SANDWICH...
HELLO? HELLO, GRACE?
DANG. LOST RECEPTION.
I'VE MADE UP MY MIND. I'M NOT OPENING IT.
JILLIAN...
I MEAN, REALLY, WE ALL KNOW IT'S ANOTHER CUTESY WOULD-BE SURPRISE.
AND QUITE FRANKLY...
I'VE HAD MORE THAN ENOUGH OF SURPRISES...
KA-PSSH

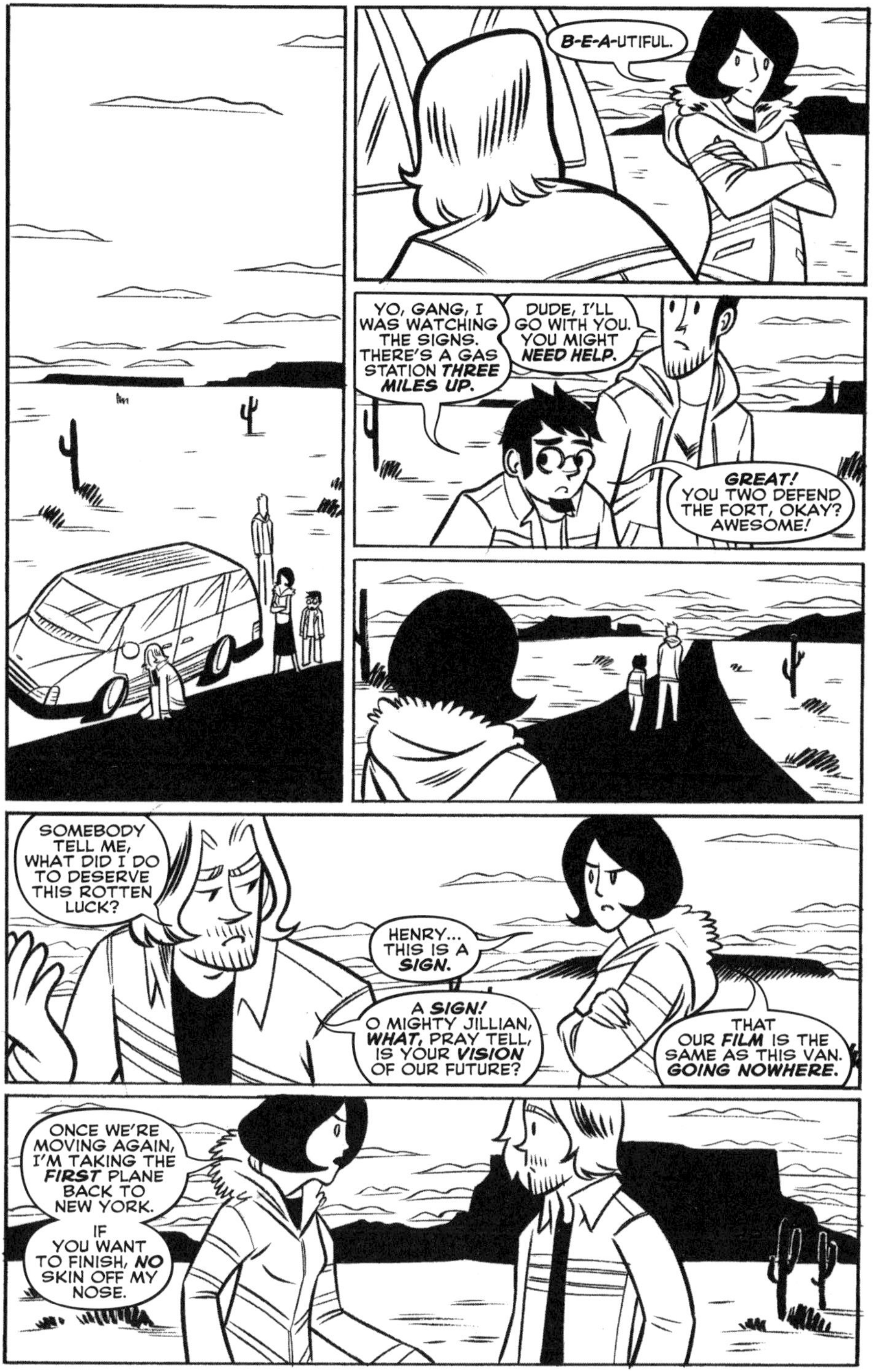
B-E-A-UTIFUL.
YO, GANG, I WAS WATCHING THE SIGNS. THERE'S A GAS STATION THREE MILES UP.
DUDE, I'LL GO WITH YOU. YOU MIGHT NEED HELP.
GREAT! YOU TWO DEFEND THE FORT, OKAY? AWESOME!
SOMEBODY TELL ME, WHAT DID I DO TO DESERVE THIS ROTTEN LUCK?
HENRY... THIS IS A SIGN.
A SIGN! O MIGHTY JILLIAN, WHAT, PRAY TELL, IS YOUR VISION OF OUR FUTURE?
THAT OUR FILM IS THE SAME AS THIS VAN. GOING NOWHERE.
ONCE WE'RE MOVING AGAIN, I'M TAKING THE FIRST PLANE BACK TO NEW YORK.
IF YOU WANT TO FINISH, NO SKIN OFF MY NOSE.

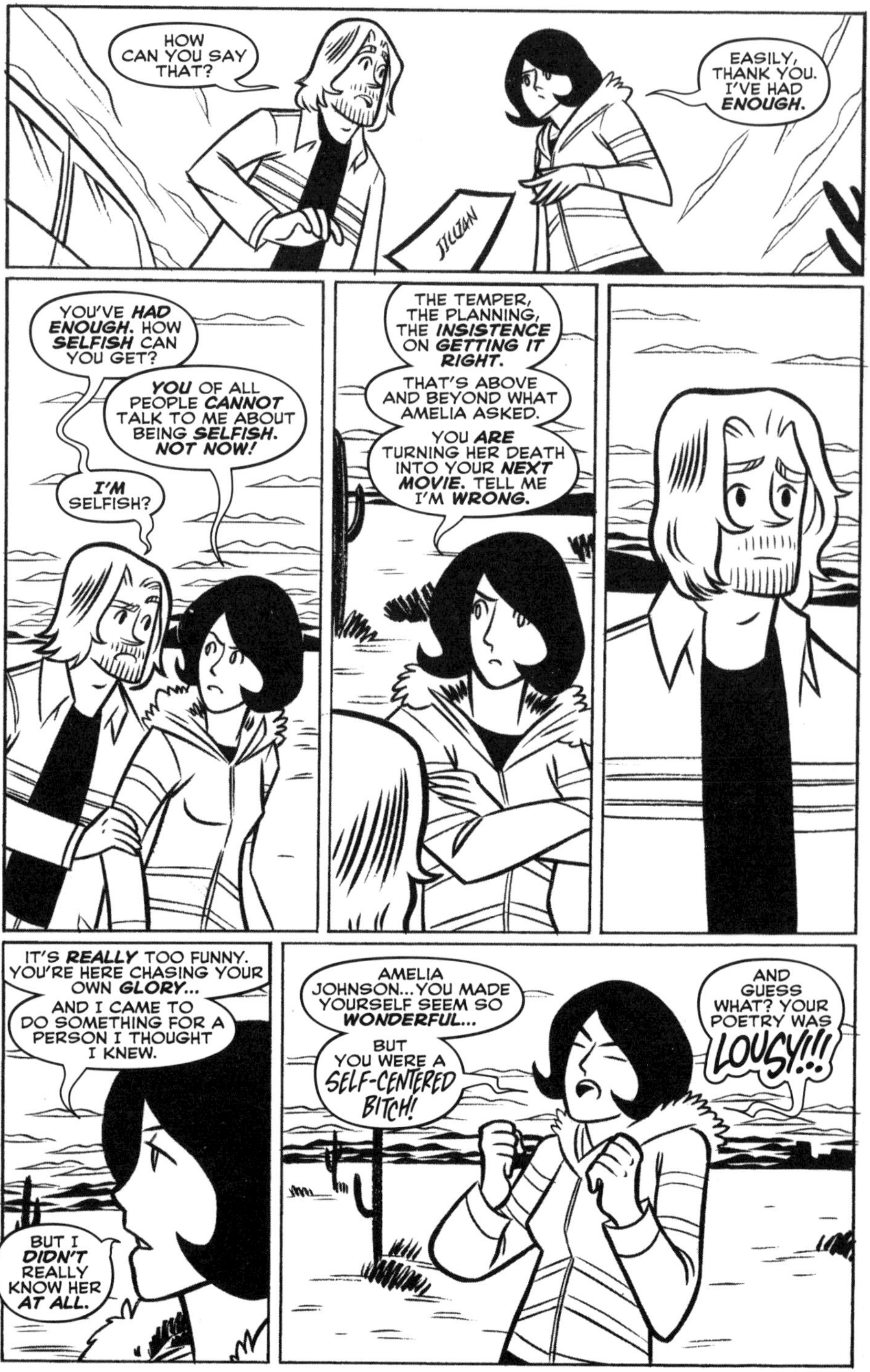
HOW CAN YOU SAY THAT?
EASILY, THANK YOU. I'VE HAD ENOUGH.
JILLIAN
YOU'VE HAD ENOUGH. HOW SELFISH CAN YOU GET?
YOU OF ALL PEOPLE CANNOT TALK TO ME ABOUT BEING SELFISH. NOT NOW!
I'M SELFISH?
THE TEMPER, THE PLANNING, THE INSISTENCE ON GETTING IT RIGHT.
THAT'S ABOVE AND BEYOND WHAT AMELIA ASKED.
YOU ARE TURNING HER DEATH INTO YOUR NEXT MOVIE. TELL ME I'M WRONG.
IT'S REALLY TOO FUNNY. YOU'RE HERE CHASING YOUR OWN GLORY...
AND I CAME TO DO SOMETHING FOR A PERSON I THOUGHT I KNEW.
BUT I DIDN'T REALLY KNOW HER AT ALL.
AMELIA JOHNSON...YOU MADE YOURSELF SEEM SO WONDERFUL...
BUT YOU WERE A SELF-CENTERED BITCH!
AND GUESS WHAT? YOUR POETRY WAS LOUSY!!!

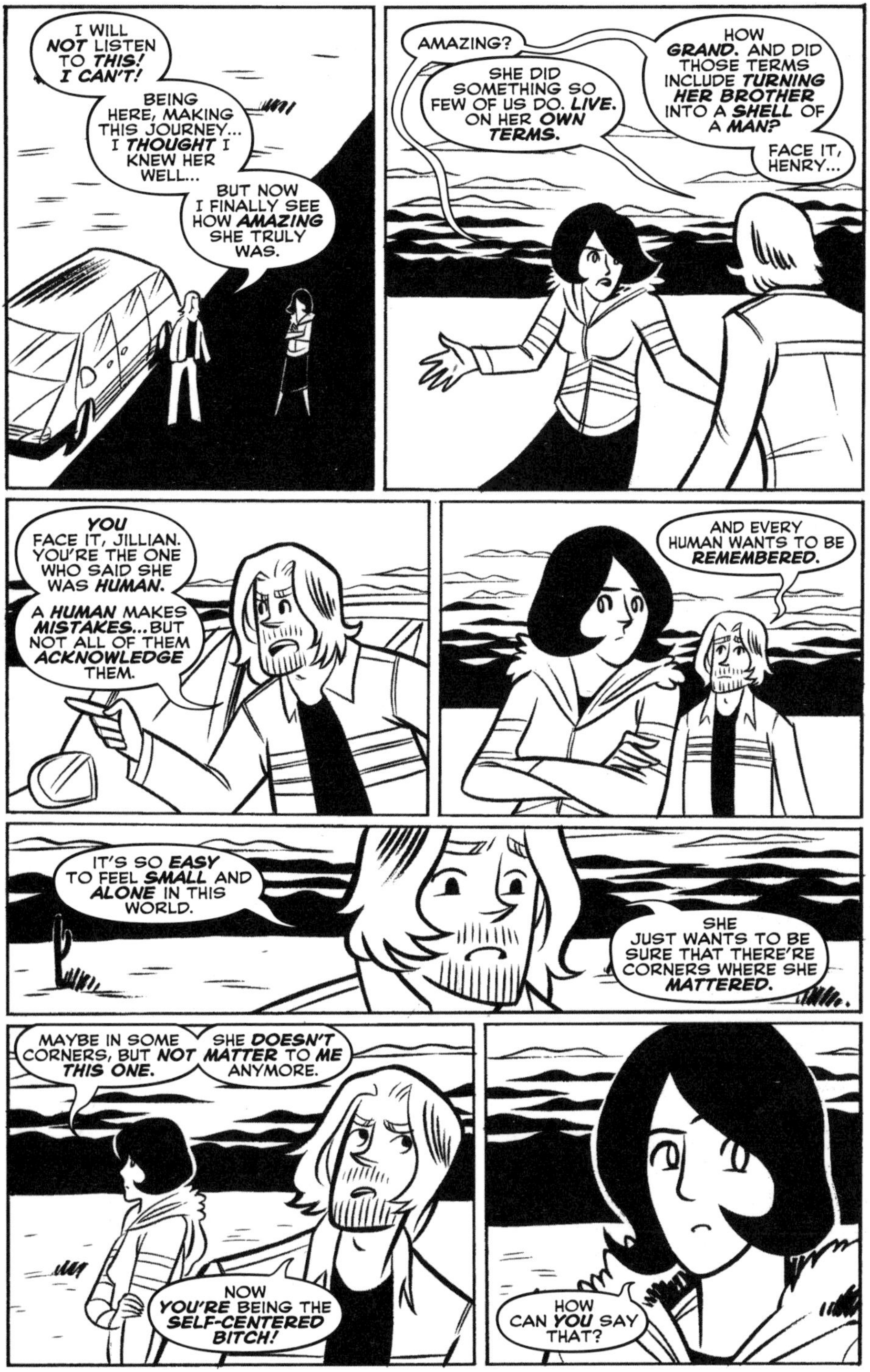
I WILL NOT LISTEN TO THIS! I CAN'T!
BEING HERE, MAKING THIS JOURNEY... I THOUGHT I KNEW HER WELL...
BUT NOW I FINALLY SEE HOW AMAZING SHE TRULY WAS.
AMAZING?
SHE DID SOMETHING SO FEW OF US DO. LIVE. ON HER OWN TERMS.
HOW GRAND. AND DID THOSE TERMS INCLUDE TURNING HER BROTHER INTO A SHELL OF A MAN?
FACE IT, HENRY...
YOU FACE IT, JILLIAN. YOU'RE THE ONE WHO SAID SHE WAS HUMAN.
A HUMAN MAKES MISTAKES...BUT NOT ALL OF THEM ACKNOWLEDGE THEM.
AND EVERY HUMAN WANTS TO BE REMEMBERED.
IT'S SO EASY TO FEEL SMALL AND ALONE IN THIS WORLD.
SHE JUST WANTS TO BE SURE THAT THERE'RE CORNERS WHERE SHE MATTERED.
MAYBE IN SOME CORNERS, BUT NOT THIS ONE.
SHE DOESN'T MATTER TO ME ANYMORE.
NOW YOU'RE BEING THE SELF-CENTERED BITCH!
HOW CAN YOU SAY THAT?

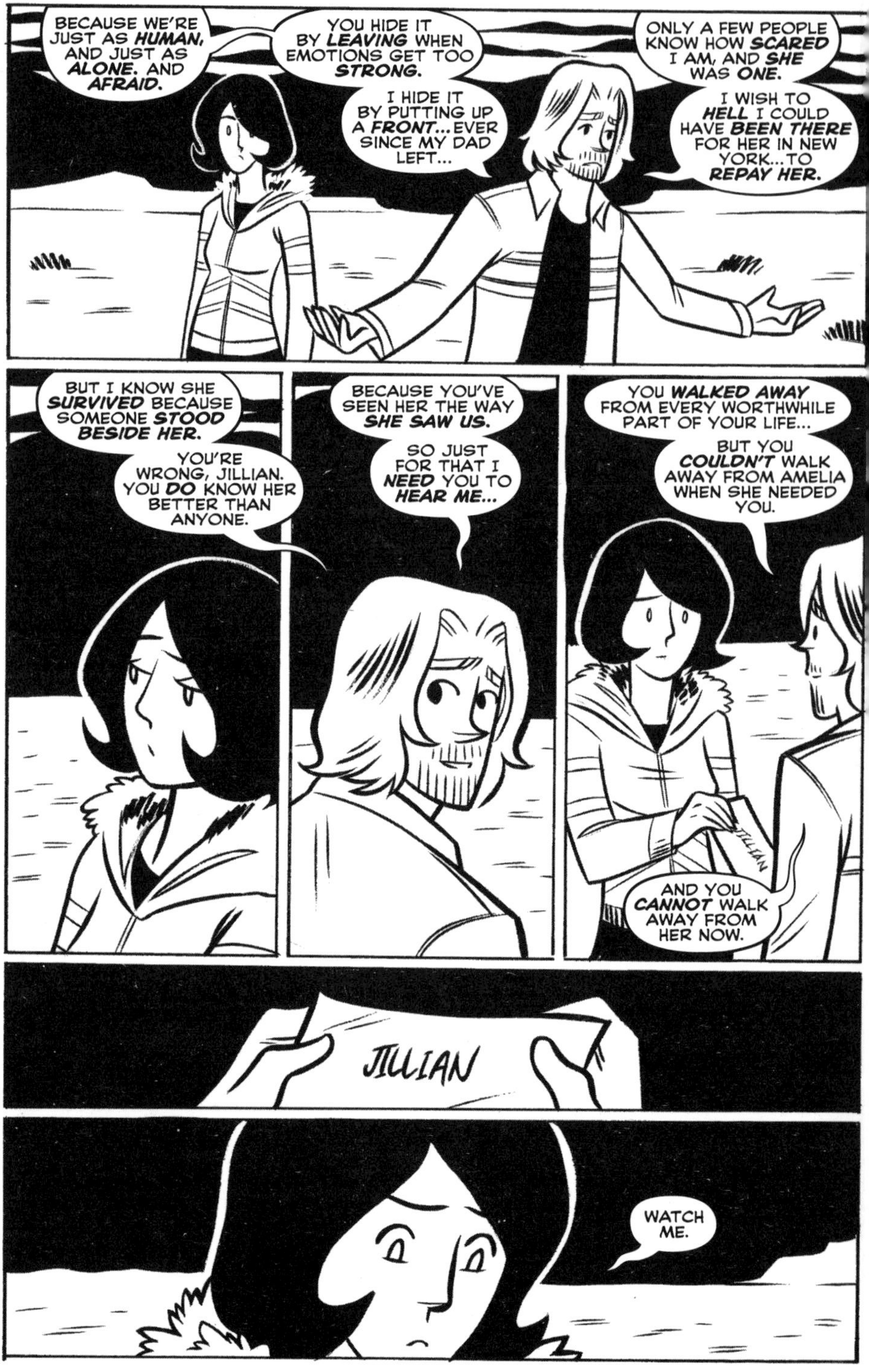
BECAUSE WE'RE JUST AS HUMAN, AND JUST AS ALONE. AND AFRAID.
YOU HIDE IT BY LEAVING WHEN EMOTIONS GET TOO STRONG.
I HIDE IT BY PUTTING UP A FRONT... EVER SINCE MY DAD LEFT...
ONLY A FEW PEOPLE KNOW HOW SCARED I AM, AND SHE WAS ONE.
I WISH TO HELL I COULD HAVE BEEN THERE FOR HER IN NEW YORK... TO REPAY HER.
BUT I KNOW SHE SURVIVED BECAUSE SOMEONE STOOD BESIDE HER.
YOU'RE WRONG, JILLIAN. YOU DO KNOW HER BETTER THAN ANYONE.
BECAUSE YOU'VE SEEN HER THE WAY SHE SAW US.
SO JUST FOR THAT I NEED YOU TO HEAR ME...
YOU WALKED AWAY FROM EVERY WORTHWHILE PART OF YOUR LIFE...
BUT YOU COULDN'T WALK AWAY FROM AMELIA WHEN SHE NEEDED YOU.
JILLIAN
AND YOU CANNOT WALK AWAY FROM HER NOW.
JILLIAN
WATCH ME.

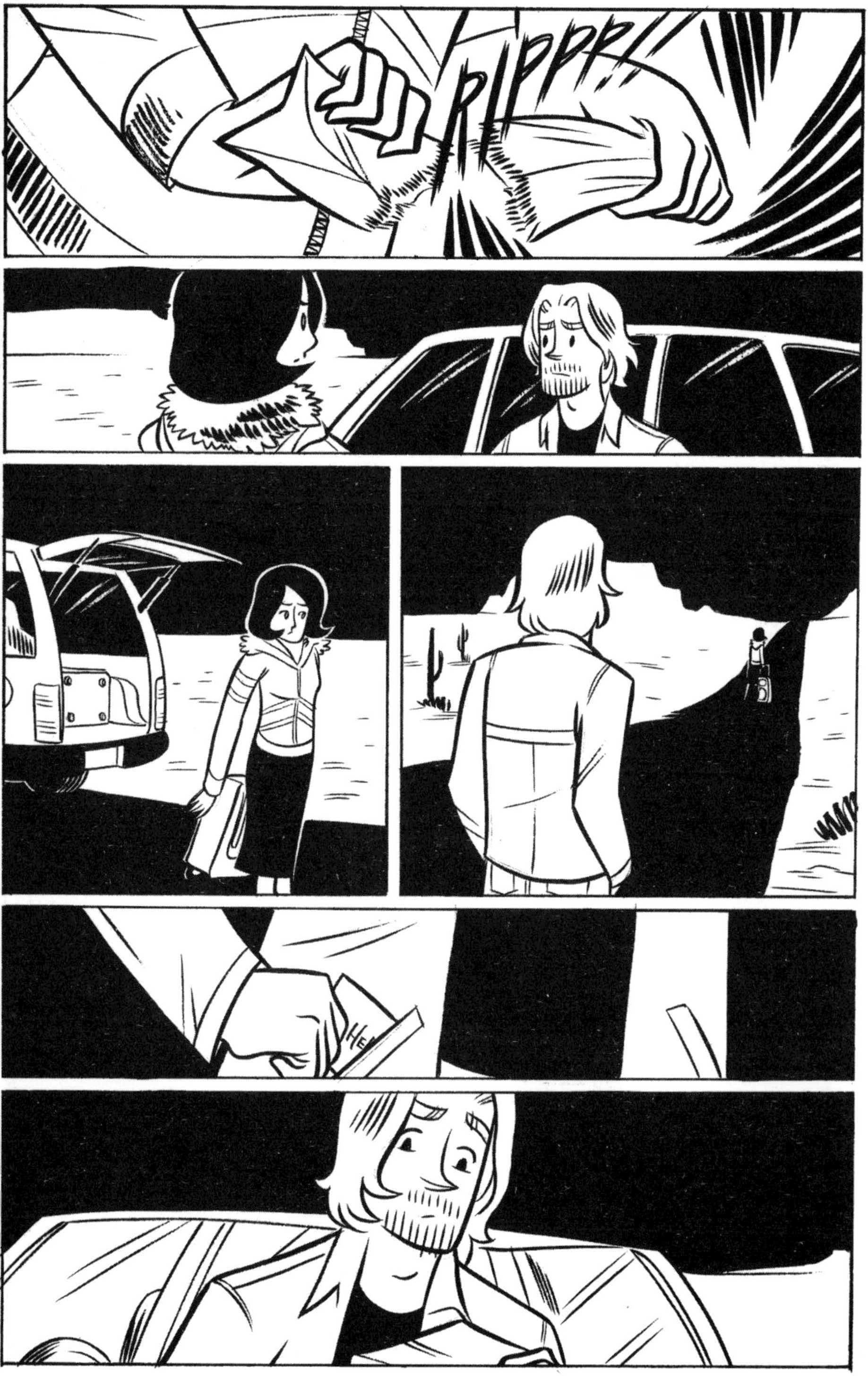
RIPPP!

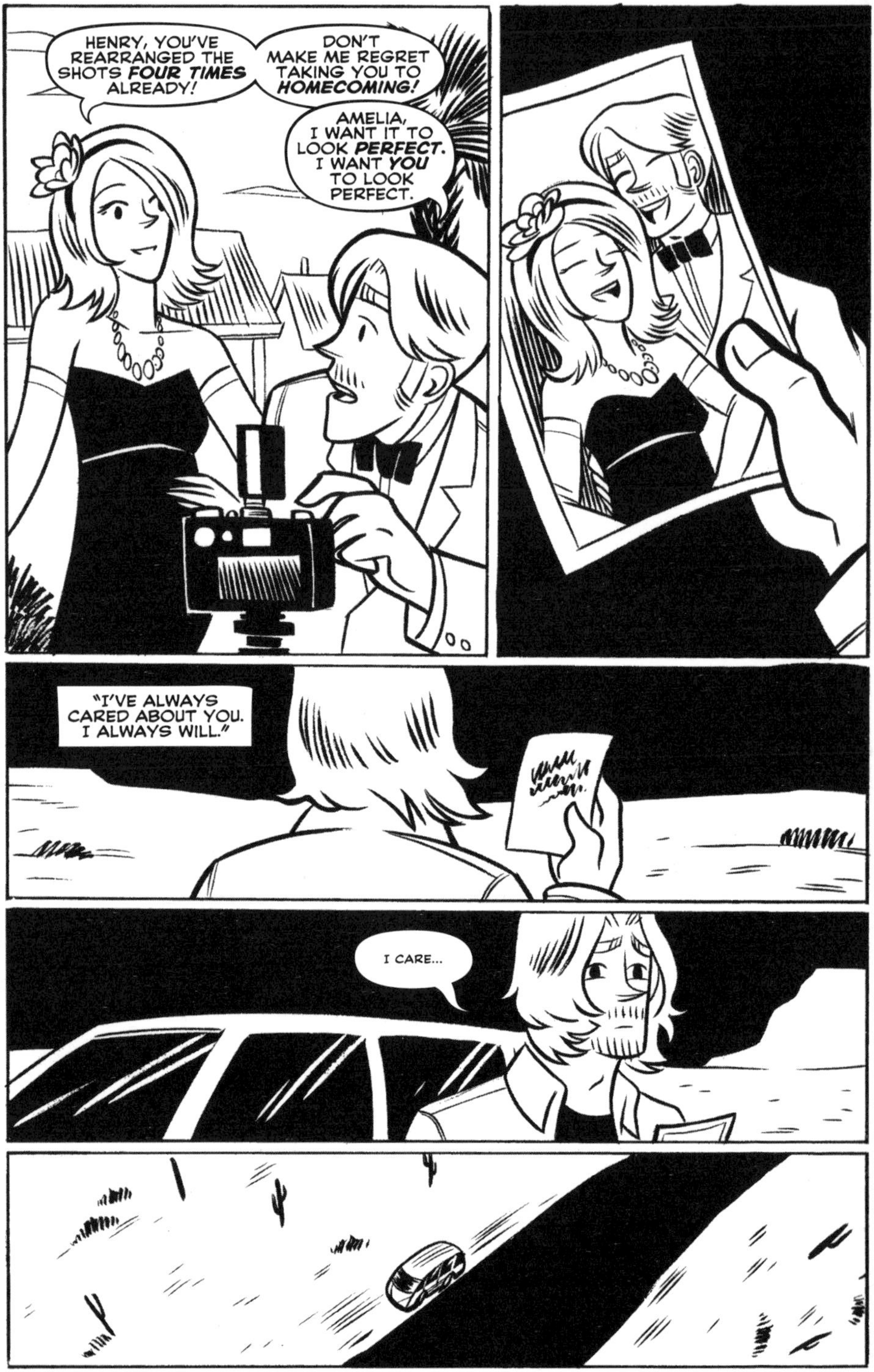
HENRY, YOU'VE REARRANGED THE SHOTS FOUR TIMES ALREADY!
DON'T MAKE ME REGRET TAKING YOU TO HOMECOMING!
AMELIA, I WANT IT TO LOOK PERFECT. I WANT YOU TO LOOK PERFECT.
"I'VE ALWAYS CARED ABOUT YOU. I ALWAYS WILL."
I CARE...

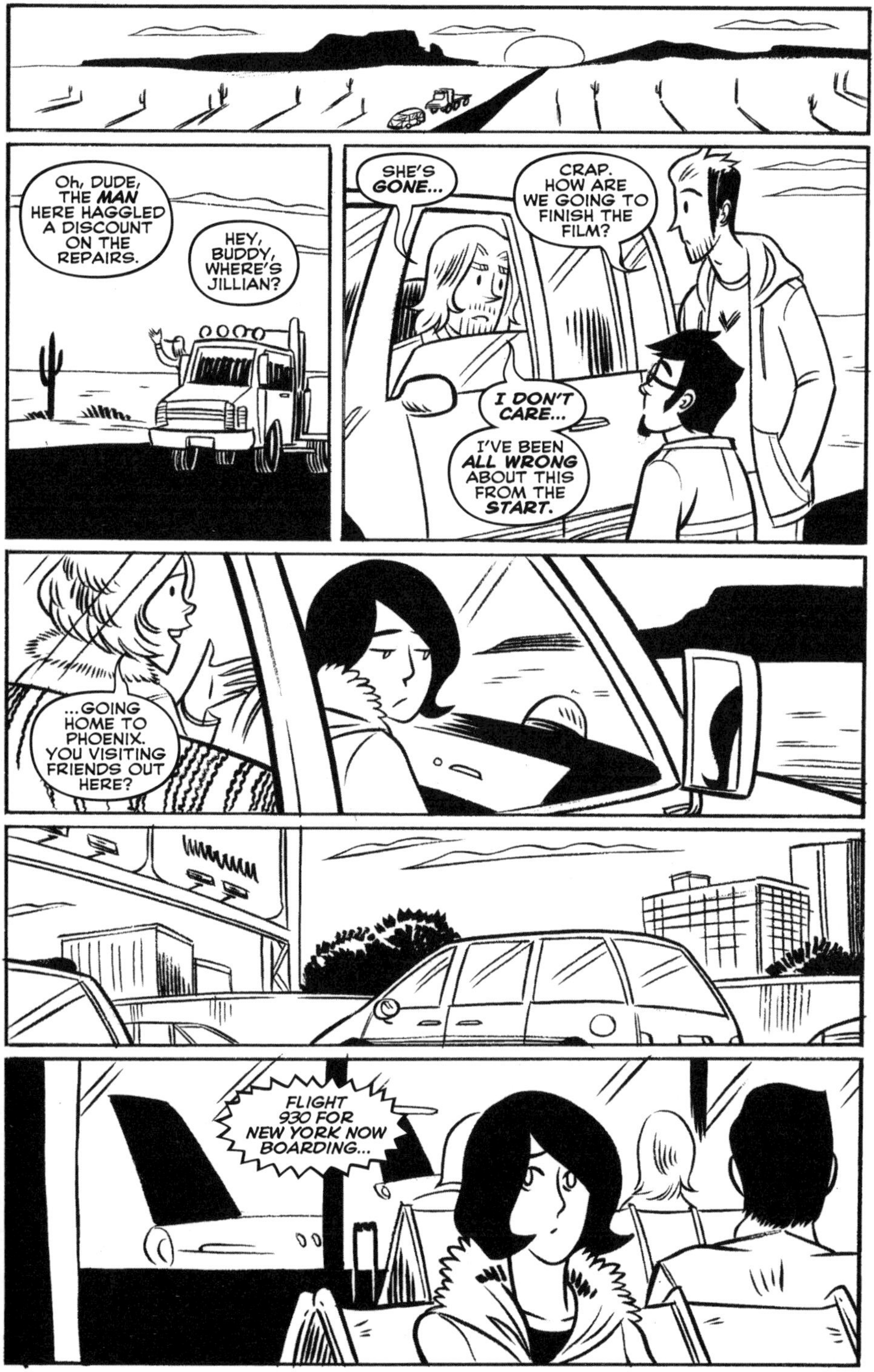
Oh, DUDE, THE MAN HERE HAGGLED A DISCOUNT ON THE REPAIRS.
HEY, BUDDY, WHERE'S JILLIAN?
SHE'S GONE...
CRAP. HOW ARE WE GOING TO FINISH THE FILM?
I DON'T CARE...
I'VE BEEN ALL WRONG ABOUT THIS FROM THE START.
...GOING HOME TO PHOENIX. YOU VISITING FRIENDS OUT HERE?
FLIGHT 930 FOR NEW YORK NOW BOARDING...

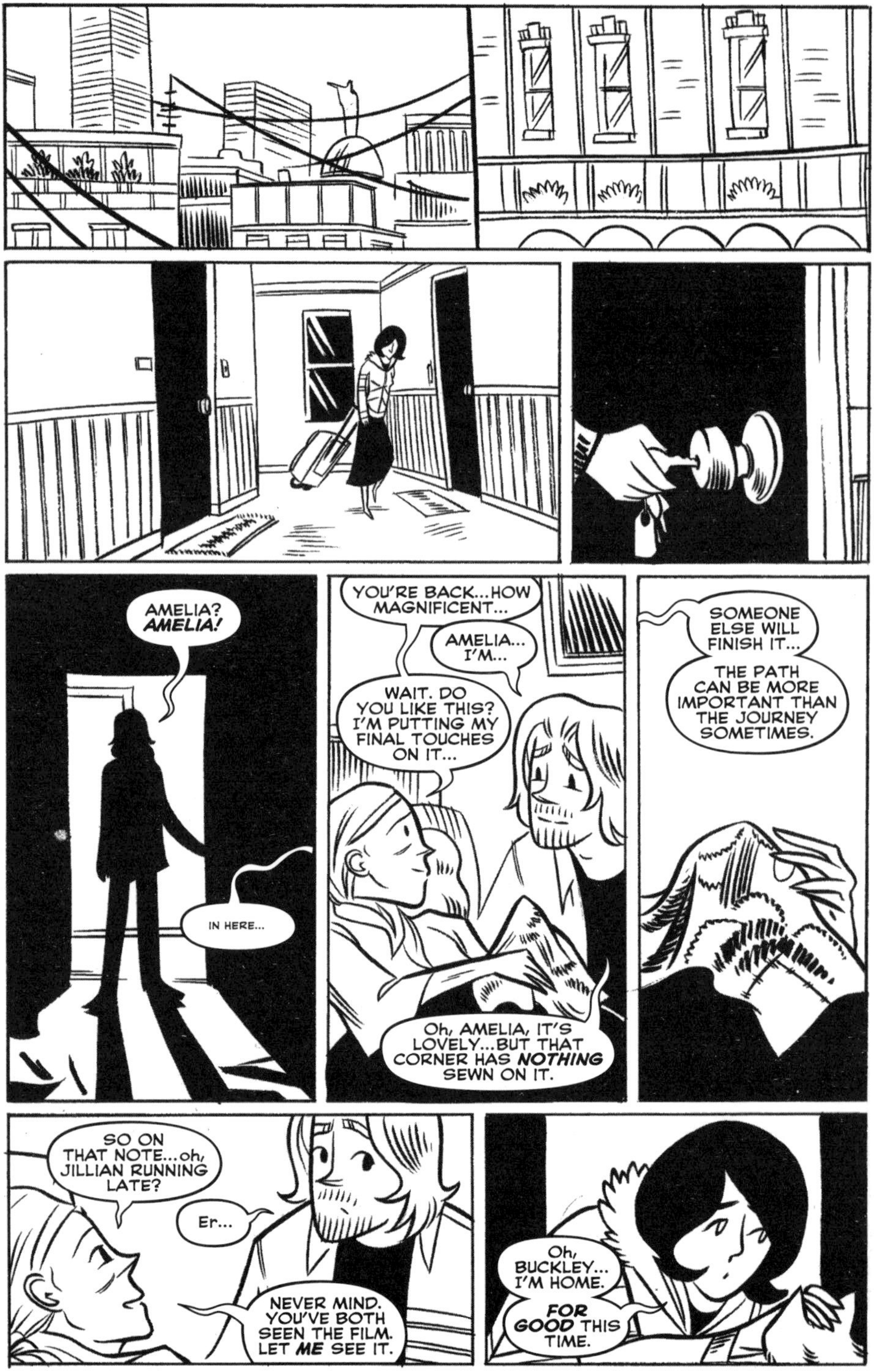
AMELIA? AMELIA!
IN HERE...
YOU'RE BACK...HOW MAGNIFICENT...
AMELIA... I'M...
WAIT. DO YOU LIKE THIS? I'M PUTTING MY FINAL TOUCHES ON IT...
Oh, AMELIA, IT'S LOVELY...BUT THAT CORNER HAS NOTHING SEWN ON IT.
SOMEONE ELSE WILL FINISH IT...
THE PATH CAN BE MORE IMPORTANT THAN THE JOURNEY SOMETIMES.
SO ON THAT NOTE...oh, JILLIAN RUNNING LATE?
Er...
NEVER MIND. YOU'VE BOTH SEEN THE FILM. LET ME SEE IT.
Oh, BUCKLEY... I'M HOME.
FOR GOOD THIS TIME.

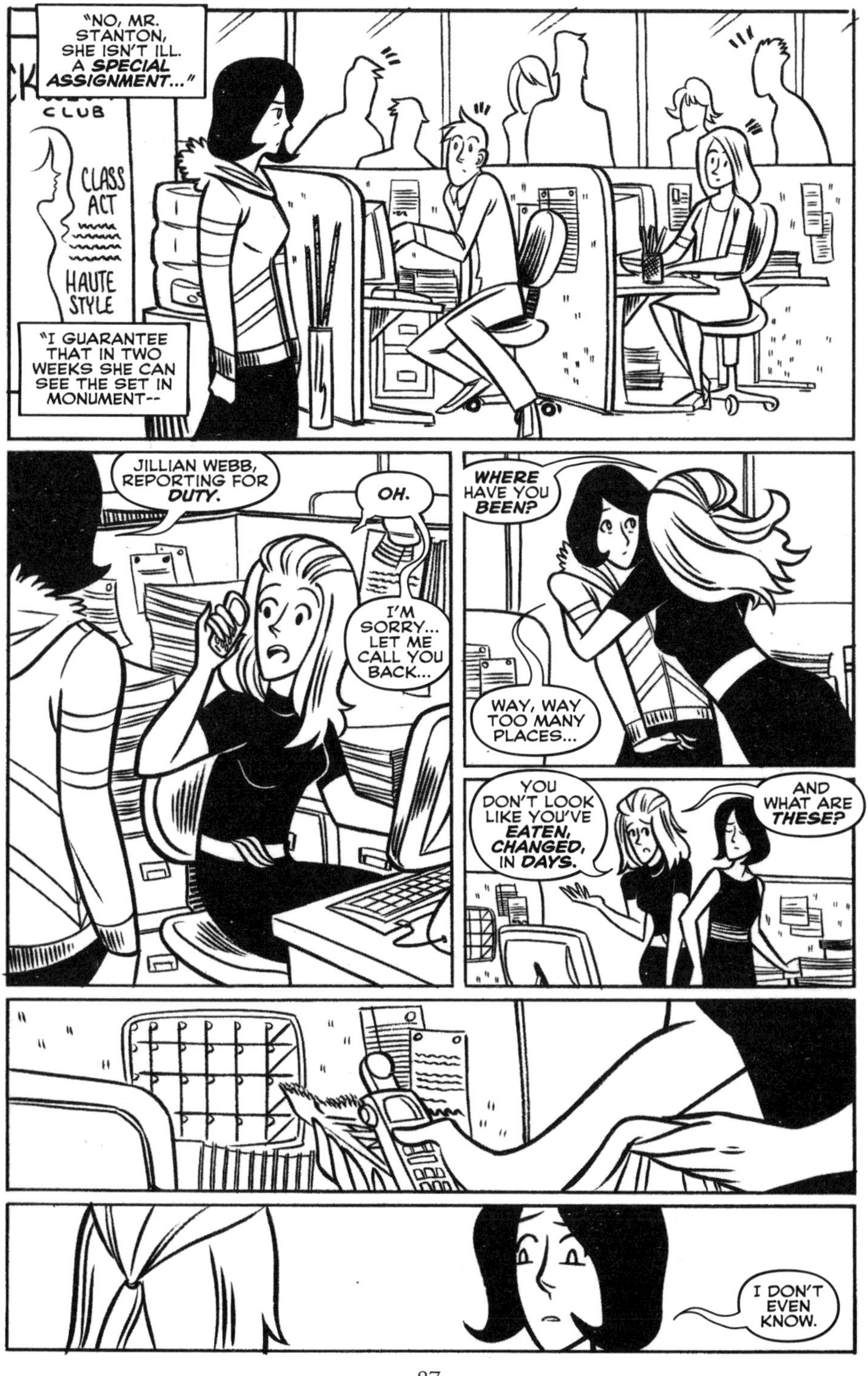
"NO, MR. STANTON, SHE ISN'T ILL. A SPECIAL ASSIGNMENT..."
CLUB
CLASS ACT
HAUTE STYLE
"I GUARANTEE THAT IN TWO WEEKS SHE CAN SEE THE SET IN MONUMENT--
JILLIAN WEBB, REPORTING FOR DUTY.
OH.
I'M SORRY... LET ME CALL YOU BACK...
WHERE HAVE YOU BEEN?
WAY, WAY TOO MANY PLACES...
YOU DON'T LOOK LIKE YOU'VE EATEN, CHANGED, IN DAYS.
AND WHAT ARE THESE?
I DON'T EVEN KNOW.

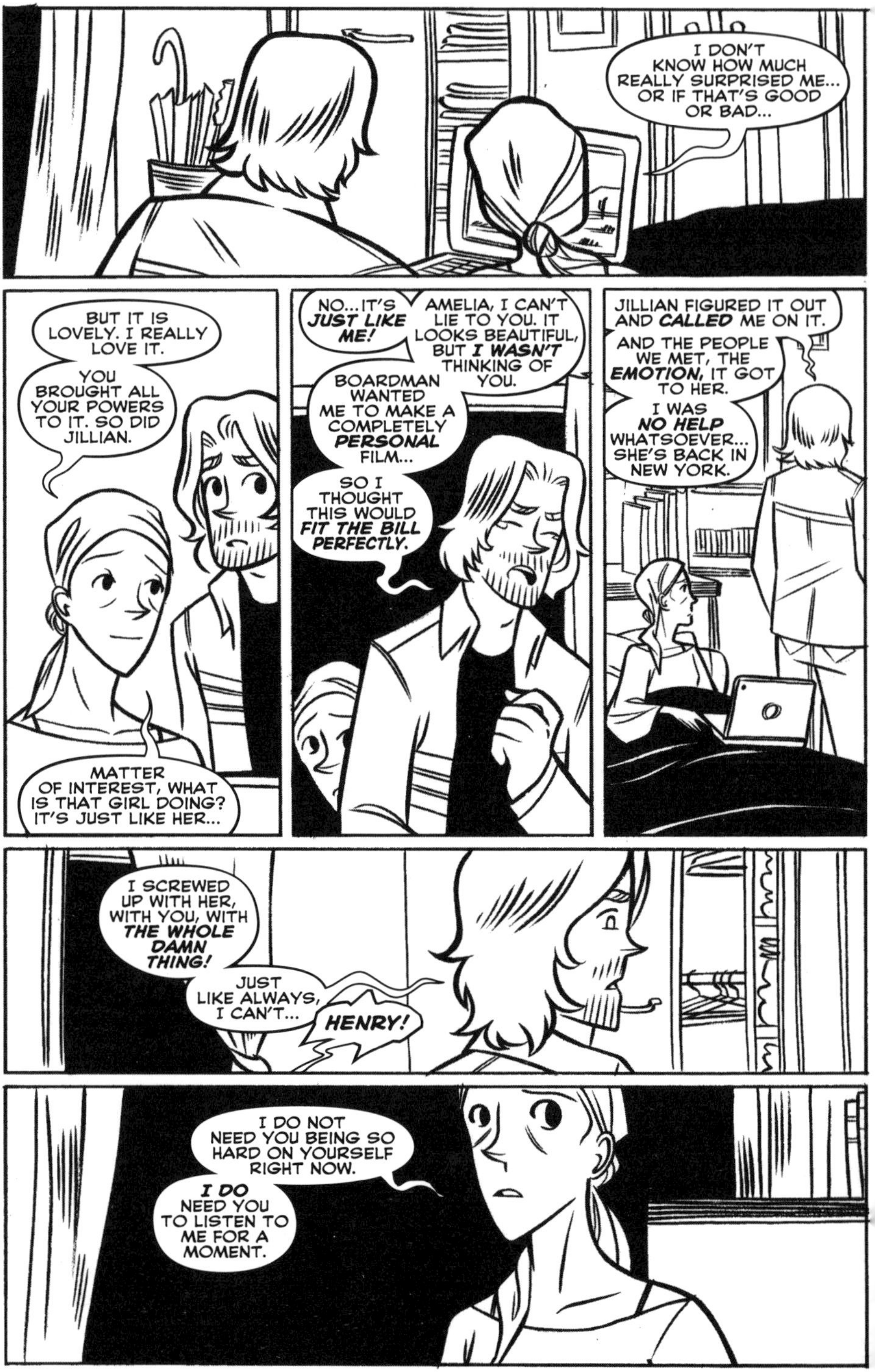
I DON'T KNOW HOW MUCH REALLY SURPRISED ME... OR IF THAT'S GOOD OR BAD...
BUT IT IS LOVELY. I REALLY LOVE IT.
YOU BROUGHT ALL YOUR POWERS TO IT. SO DID JILLIAN.
MATTER OF INTEREST, WHAT IS THAT GIRL DOING? IT'S JUST LIKE HER...
NO... IT'S JUST LIKE ME!
AMELIA, I CAN'T LIE TO YOU. IT LOOKS BEAUTIFUL, BUT I WASN'T THINKING OF YOU.
BOARDMAN WANTED ME TO MAKE A COMPLETELY PERSONAL FILM...
SO I THOUGHT THIS WOULD FIT THE BILL PERFECTLY.
JILLIAN FIGURED IT OUT AND CALLED ME ON IT.
AND THE PEOPLE WE MET, THE EMOTION, IT GOT TO HER.
I WAS NO HELP WHATSOEVER... SHE'S BACK IN NEW YORK.
I SCREWED UP WITH HER, WITH YOU, WITH THE WHOLE DAMN THING!
JUST LIKE ALWAYS, I CAN'T...
HENRY!
I DO NOT NEED YOU BEING SO HARD ON YOURSELF RIGHT NOW.
I DO NEED YOU TO LISTEN TO ME FOR A MOMENT.

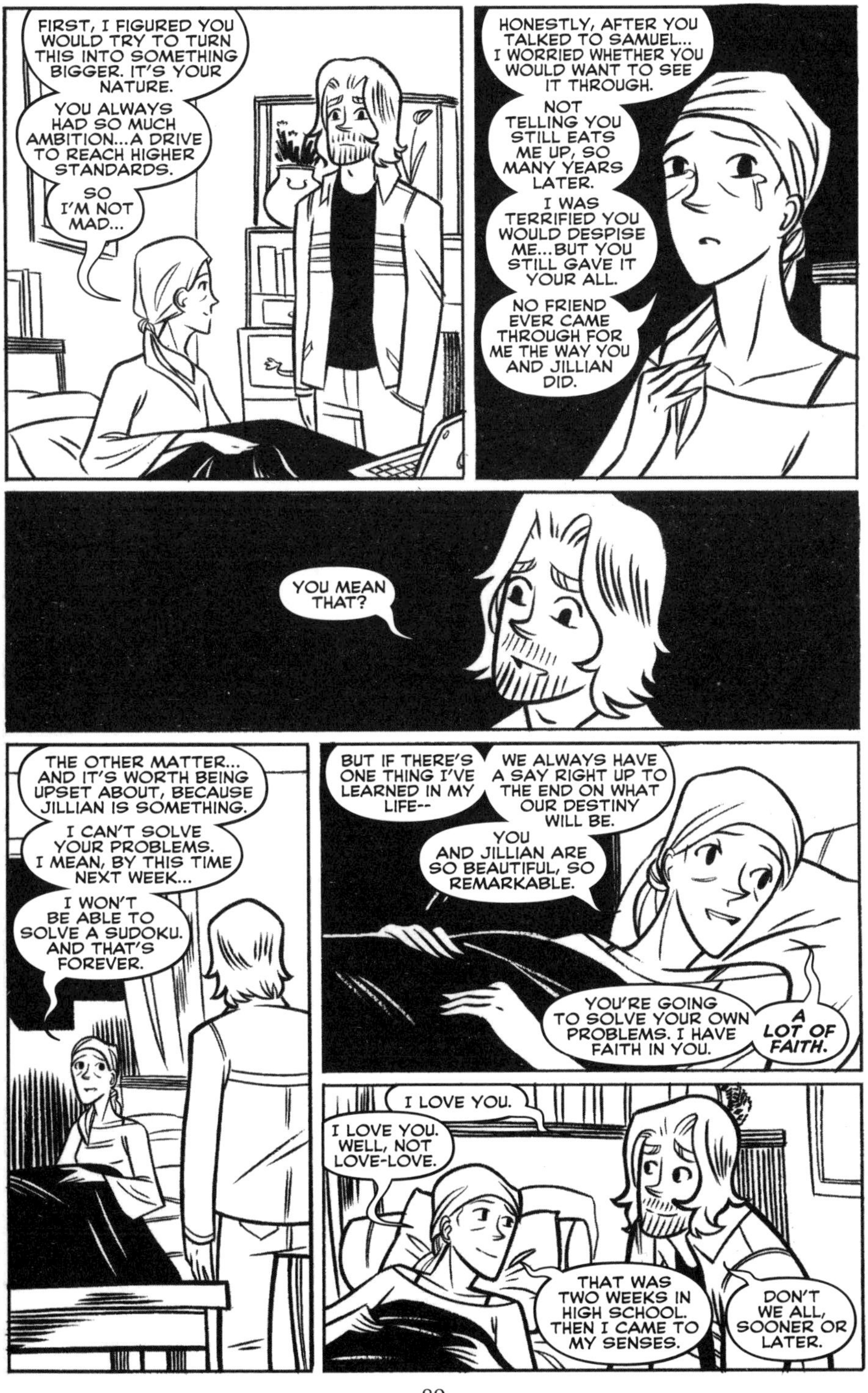
FIRST, I FIGURED YOU WOULD TRY TO TURN THIS INTO SOMETHING BIGGER. IT'S YOUR NATURE.
YOU ALWAYS HAD SO MUCH AMBITION...A DRIVE TO REACH HIGHER STANDARDS.
SO I'M NOT MAD...
HONESTLY, AFTER YOU TALKED TO SAMUEL... I WORRIED WHETHER YOU WOULD WANT TO SEE IT THROUGH.
NOT TELLING YOU STILL EATS ME UP, SO MANY YEARS LATER.
I WAS TERRIFIED YOU WOULD DESPISE ME...BUT YOU STILL GAVE IT YOUR ALL.
NO FRIEND EVER CAME THROUGH FOR ME THE WAY YOU AND JILLIAN DID.
YOU MEAN THAT?
THE OTHER MATTER... AND IT'S WORTH BEING UPSET ABOUT, BECAUSE JILLIAN IS SOMETHING.
I CAN'T SOLVE YOUR PROBLEMS. I MEAN, BY THIS TIME NEXT WEEK...
I WON'T BE ABLE TO SOLVE A SUDOKU. AND THAT'S FOREVER.
BUT IF THERE'S ONE THING I'VE LEARNED IN MY LIFE--
WE ALWAYS HAVE A SAY RIGHT UP TO THE END ON WHAT OUR DESTINY WILL BE.
YOU AND JILLIAN ARE SO BEAUTIFUL, SO REMARKABLE.
YOU'RE GOING TO SOLVE YOUR OWN PROBLEMS. I HAVE FAITH IN YOU.
A LOT OF FAITH.
I LOVE YOU.
I LOVE YOU. WELL, NOT LOVE-LOVE.
THAT WAS TWO WEEKS IN HIGH SCHOOL. THEN I CAME TO MY SENSES.
DON'T WE ALL, SOONER OR LATER.

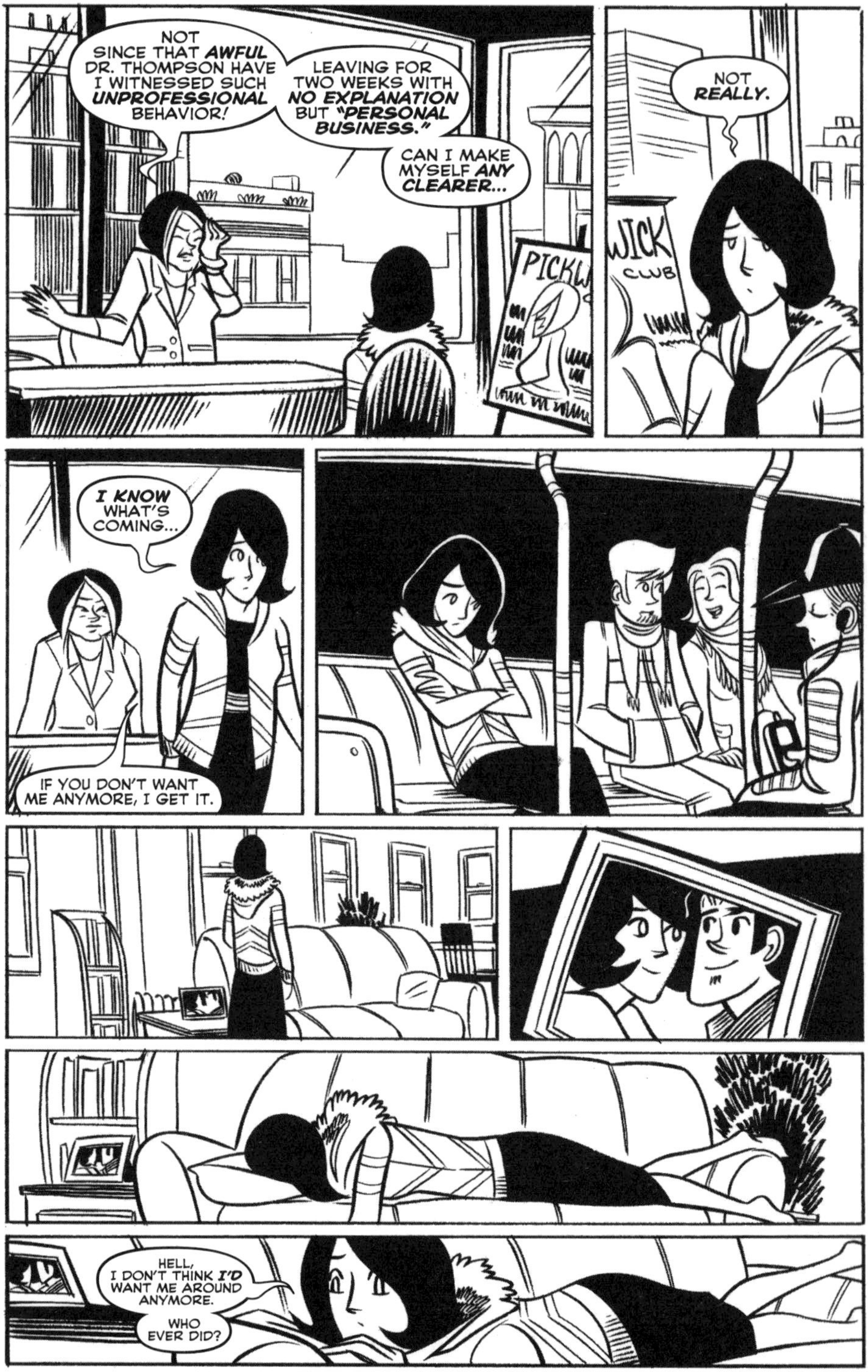
NOT SINCE THAT AWFUL DR. THOMPSON HAVE I WITNESSED SUCH UNPROFESSIONAL BEHAVIOR!
LEAVING FOR TWO WEEKS WITH NO EXPLANATION BUT "PERSONAL BUSINESS."
CAN I MAKE MYSELF ANY CLEARER...
PICKW
NOT REALLY.
WICK CLUB
I KNOW WHAT'S COMING...
IF YOU DON'T WANT ME ANYMORE, I GET IT.
HELL, I DON'T THINK I'D WANT ME AROUND ANYMORE.
WHO EVER DID?

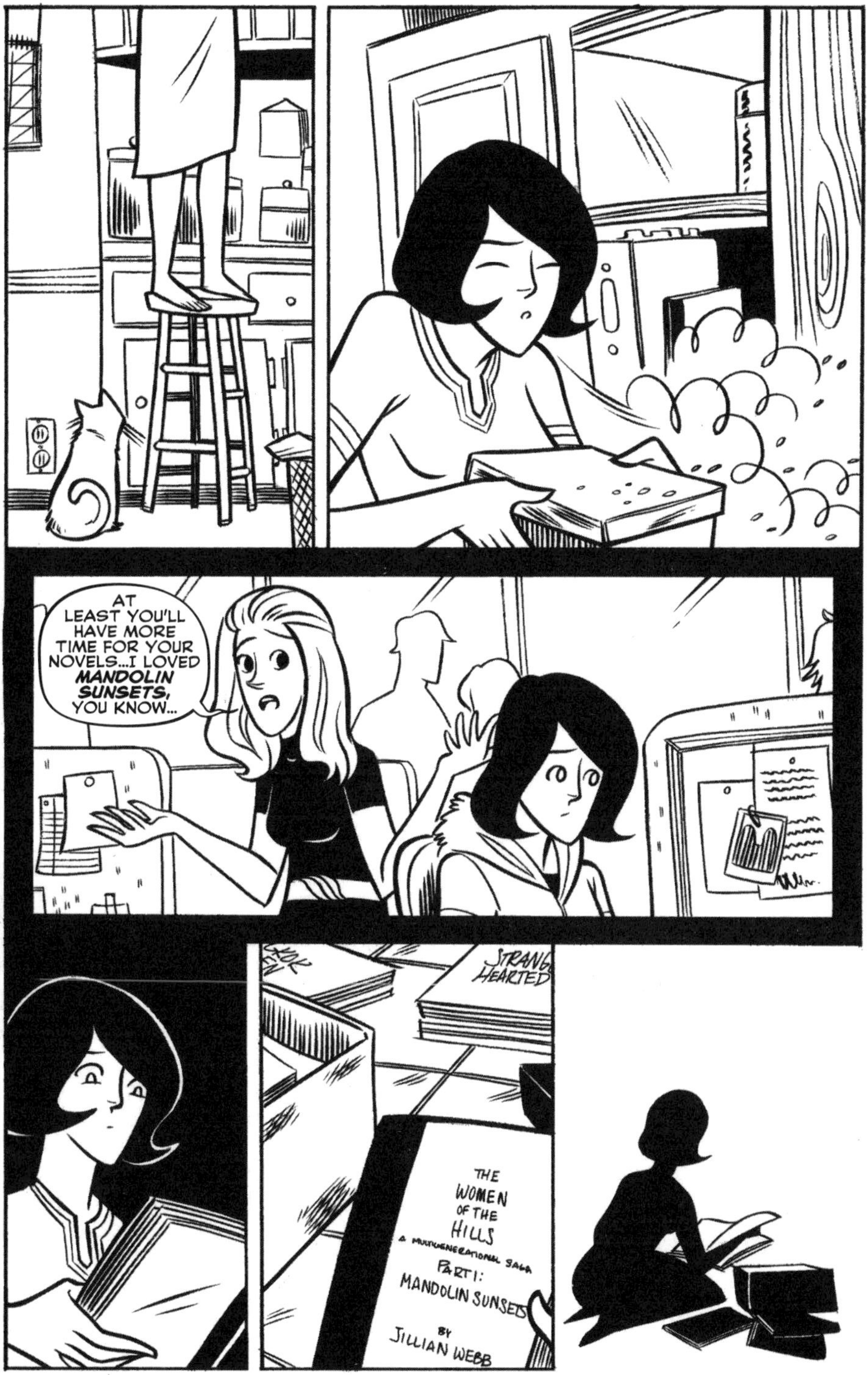
AT LEAST YOU'LL HAVE MORE TIME FOR YOUR NOVELS...I LOVED **MANDOLIN SUNSETS,** YOU KNOW...
THE WOMEN OF THE HILLS
A MULTIGENERATIONAL SAGA
PART I: MANDOLIN SUNSETS
BY JILLIAN WEBB

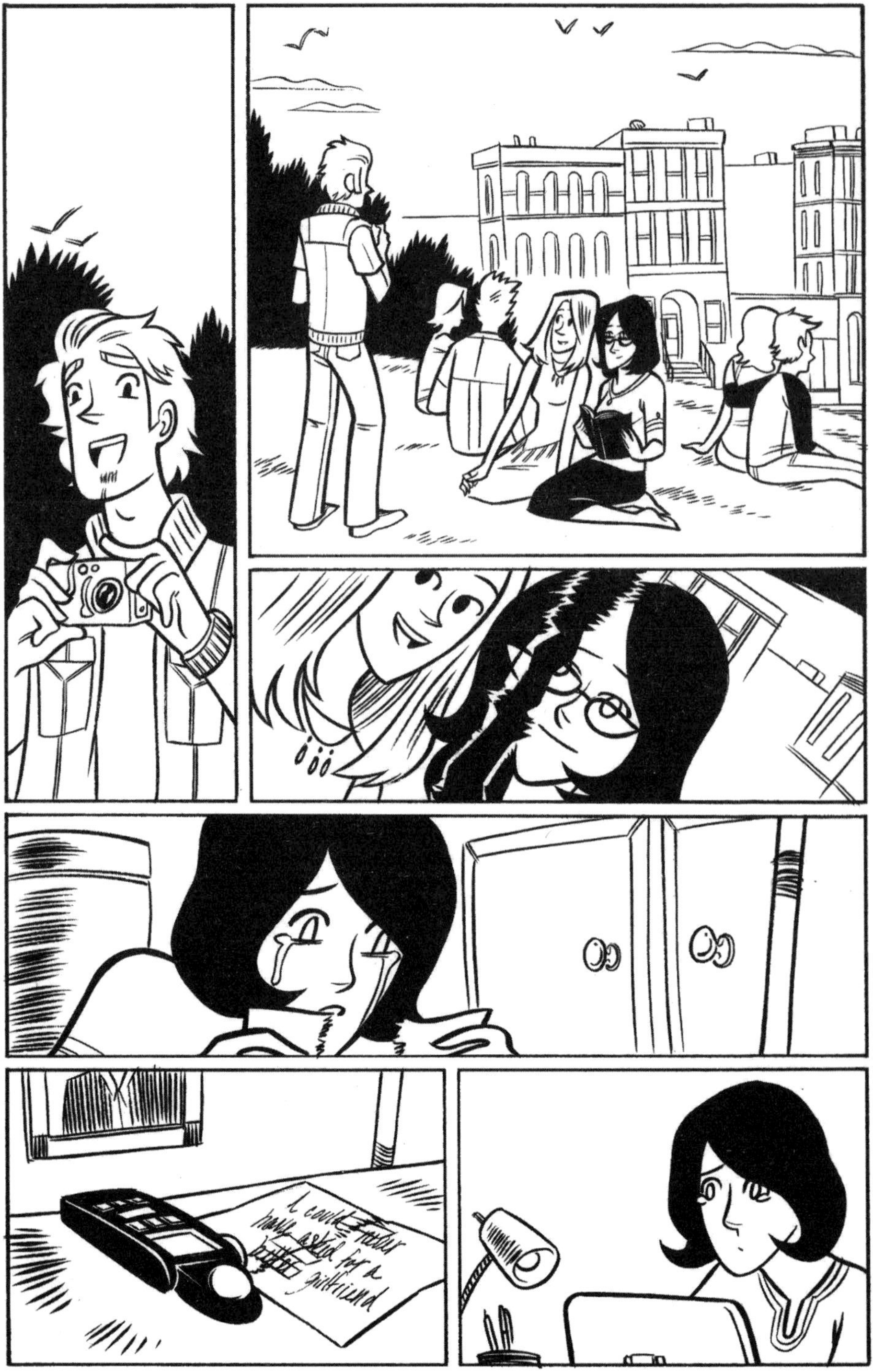
I could
have asked for a
girlfriend

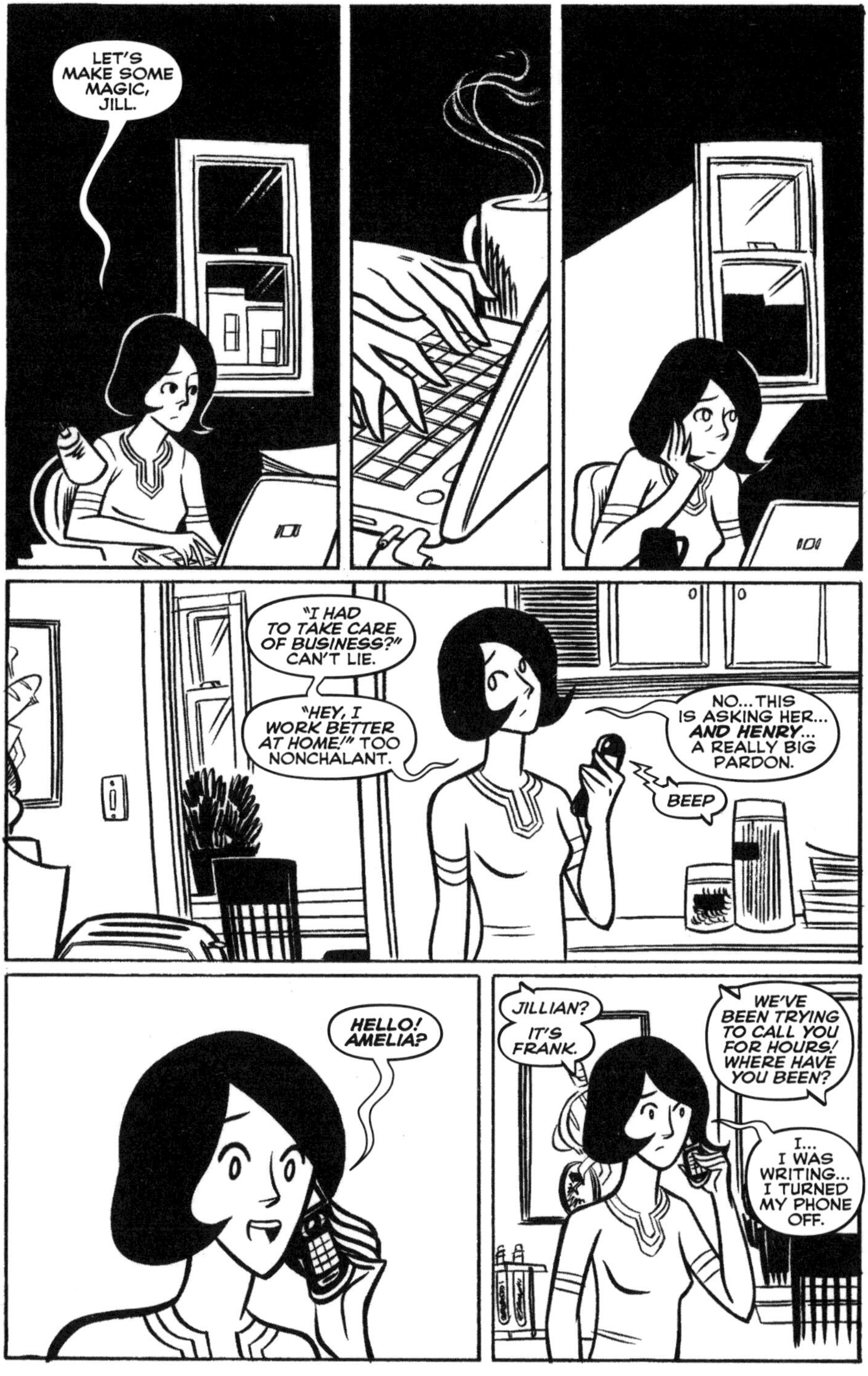
LET'S MAKE SOME MAGIC, JILL.
"I HAD TO TAKE CARE OF BUSINESS?" CAN'T LIE.
"HEY, I WORK BETTER AT HOME!" TOO NONCHALANT.
NO... THIS IS ASKING HER... AND HENRY... A REALLY BIG PARDON.
BEEP
HELLO! AMELIA?
JILLIAN? IT'S FRANK.
WE'VE BEEN TRYING TO CALL YOU FOR HOURS! WHERE HAVE YOU BEEN?
I... I WAS WRITING... I TURNED MY PHONE OFF.

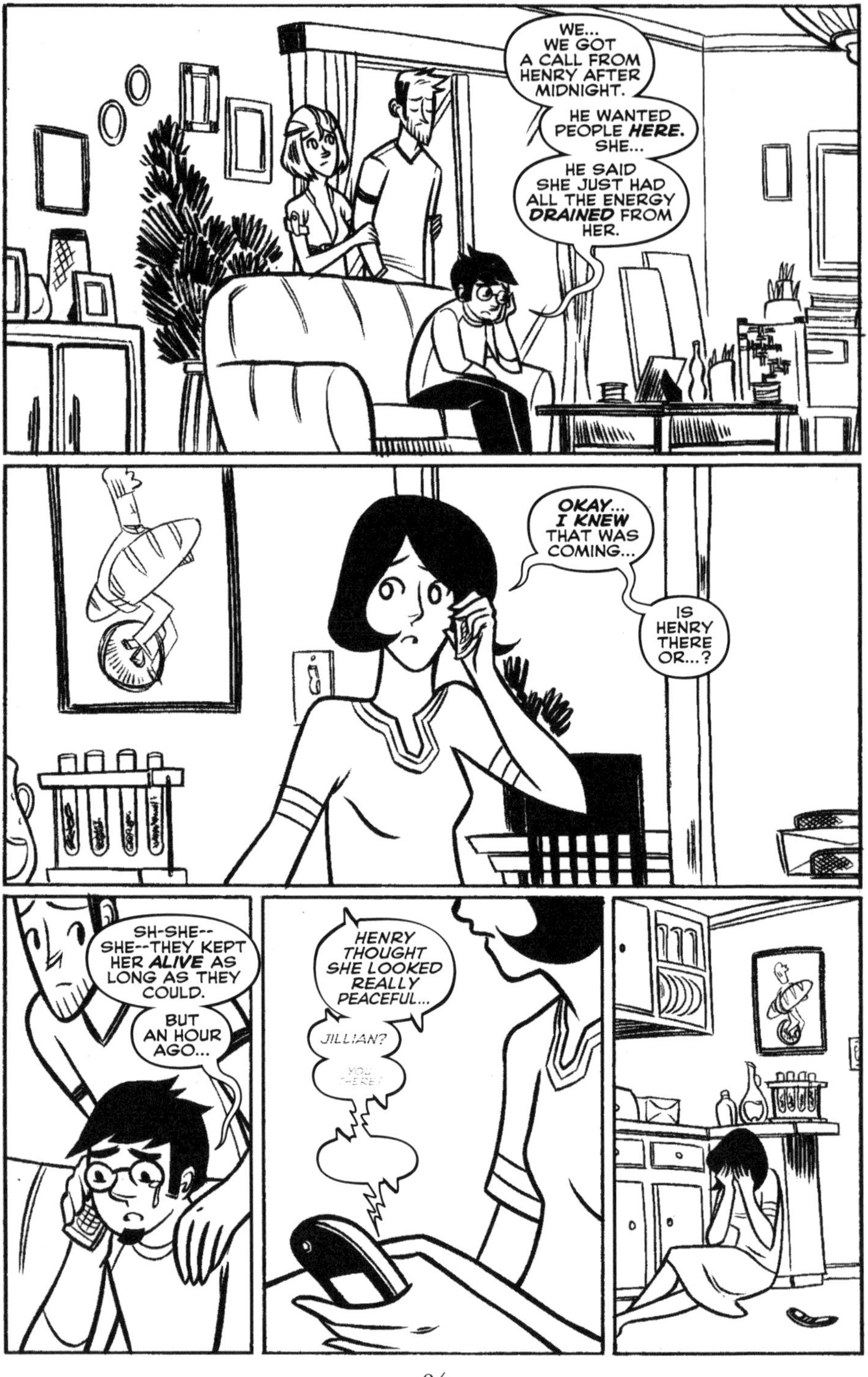
WE... WE GOT A CALL FROM HENRY AFTER MIDNIGHT.
HE WANTED PEOPLE ***HERE.*** SHE...
HE SAID SHE JUST HAD ALL THE ENERGY ***DRAINED*** FROM HER.
OKAY... I KNEW THAT WAS COMING...
IS HENRY THERE OR...?
SH-SHE-- SHE--THEY KEPT HER ***ALIVE*** AS LONG AS THEY COULD.
BUT AN HOUR AGO...
HENRY THOUGHT SHE LOOKED REALLY PEACEFUL...
JILLIAN?
YOU THERE?

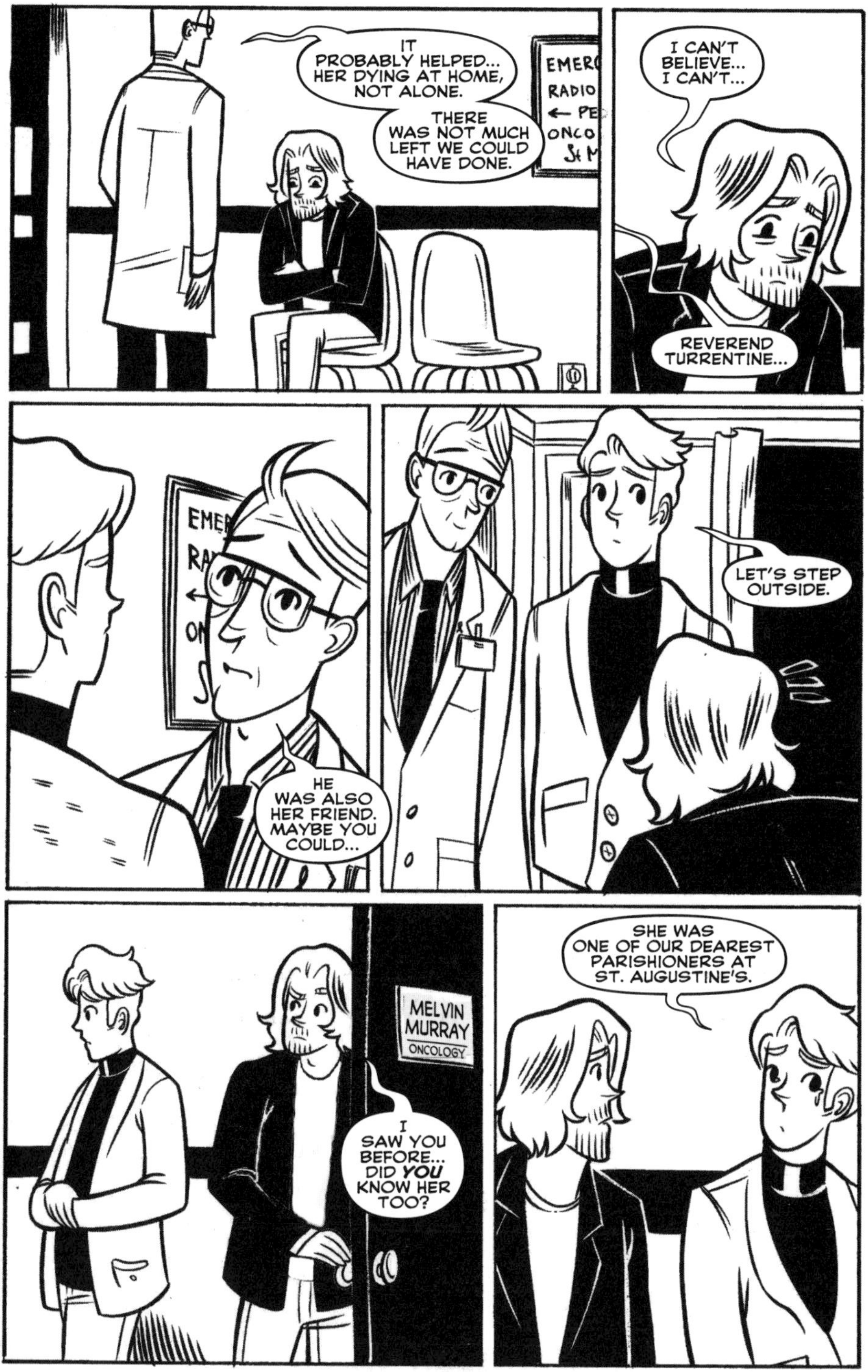
IT PROBABLY HELPED... HER DYING AT HOME, NOT ALONE.
THERE WAS NOT MUCH LEFT WE COULD HAVE DONE.
I CAN'T BELIEVE... I CAN'T...
REVEREND TURRENTINE...
HE WAS ALSO HER FRIEND. MAYBE YOU COULD...
LET'S STEP OUTSIDE.
MELVIN MURRAY
ONCOLOGY
I SAW YOU BEFORE... DID *YOU* KNOW HER TOO?
SHE WAS ONE OF OUR DEAREST PARISHIONERS AT ST. AUGUSTINE'S.

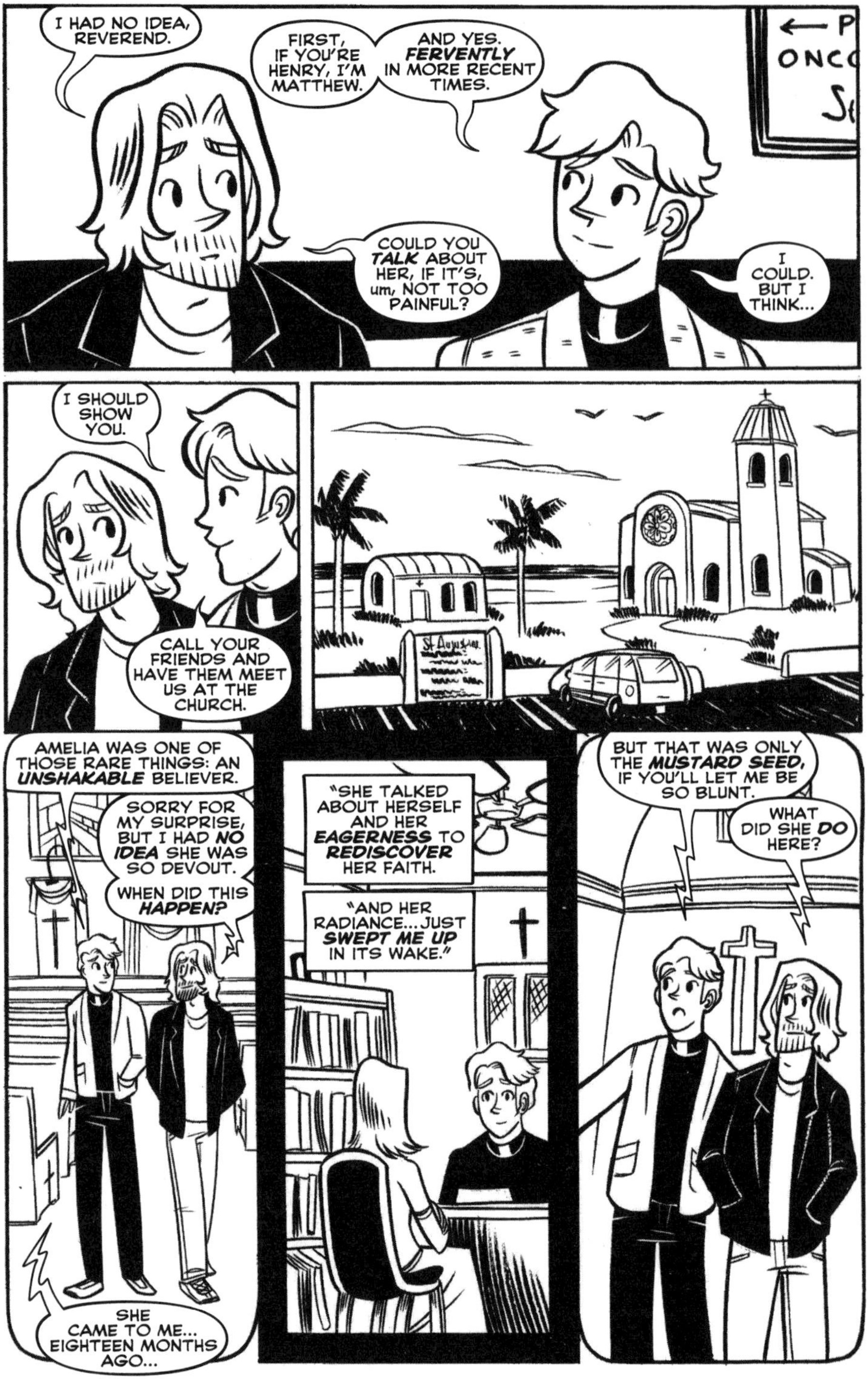

I HAD NO IDEA, REVEREND.
FIRST, IF YOU'RE HENRY, I'M MATTHEW.
AND YES. FERVENTLY IN MORE RECENT TIMES.
COULD YOU TALK ABOUT HER, IF IT'S, um, NOT TOO PAINFUL?
I COULD. BUT I THINK...
I SHOULD SHOW YOU.
CALL YOUR FRIENDS AND HAVE THEM MEET US AT THE CHURCH.
AMELIA WAS ONE OF THOSE RARE THINGS: AN UNSHAKABLE BELIEVER.
SORRY FOR MY SURPRISE, BUT I HAD NO IDEA SHE WAS SO DEVOUT.
WHEN DID THIS HAPPEN?
SHE CAME TO ME... EIGHTEEN MONTHS AGO...
"SHE TALKED ABOUT HERSELF AND HER EAGERNESS TO REDISCOVER HER FAITH.
"AND HER RADIANCE... JUST SWEPT ME UP IN ITS WAKE."
BUT THAT WAS ONLY THE MUSTARD SEED, IF YOU'LL LET ME BE SO BLUNT.
WHAT DID SHE DO HERE?

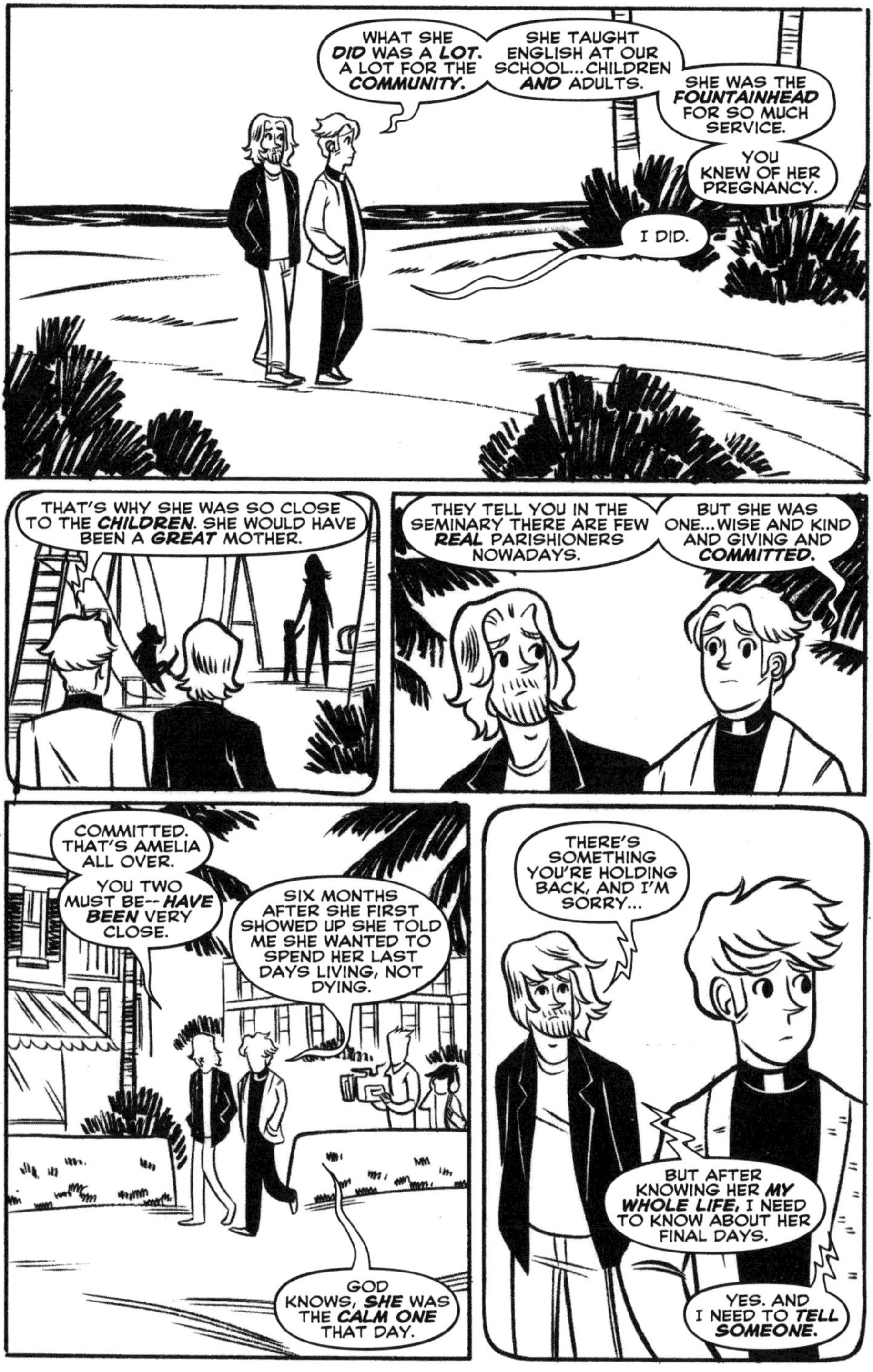
WHAT SHE DID WAS A LOT. A LOT FOR THE COMMUNITY.
SHE TAUGHT ENGLISH AT OUR SCHOOL...CHILDREN AND ADULTS.
SHE WAS THE FOUNTAINHEAD FOR SO MUCH SERVICE.
YOU KNEW OF HER PREGNANCY.
I DID.
THAT'S WHY SHE WAS SO CLOSE TO THE CHILDREN. SHE WOULD HAVE BEEN A GREAT MOTHER.
THEY TELL YOU IN THE SEMINARY THERE ARE FEW REAL PARISHIONERS NOWADAYS.
BUT SHE WAS ONE...WISE AND KIND AND GIVING AND COMMITTED.
COMMITTED. THAT'S AMELIA ALL OVER.
YOU TWO MUST BE-- HAVE BEEN VERY CLOSE.
SIX MONTHS AFTER SHE FIRST SHOWED UP SHE TOLD ME SHE WANTED TO SPEND HER LAST DAYS LIVING, NOT DYING.
GOD KNOWS, SHE WAS THE CALM ONE THAT DAY.
THERE'S SOMETHING YOU'RE HOLDING BACK, AND I'M SORRY...
BUT AFTER KNOWING HER MY WHOLE LIFE, I NEED TO KNOW ABOUT HER FINAL DAYS.
YES. AND I NEED TO TELL SOMEONE.

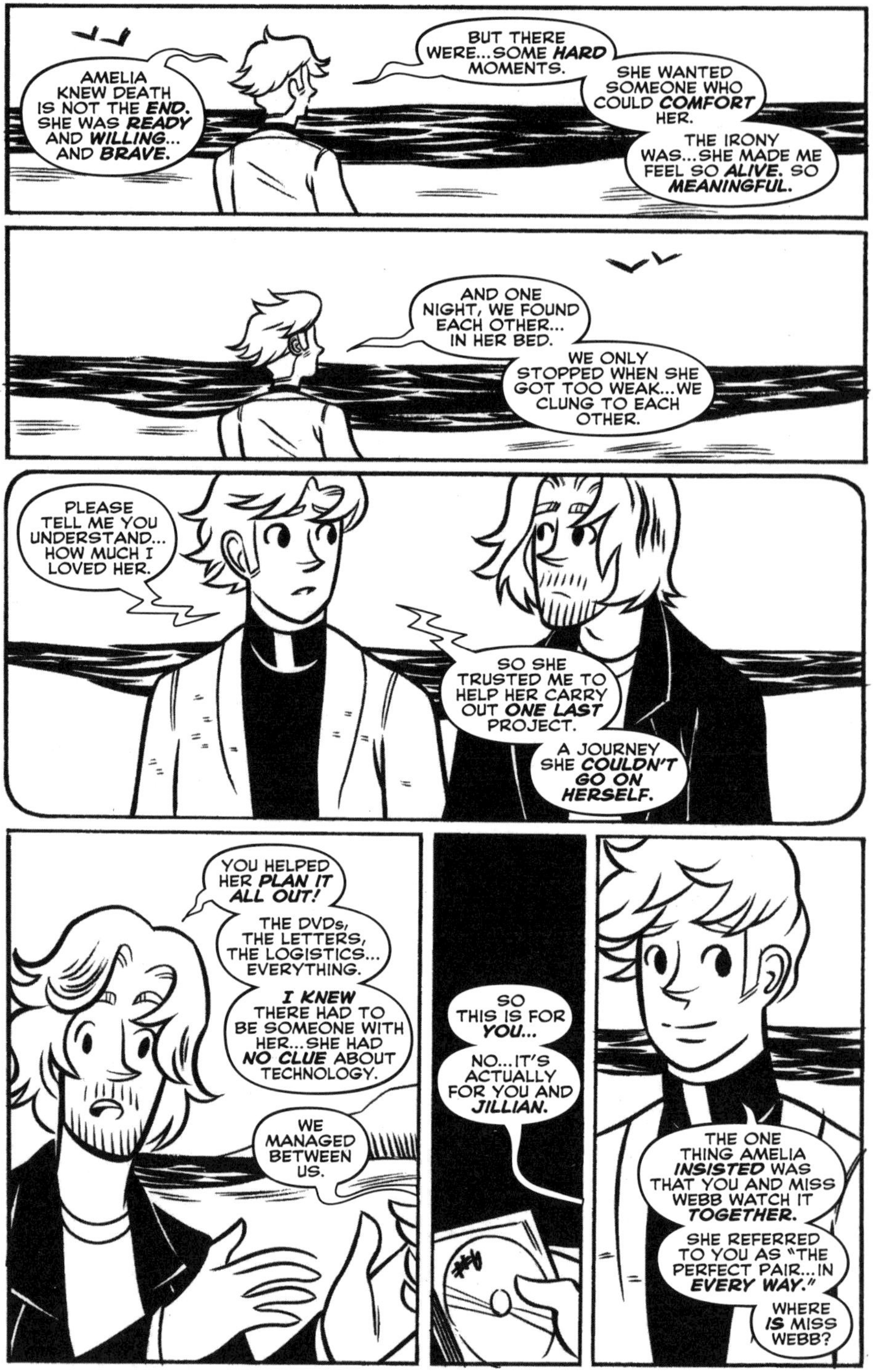
AMELIA KNEW DEATH IS NOT THE END. SHE WAS READY AND WILLING... AND BRAVE.
BUT THERE WERE...SOME HARD MOMENTS.
SHE WANTED SOMEONE WHO COULD COMFORT HER.
THE IRONY WAS...SHE MADE ME FEEL SO ALIVE. SO MEANINGFUL.
AND ONE NIGHT, WE FOUND EACH OTHER... IN HER BED.
WE ONLY STOPPED WHEN SHE GOT TOO WEAK...WE CLUNG TO EACH OTHER.
PLEASE TELL ME YOU UNDERSTAND... HOW MUCH I LOVED HER.
SO SHE TRUSTED ME TO HELP HER CARRY OUT ONE LAST PROJECT.
A JOURNEY SHE COULDN'T GO ON HERSELF.
YOU HELPED HER PLAN IT ALL OUT!
THE DVDs, THE LETTERS, THE LOGISTICS... EVERYTHING.
I KNEW THERE HAD TO BE SOMEONE WITH HER...SHE HAD NO CLUE ABOUT TECHNOLOGY.
WE MANAGED BETWEEN US.
SO THIS IS FOR YOU...
NO...IT'S ACTUALLY FOR YOU AND JILLIAN.
THE ONE THING AMELIA INSISTED WAS THAT YOU AND MISS WEBB WATCH IT TOGETHER.
SHE REFERRED TO YOU AS "THE PERFECT PAIR...IN EVERY WAY."
WHERE IS MISS WEBB?

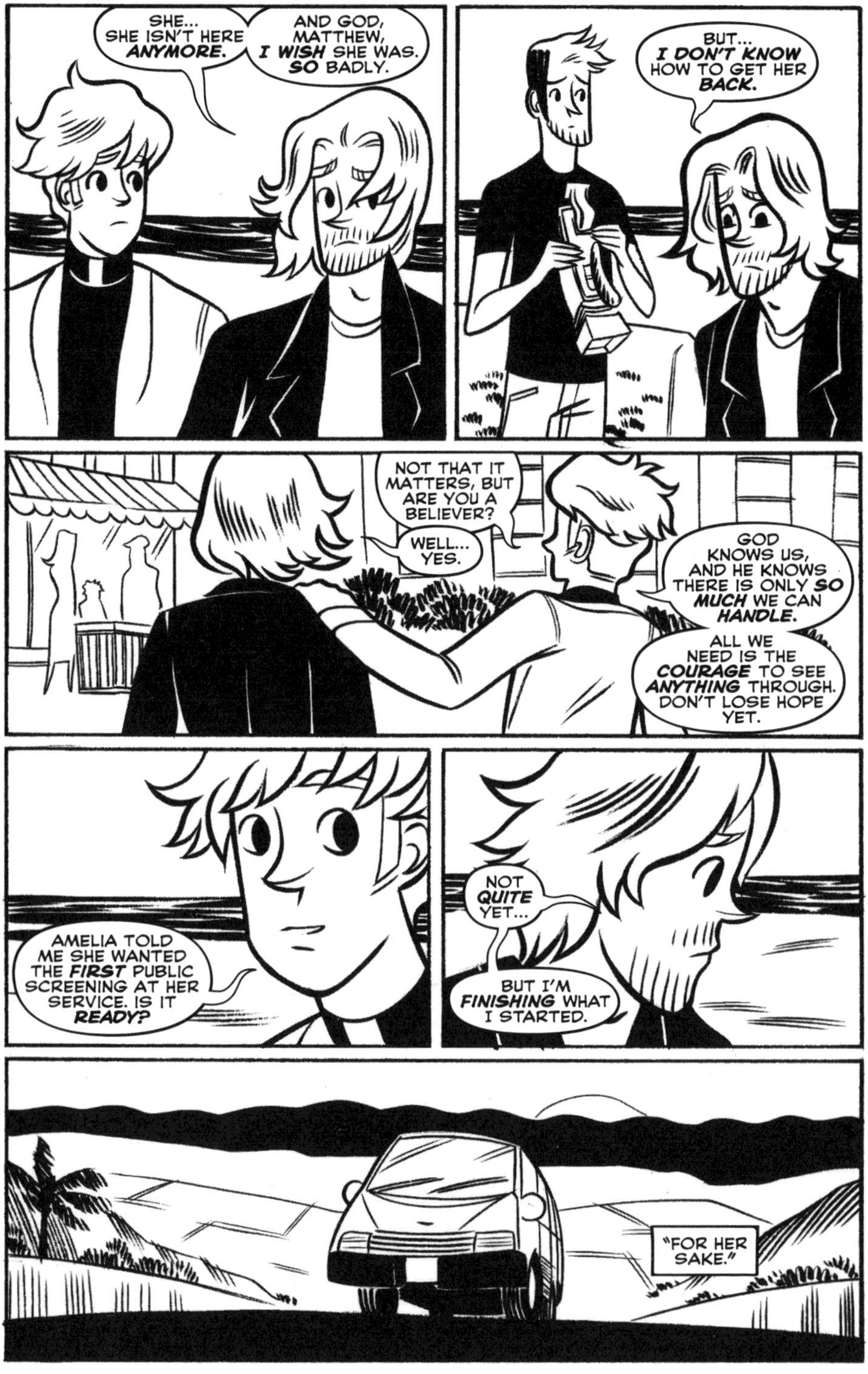
SHE... SHE ISN'T HERE ANYMORE.
AND GOD, MATTHEW, I WISH SHE WAS. SO BADLY.
BUT... I DON'T KNOW HOW TO GET HER BACK.
NOT THAT IT MATTERS, BUT ARE YOU A BELIEVER?
WELL... YES.
GOD KNOWS US, AND HE KNOWS THERE IS ONLY SO MUCH WE CAN HANDLE.
ALL WE NEED IS THE COURAGE TO SEE ANYTHING THROUGH. DON'T LOSE HOPE YET.
AMELIA TOLD ME SHE WANTED THE FIRST PUBLIC SCREENING AT HER SERVICE. IS IT READY?
NOT QUITE YET...
BUT I'M FINISHING WHAT I STARTED.
"FOR HER SAKE."

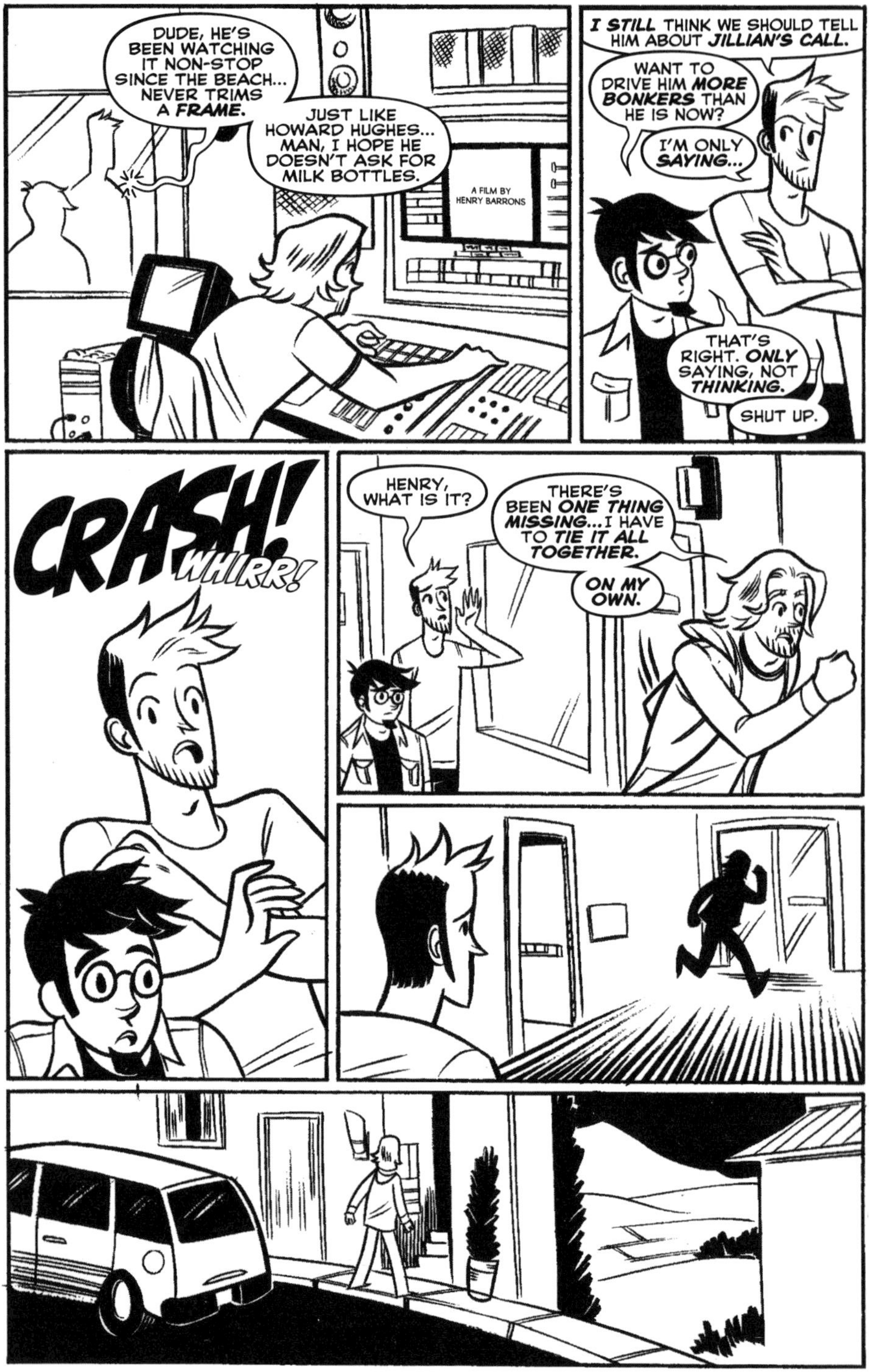
DUDE, HE'S BEEN WATCHING IT NON-STOP SINCE THE BEACH... NEVER TRIMS A FRAME.
JUST LIKE HOWARD HUGHES... MAN, I HOPE HE DOESN'T ASK FOR MILK BOTTLES.
A FILM BY HENRY BARRONS
I STILL THINK WE SHOULD TELL HIM ABOUT JILLIAN'S CALL.
WANT TO DRIVE HIM MORE BONKERS THAN HE IS NOW?
I'M ONLY SAYING...
THAT'S RIGHT. ONLY SAYING, NOT THINKING.
SHUT UP.
CRASH!
WHIRR!
HENRY, WHAT IS IT?
THERE'S BEEN ONE THING MISSING...I HAVE TO TIE IT ALL TOGETHER.
ON MY OWN.

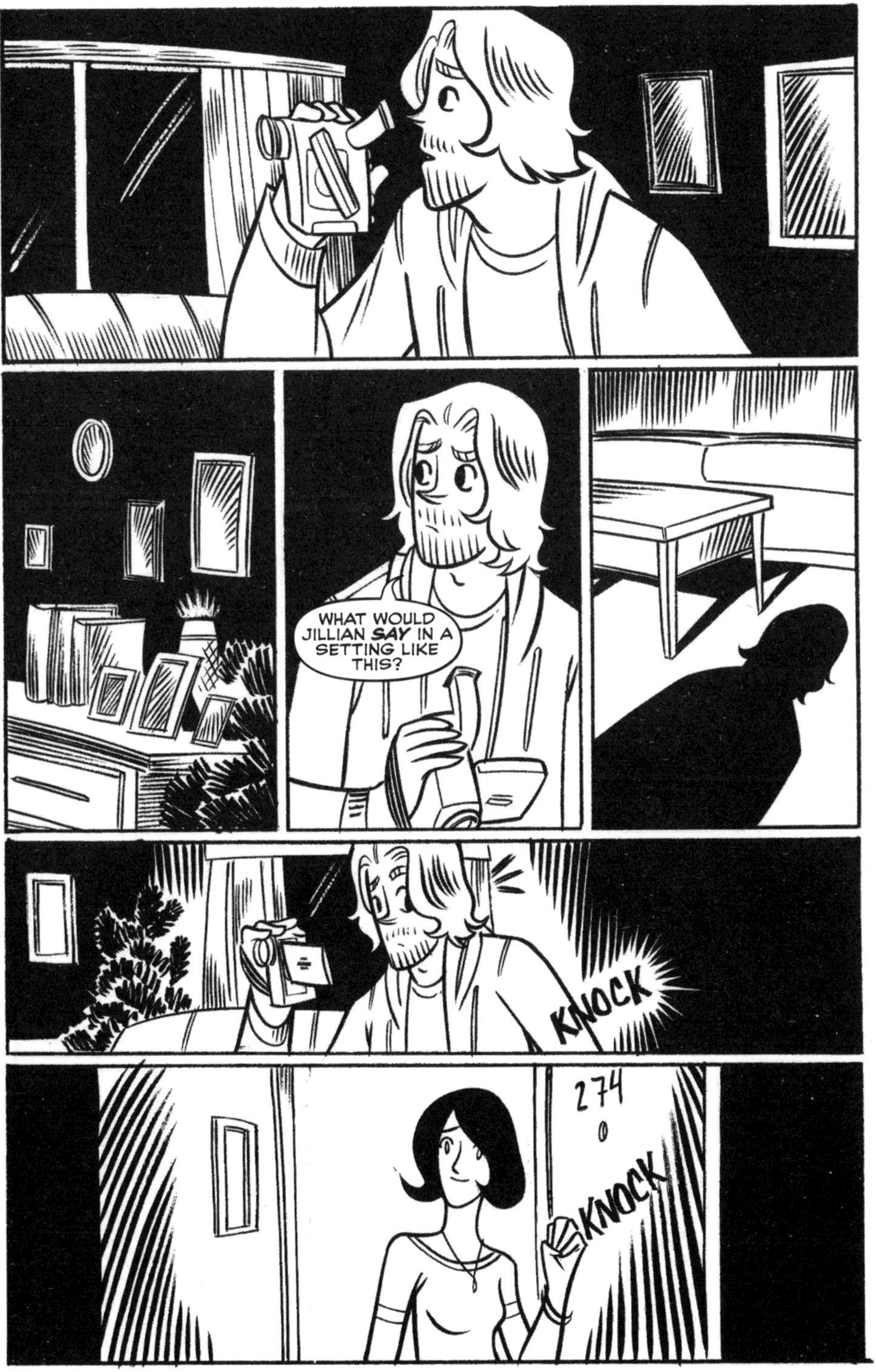
WHAT WOULD JILLIAN SAY IN A SETTING LIKE THIS?
KNOCK
274
KNOCK

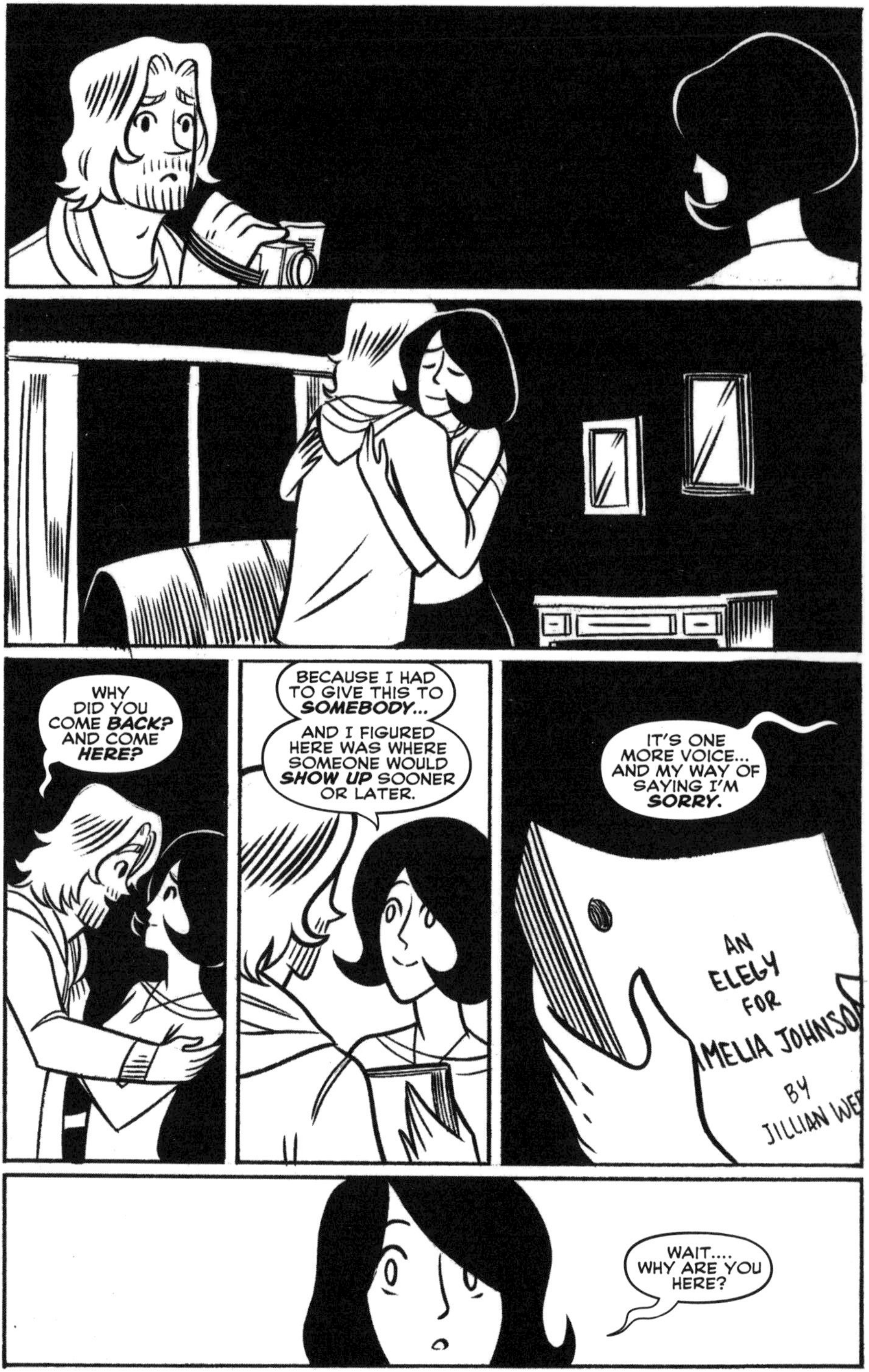
WHY DID YOU COME BACK? AND COME HERE?
BECAUSE I HAD TO GIVE THIS TO SOMEBODY...
AND I FIGURED HERE WAS WHERE SOMEONE WOULD SHOW UP SOONER OR LATER.
IT'S ONE MORE VOICE... AND MY WAY OF SAYING I'M SORRY.
AN ELEGY FOR
MELIA JOHNSO
BY
JILLIAN WE
WAIT.... WHY ARE YOU HERE?

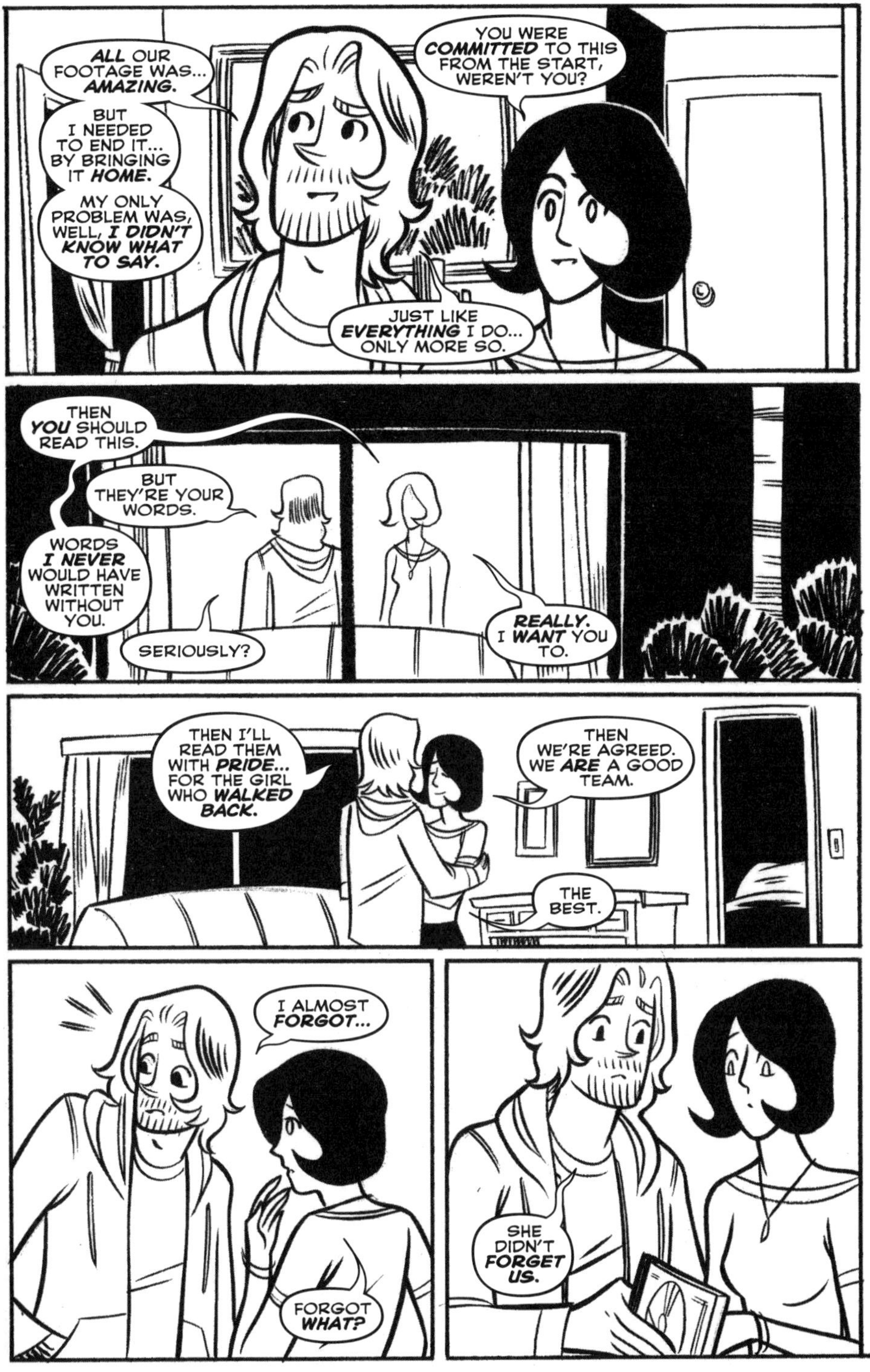
ALL OUR FOOTAGE WAS... AMAZING.
BUT I NEEDED TO END IT... BY BRINGING IT HOME.
MY ONLY PROBLEM WAS, WELL, I DIDN'T KNOW WHAT TO SAY.
YOU WERE COMMITTED TO THIS FROM THE START, WEREN'T YOU?
JUST LIKE EVERYTHING I DO... ONLY MORE SO.
THEN YOU SHOULD READ THIS.
BUT THEY'RE YOUR WORDS.
WORDS I NEVER WOULD HAVE WRITTEN WITHOUT YOU.
SERIOUSLY?
REALLY. I WANT YOU TO.
THEN I'LL READ THEM WITH PRIDE... FOR THE GIRL WHO WALKED BACK.
THEN WE'RE AGREED. WE ARE A GOOD TEAM.
THE BEST.
I ALMOST FORGOT...
FORGOT WHAT?
SHE DIDN'T FORGET US.

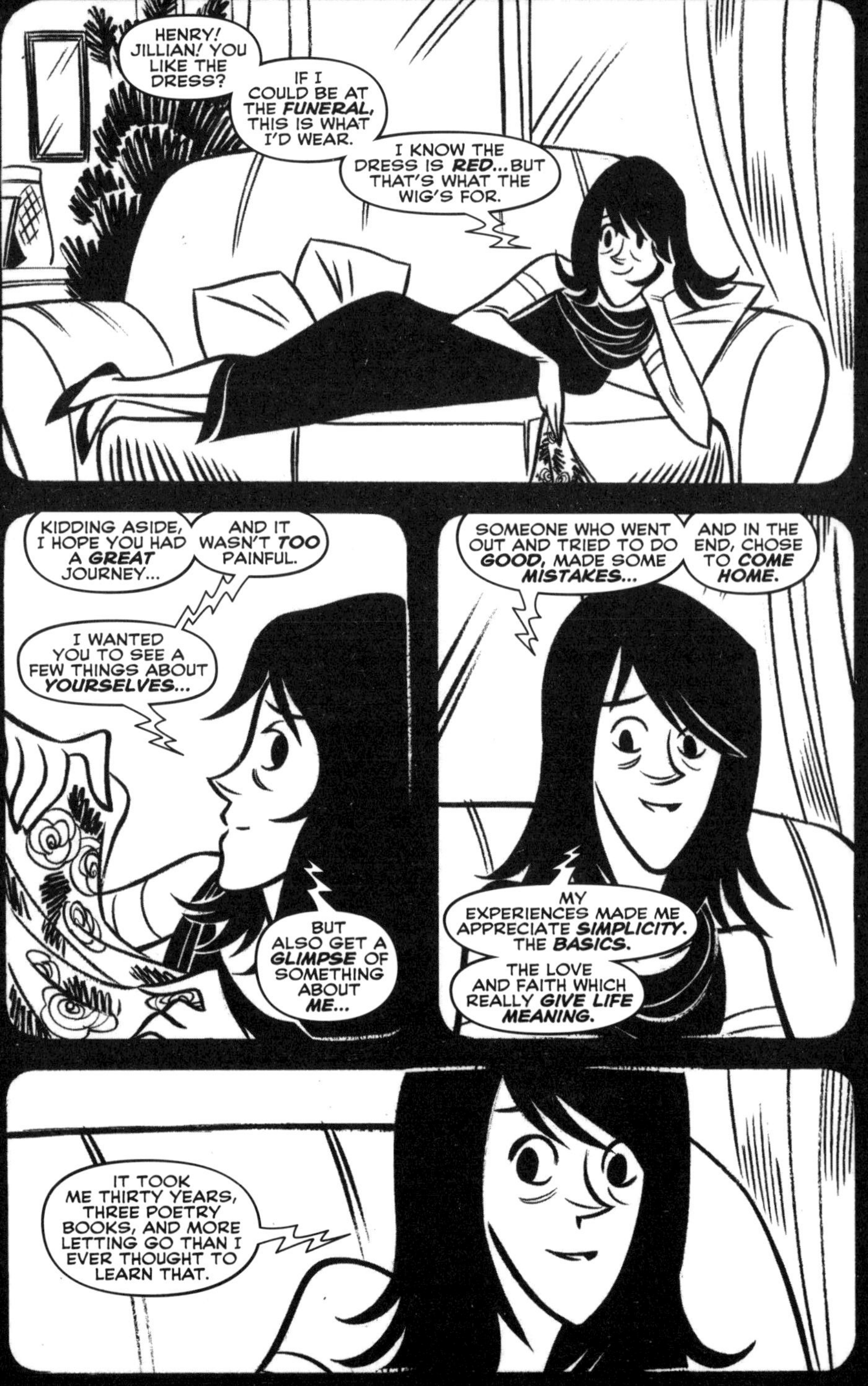
HENRY! JILLIAN! YOU LIKE THE DRESS?
IF I COULD BE AT THE FUNERAL, THIS IS WHAT I'D WEAR.
I KNOW THE DRESS IS RED... BUT THAT'S WHAT THE WIG'S FOR.
KIDDING ASIDE, I HOPE YOU HAD A GREAT JOURNEY...
AND IT WASN'T TOO PAINFUL.
I WANTED YOU TO SEE A FEW THINGS ABOUT YOURSELVES...
BUT ALSO GET A GLIMPSE OF SOMETHING ABOUT ME...
SOMEONE WHO WENT OUT AND TRIED TO DO GOOD, MADE SOME MISTAKES...
AND IN THE END, CHOSE TO COME HOME.
MY EXPERIENCES MADE ME APPRECIATE SIMPLICITY. THE BASICS.
THE LOVE AND FAITH WHICH REALLY GIVE LIFE MEANING.
IT TOOK ME THIRTY YEARS, THREE POETRY BOOKS, AND MORE LETTING GO THAN I EVER THOUGHT TO LEARN THAT.

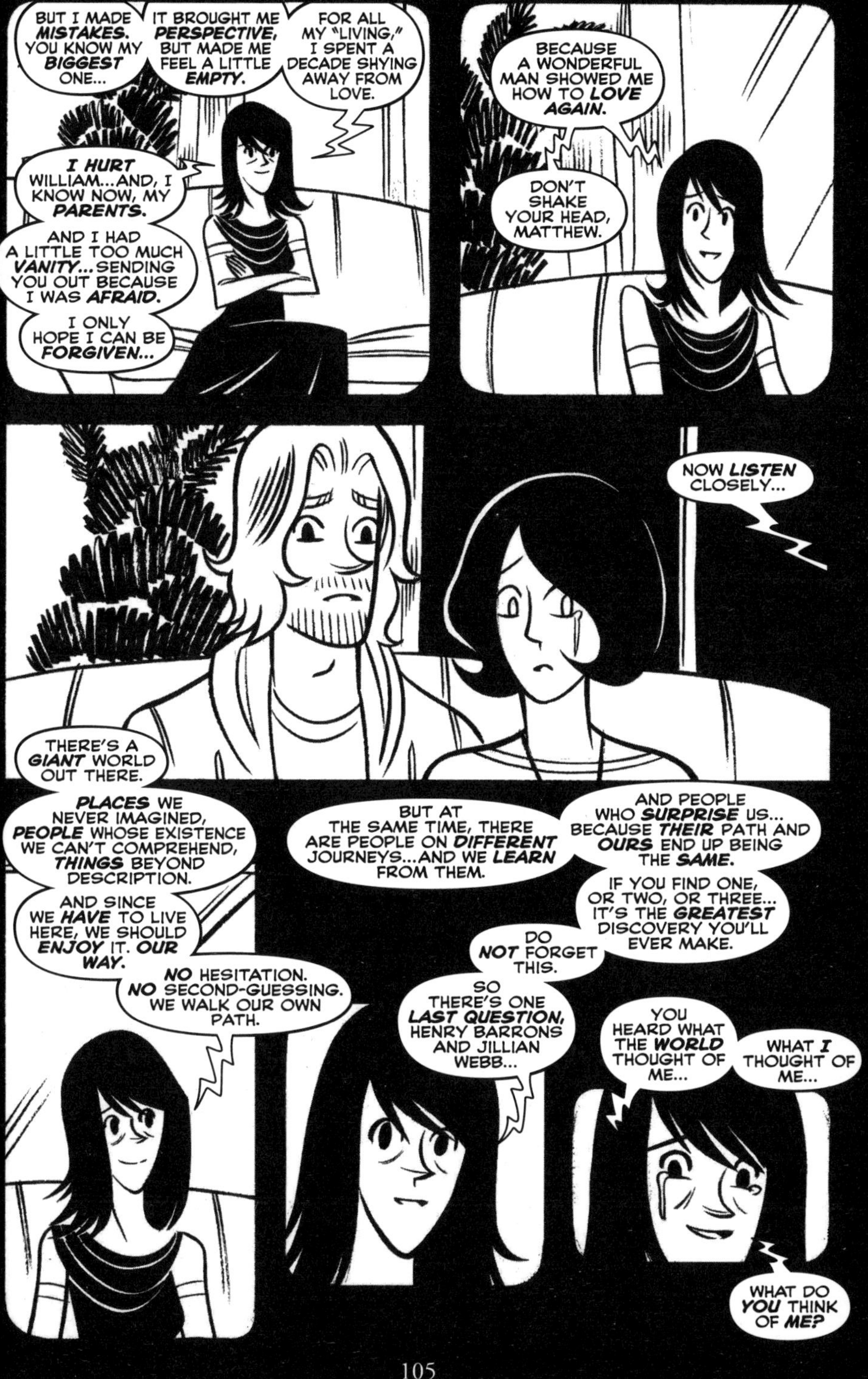
BUT I MADE MISTAKES. YOU KNOW MY BIGGEST ONE...
IT BROUGHT ME PERSPECTIVE, BUT MADE ME FEEL A LITTLE EMPTY.
FOR ALL MY "LIVING," I SPENT A DECADE SHYING AWAY FROM LOVE.
I HURT WILLIAM...AND, I KNOW NOW, MY PARENTS.
AND I HAD A LITTLE TOO MUCH VANITY...SENDING YOU OUT BECAUSE I WAS AFRAID.
I ONLY HOPE I CAN BE FORGIVEN...
BECAUSE A WONDERFUL MAN SHOWED ME HOW TO LOVE AGAIN.
DON'T SHAKE YOUR HEAD, MATTHEW.
NOW LISTEN CLOSELY...
THERE'S A GIANT WORLD OUT THERE.
PLACES WE NEVER IMAGINED, PEOPLE WHOSE EXISTENCE WE CAN'T COMPREHEND, THINGS BEYOND DESCRIPTION.
AND SINCE WE HAVE TO LIVE HERE, WE SHOULD ENJOY IT. OUR WAY.
NO HESITATION. NO SECOND-GUESSING. WE WALK OUR OWN PATH.
BUT AT THE SAME TIME, THERE ARE PEOPLE ON DIFFERENT JOURNEYS...AND WE LEARN FROM THEM.
AND PEOPLE WHO SURPRISE US... BECAUSE THEIR PATH AND OURS END UP BEING THE SAME.
IF YOU FIND ONE, OR TWO, OR THREE... IT'S THE GREATEST DISCOVERY YOU'LL EVER MAKE.
DO NOT FORGET THIS.
SO THERE'S ONE LAST QUESTION, HENRY BARRONS AND JILLIAN WEBB...
YOU HEARD WHAT THE WORLD THOUGHT OF ME...
WHAT I THOUGHT OF ME...
WHAT DO YOU THINK OF ME?

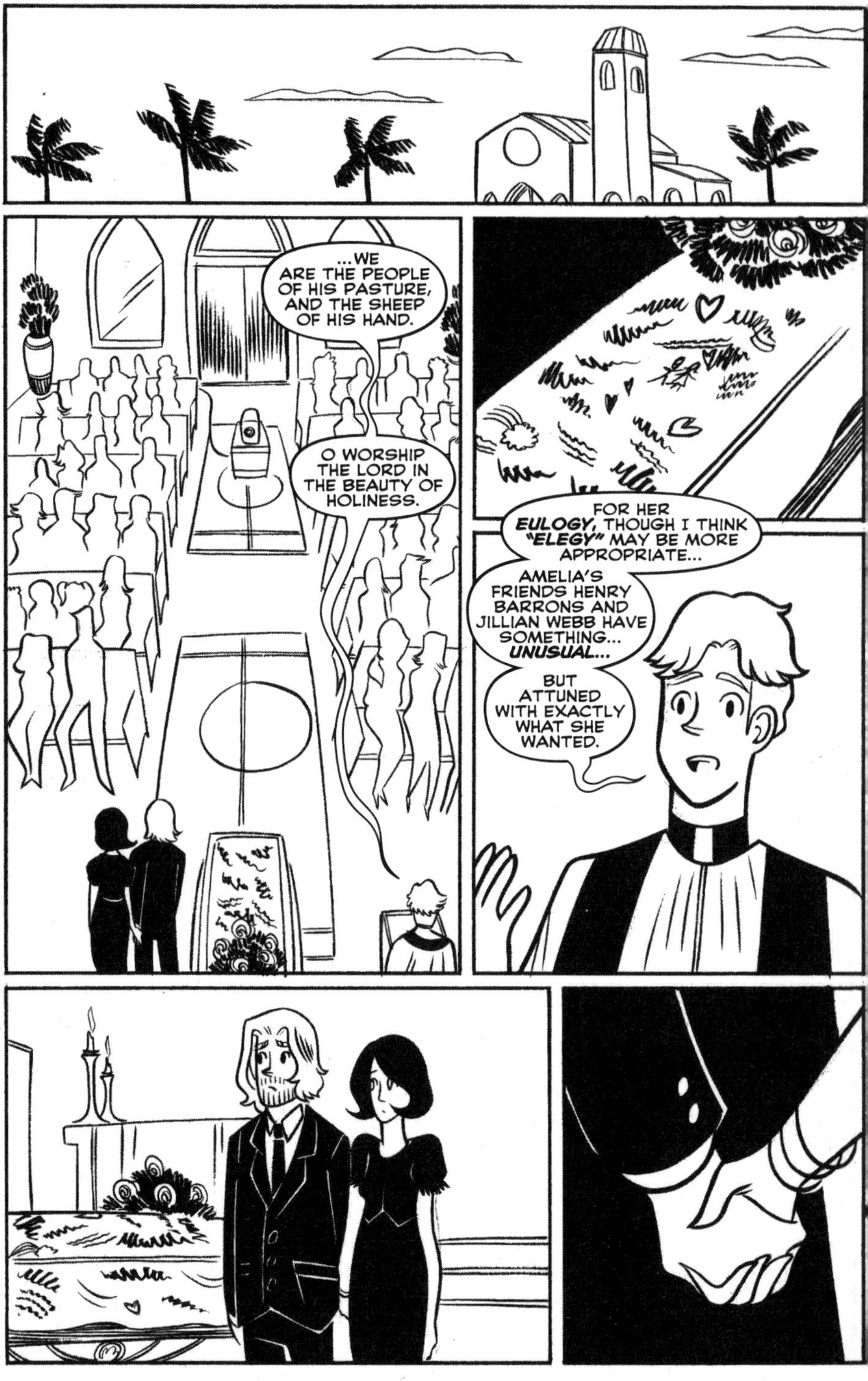
...WE ARE THE PEOPLE OF HIS PASTURE, AND THE SHEEP OF HIS HAND.
O WORSHIP THE LORD IN THE BEAUTY OF HOLINESS.
FOR HER *EULOGY,* THOUGH I THINK *"ELEGY"* MAY BE MORE APPROPRIATE...
AMELIA'S FRIENDS HENRY BARRONS AND JILLIAN WEBB HAVE SOMETHING... *UNUSUAL...*
BUT ATTUNED WITH EXACTLY WHAT SHE WANTED.

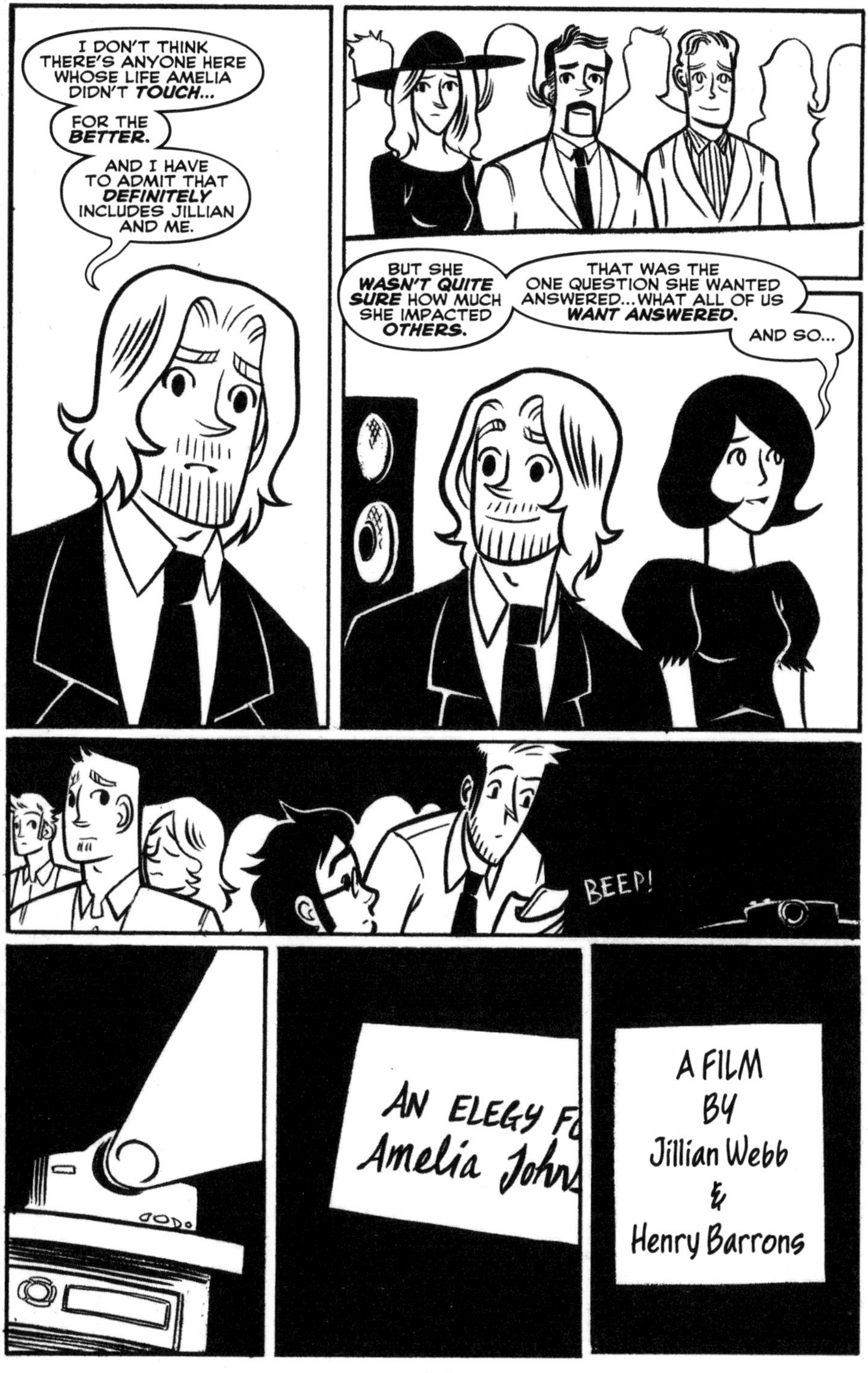
I DON'T THINK THERE'S ANYONE HERE WHOSE LIFE AMELIA DIDN'T **TOUCH...**
FOR THE **BETTER.**
AND I HAVE TO ADMIT THAT **DEFINITELY** INCLUDES JILLIAN AND ME.
BUT SHE **WASN'T QUITE SURE** HOW MUCH SHE IMPACTED **OTHERS.**
THAT WAS THE ONE QUESTION SHE WANTED ANSWERED...WHAT ALL OF US **WANT ANSWERED.**
AND SO...
BEEP!
AN ELEGY F
Amelia John
A FILM BY Jillian Webb & Henry Barrons

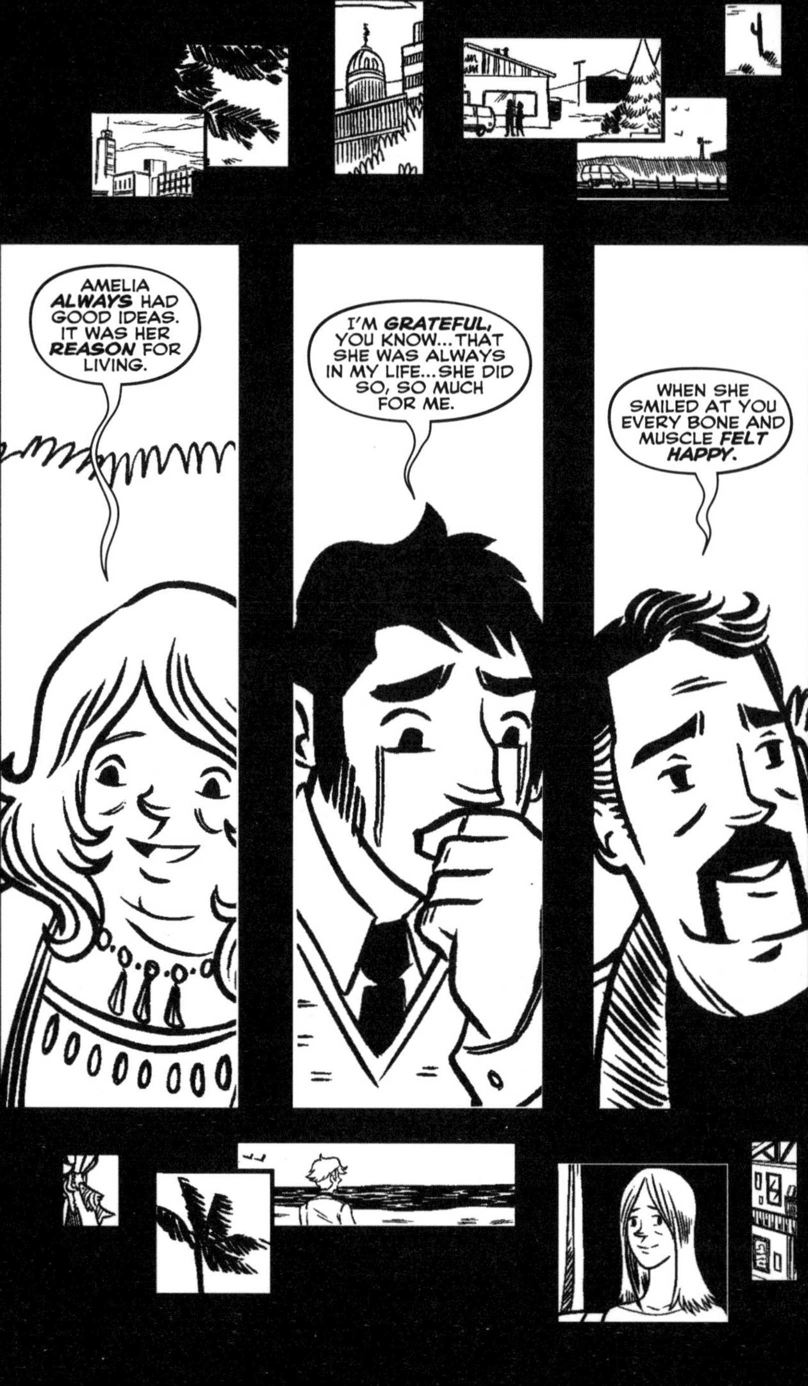
AMELIA ALWAYS HAD GOOD IDEAS. IT WAS HER REASON FOR LIVING.
I'M GRATEFUL, YOU KNOW... THAT SHE WAS ALWAYS IN MY LIFE... SHE DID SO, SO MUCH FOR ME.
WHEN SHE SMILED AT YOU EVERY BONE AND MUSCLE FELT HAPPY.

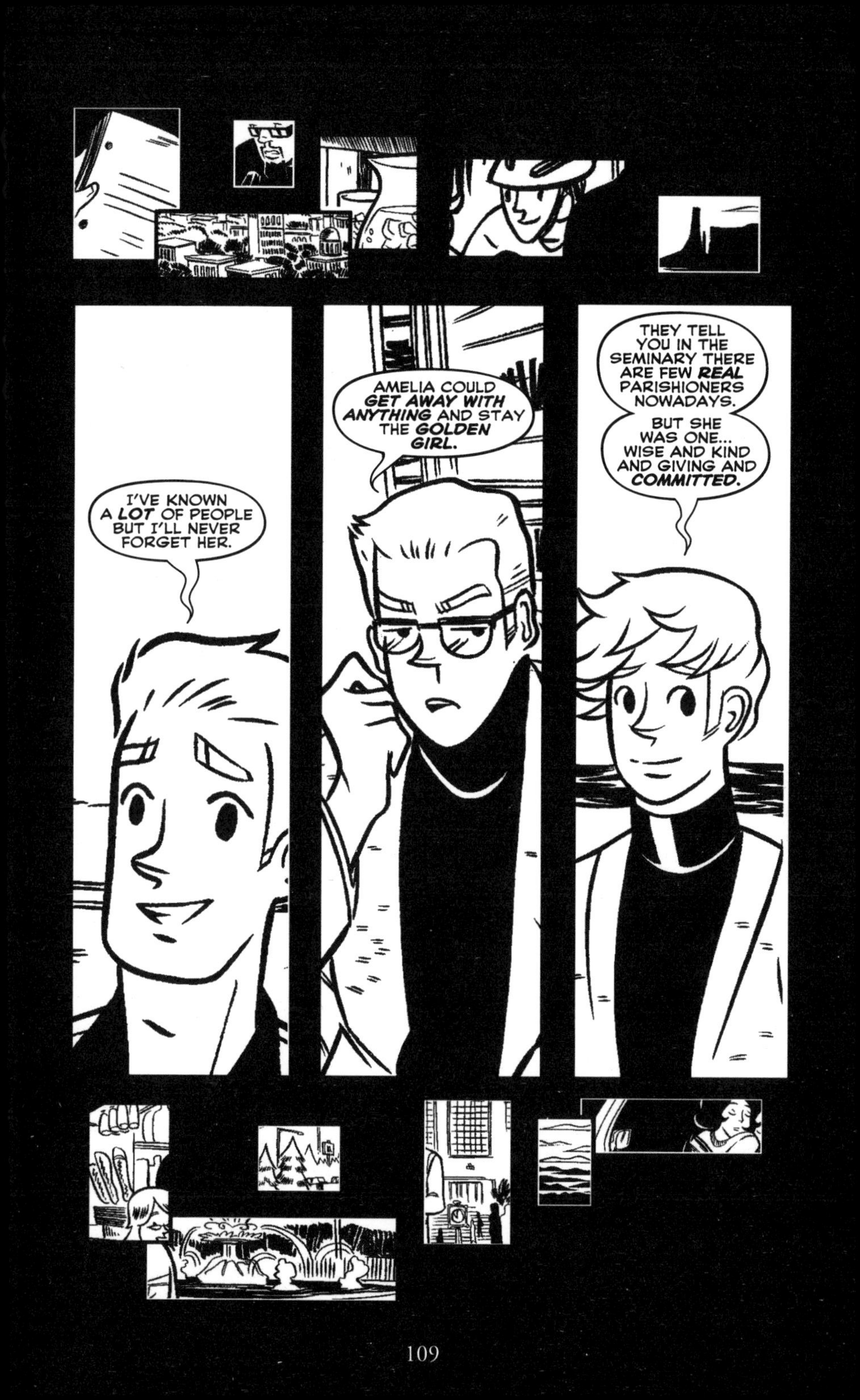
I'VE KNOWN A LOT OF PEOPLE BUT I'LL NEVER FORGET HER.
AMELIA COULD GET AWAY WITH ANYTHING AND STAY THE GOLDEN GIRL.
THEY TELL YOU IN THE SEMINARY THERE ARE FEW REAL PARISHIONERS NOWADAYS.
BUT SHE WAS ONE... WISE AND KIND AND GIVING AND COMMITTED.

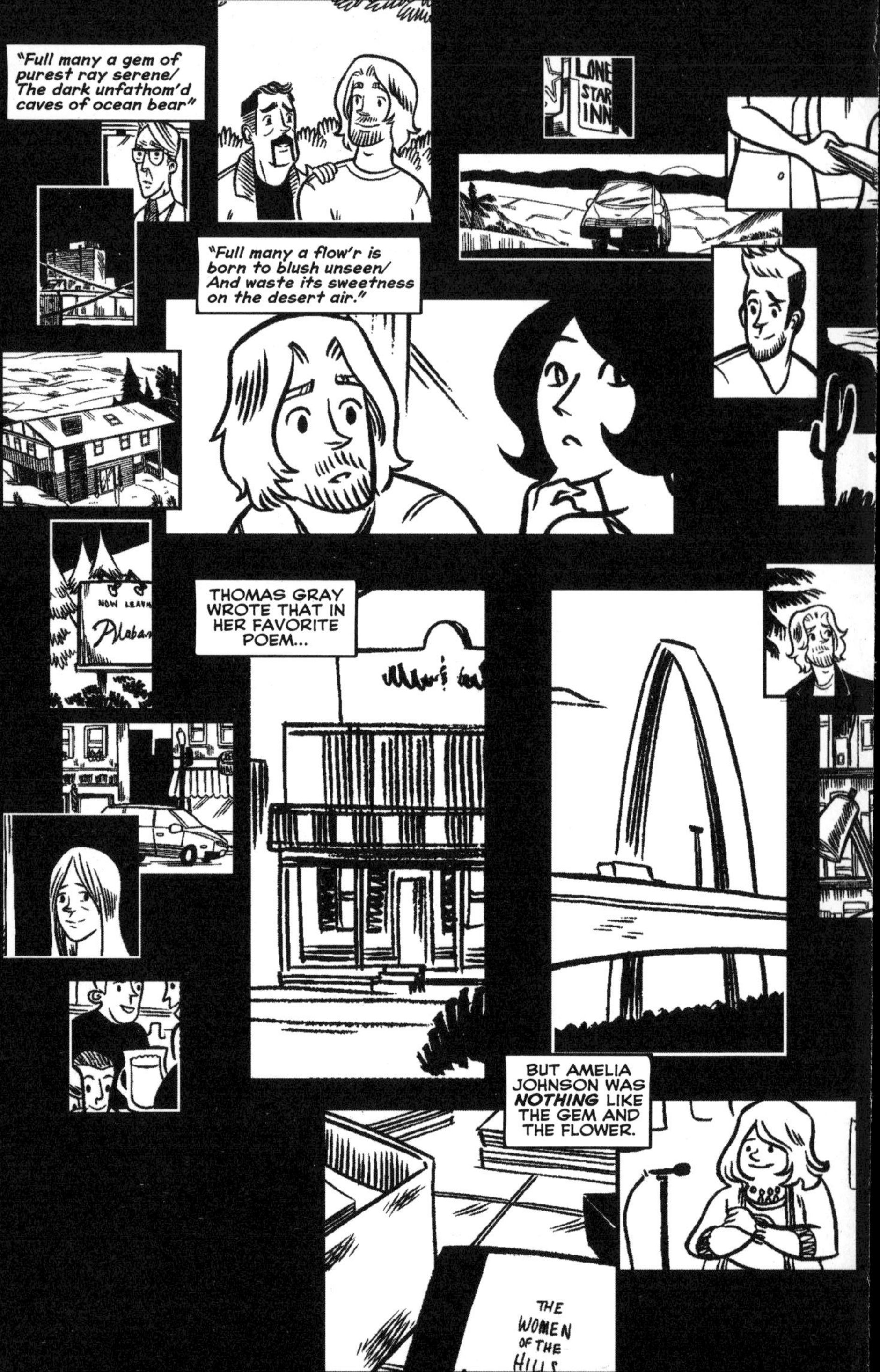
"Full many a gem of purest ray serene/ The dark unfathom'd caves of ocean bear"
LONE STAR INN
"Full many a flow'r is born to blush unseen/ And waste its sweetness on the desert air."
NOW LEAVING
THOMAS GRAY WROTE THAT IN HER FAVORITE POEM...
BUT AMELIA JOHNSON WAS NOTHING LIKE THE GEM AND THE FLOWER.
THE WOMEN OF THE

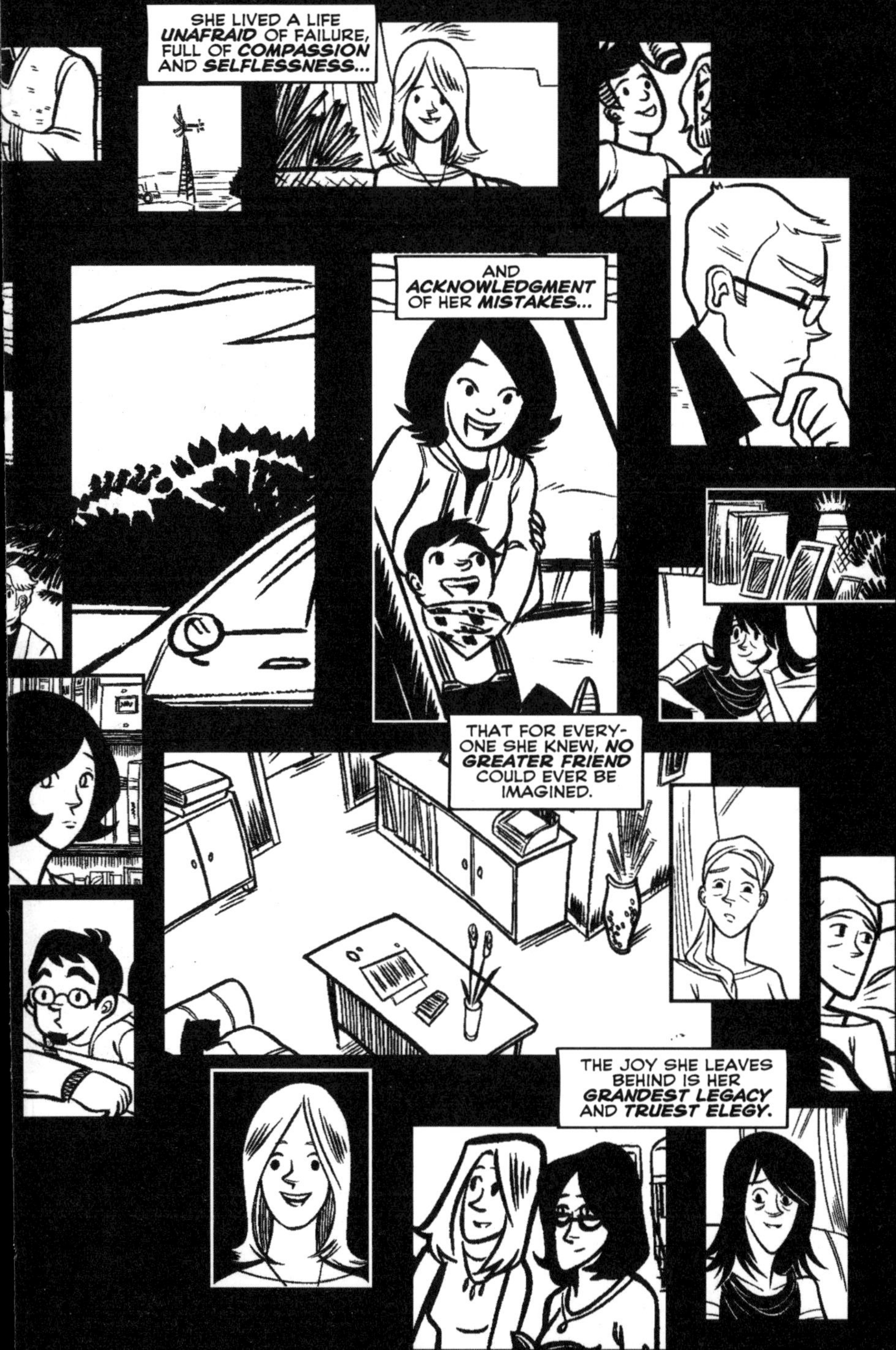
SHE LIVED A LIFE *UNAFRAID* OF FAILURE, FULL OF *COMPASSION* AND *SELFLESSNESS...*
AND *ACKNOWLEDGMENT* OF HER *MISTAKES...*
THAT FOR EVERY-ONE SHE KNEW, *NO GREATER FRIEND* COULD EVER BE IMAGINED.
THE JOY SHE LEAVES BEHIND IS HER *GRANDEST LEGACY* AND *TRUEST ELEGY*.

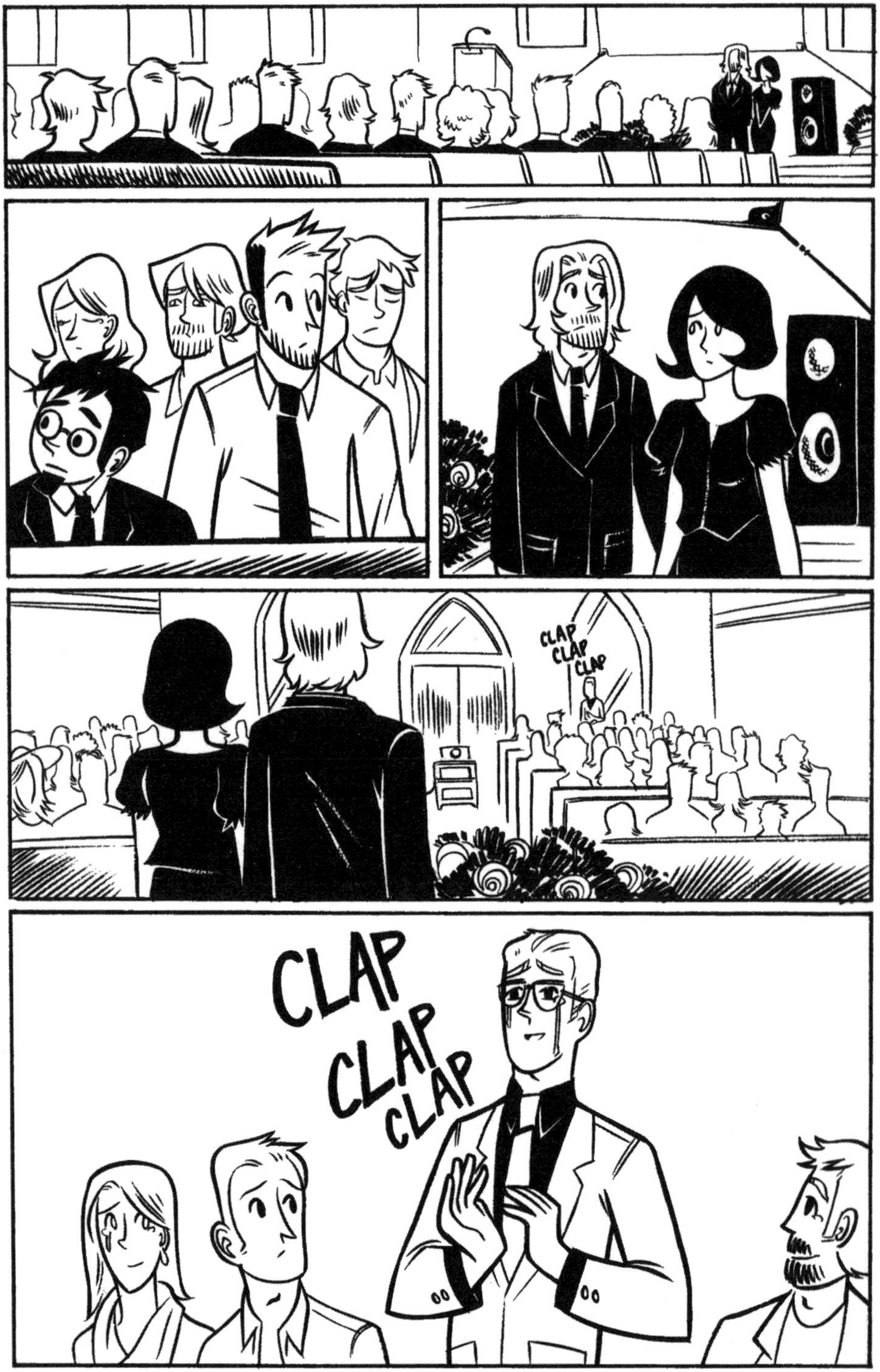
CLAP
CLAP
CLAP
CLAP
CLAP
CLAP

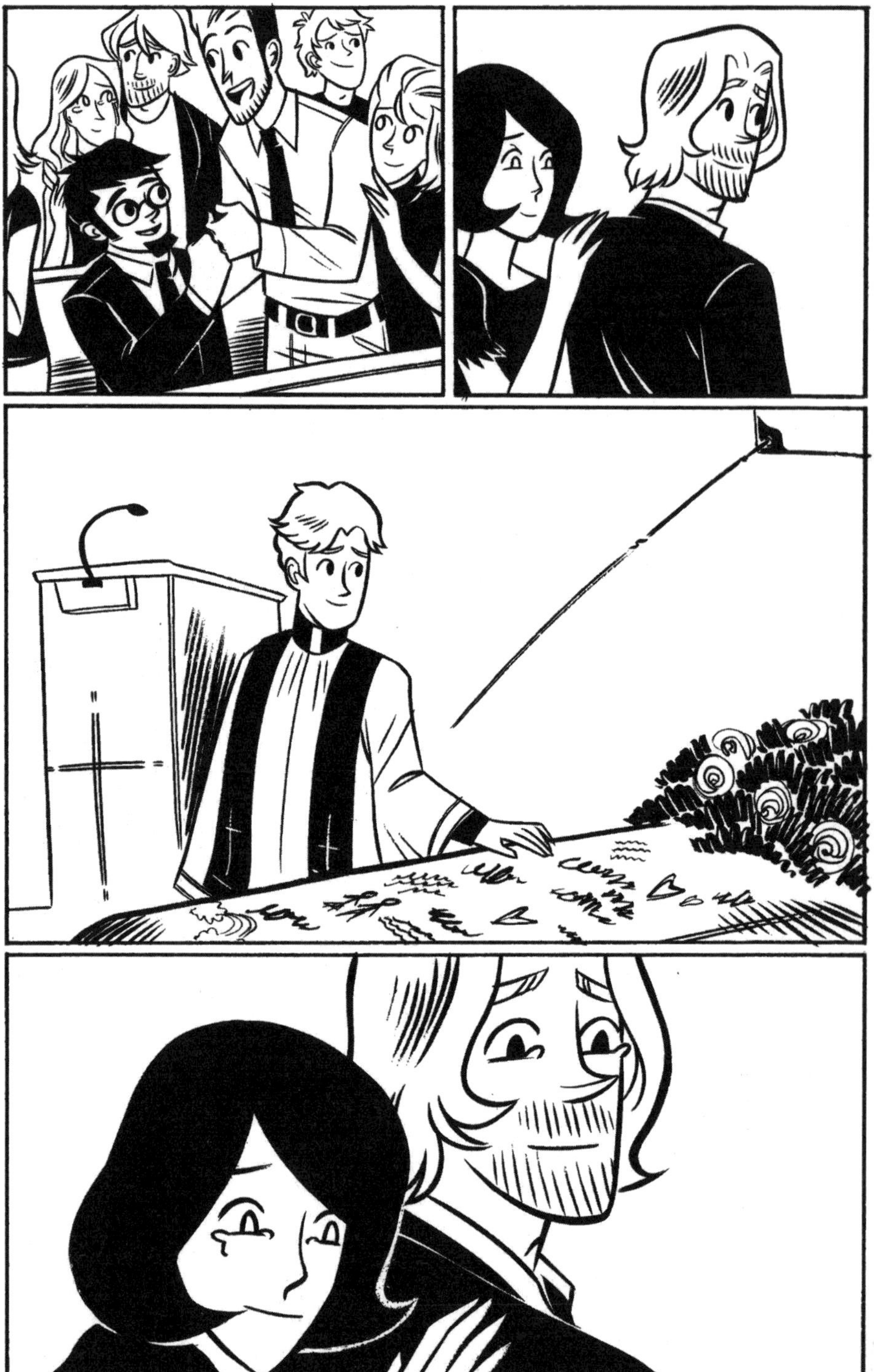

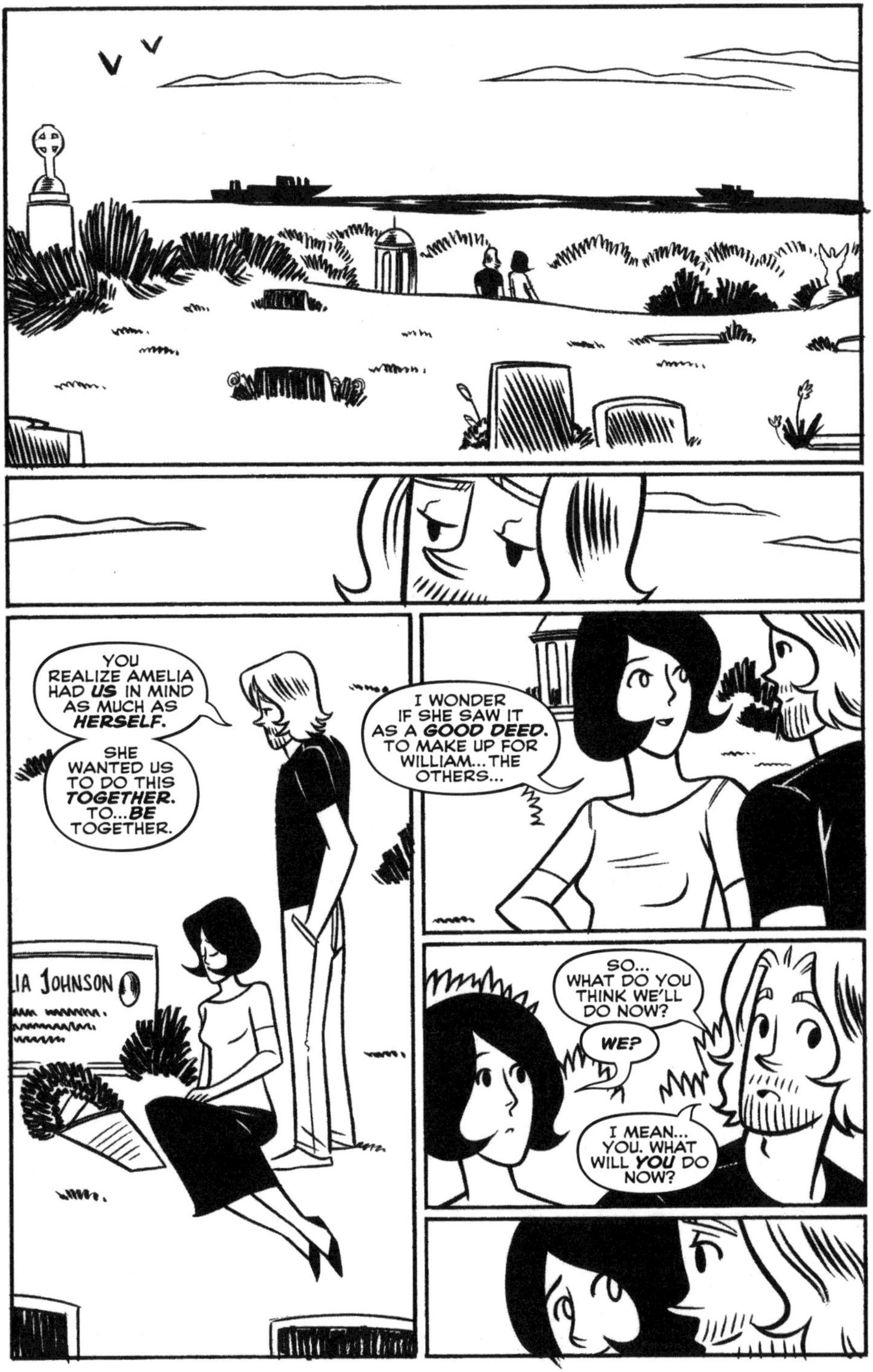
YOU REALIZE AMELIA HAD **US** IN MIND AS MUCH AS ***HERSELF.***
SHE WANTED US TO DO THIS ***TOGETHER.*** TO...***BE*** TOGETHER.
LIA JOHNSON
I WONDER IF SHE SAW IT AS A ***GOOD DEED.*** TO MAKE UP FOR WILLIAM...THE OTHERS...
SO... WHAT DO YOU THINK WE'LL DO NOW?
WE?
I MEAN... YOU. WHAT WILL ***YOU*** DO NOW?

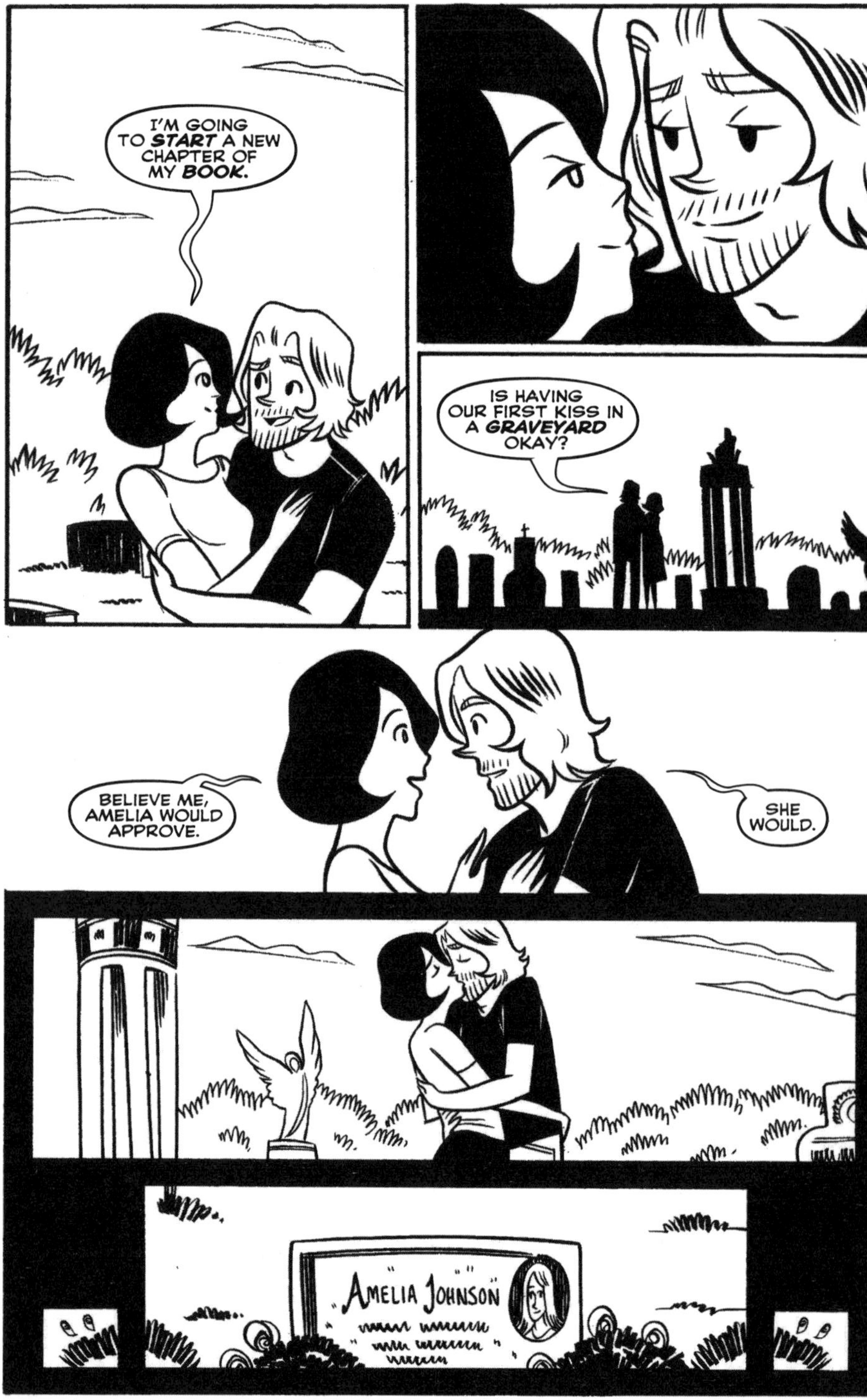
I'M GOING TO START A NEW CHAPTER OF MY BOOK.
IS HAVING OUR FIRST KISS IN A GRAVEYARD OKAY?
BELIEVE ME, AMELIA WOULD APPROVE.
SHE WOULD.
AMELIA JOHNSON

THE END

AFTERWORD

The idea for *An Elegy for Amelia Johnson* occurred to me one warm August evening in 2007. I was walking down a street in Santa Monica, musing on how one can tell a story about two elements: love and time. Suddenly, "death" popped into my head. Isn't death the be-all and end-all of time, and also usually present in many of the greatest love stories?

I'm an optimist, so I decided to run with this thought in a way which would ultimately be optimistic: one person's death results in two others falling in love. Through over three years of writing and rewriting, the plot and characters continually changed, but that one idea remained the same.

There were three people who brought it to fruition. I am merely a vessel for a few words. Dave Valeza is an artist beyond compare who requires no words at all. There have been few greater thrills in my life than seeing Dave's original sketches and page layouts coming in, a chunk at a time, and realizing he could have told the whole story without any help from me.

Moreover, he is an astoundingly positive person whose energy is infectious and inspiring.

When unexpected circumstances required Dave to move on to other projects before the book was ready, Kate Kasenow came from either nowhere or providence, whatever you like, to add the final touches. I have rarely seen anyone work as hard as Kate over so short a period of time… or as aesthetically magnificent.

And I never would have worked with Dave and Kate if not for Stephen Christy, our erstwhile editor, one of the hardest-working men in Los Angeles, the man who first conceived of meshing love and time together… and this book's most strident champion from the get-go. While juggling twenty or thirty other projects, Stephen always made me feel like this was his only book… and his insights and suggestions as to how to change plot and character were crucial. Moreover, he is a wonderful friend who has been there for me personally and professionally through every stroke of the keyboard.

Finally, I must thank and acknowledge:

…God, without Whom I am nothing, and Who gave me my ability to write in the first place.

…Robert, Nancy, and Marc Rostan, the greatest family anyone ever asked for, who give me the courage and freedom to follow even my craziest whims.

…Jonathan Ade, Kal-El Bogdanove, Paul Brindley, Brad Champagne, Dave Child, Chris Faiella, and Mike Pintar for their invaluable friendship and insights during the composition.

…Lisa Huberman, Carlee Tressel, Anna Haas, Aimee Ranger, and Katerina Schmidt for close-to-divine inspiration.

…Toby Schwartz, who didn't come into my life until the final revisions but is Amelia Johnson in the flesh.

…And anyone who ever reads this book and feels moved to let someone special to them know they are loved or forgiven.

—ANDREW J. ROSTAN
2011

ABOUT *the* AUTHORS

ANDREW J. ROSTAN was born in Youngstown, Ohio, went to college in Boston and a small town in the Netherlands, and wrote the vast majority of *An Elegy For Amelia Johnson* in Los Angeles, where he lived from 2007 to 2009. He concurrently produced several unpublished and very, very bad projects, which he was able to do thanks to five victories on Jeopardy! After receiving a moment of clarity at a monastery which later burned to the ground, Rostan moved to Chicago and earned his master's degree in the Humanities, therefore qualifying him for any job on the market. Today Rostan still lives in Chicago where, when not working on his next books, he represents Aflac, cooks near-gourmet meals, and amuses his girlfriend. His inspirations are his parents, Harry Chapin, Robert Bolt, Woody Allen, and Anthony Trollope. He will talk about old movies, classic rock, fiction, and baseball for hours if you get him started.

DAVE VALEZA is inspired by human relationships, science fiction, and shenanigans. He studied illustration and comics at SCAD, and currently lives in the L.A. area.

KATE KASENOW loves nature, comics, and JRR Tolkien. Though most people think that she runs around hugging trees all day, she actually spends most of her time writing, drawing, and pursuing her MFA at Savannah College of Art and Design. She expects to graduate in March of 2011. You can find more of her work at *romanykate.deviantart.com* or at *katekaz. blogspot.com.*

DAVE LANPHEAR is a veteran designer and comic book letterer whose credits include *Batman: The Long Halloween, Marvel Fairy Tales* and Crossgen's *Ruse.*

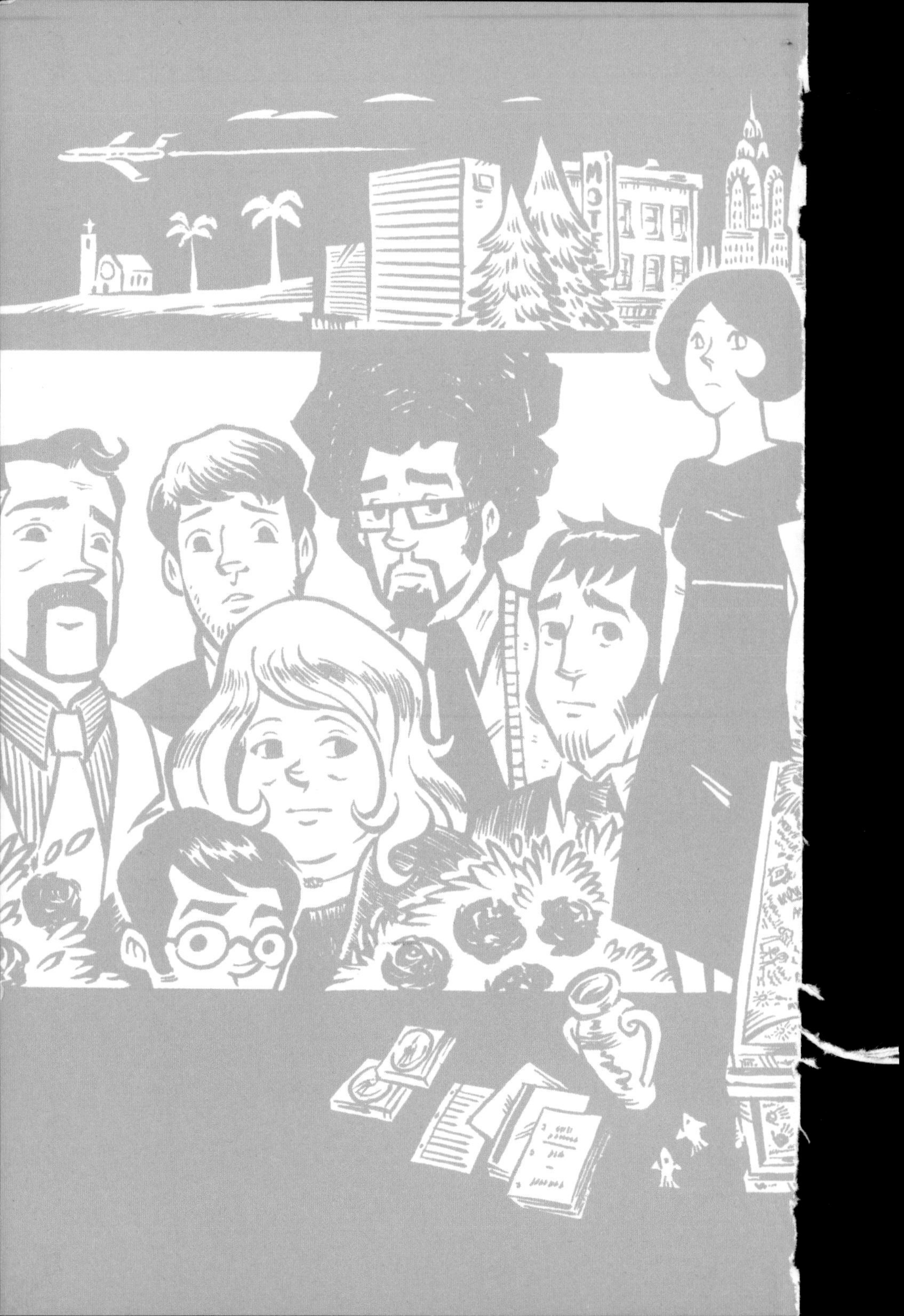